Callused Hands Hungry Heart

The Life of a Fisherman-Farmer

by
Jim Lawrence

Callused Hands Hungry Heart
The life of a fisherman-farmer

First Edition

Thirsty Goose Farms
Friday Harbor, WA 98250

Contact Jim Lawrence: jimjet@rockisland.com

Cover photo and design: Lisa Lawrence
Photo credit on back cover- Abbie Sewall
Interior layout and publishing services by W. Bruce Conway

Printed in the U.S.A. on recycled paper

ISBN: 978-1-4507-5016-5

Library of Congress Control Number is available from publisher upon request.

Dedicated
to

Lisa M, Natalia S, Mara W, and Charley S
My brother Hugh

And to all those people looking for a life of meaning
while walking the path less traveled

Table of Contents

Chapter 1

Ozette

I left Seattle pissed off at everything. I threw what few belongings I owned into my '67 VW van, strapped my kayak to the roof, loaded my devoted dog and just drove away the week before finals my junior year. College felt like the ultimate contradiction. It was a combination of little relevance and being an abysmal student.

The year was 1972 and I'd just escaped the ravenous jaws of the military draft for Vietnam. The University of Washington campus was alive with discussion on our corrupt society, the evils of capitalism, the war machine and lists of injustices too numerous to keep track of, but the bottom line was everyone was dissatisfied, the country angry and I was no exception. Everything needed changing.

So why were we all going to school, learning the same crap over and over again, continually complaining about it and not doing anything different? We all talked about a new life in the country but no one was leaving. I had spent way too many nights up until dawn arguing the finer points of a new society, generally through a hazy cocktail of dope and beer. At three or four in the morning, between the poignant lyrics of Bob Dylan, my friends and I came to some basic truths generally agreeing that most things were pretty messed up including the women we never seemed to meet. It was time for a change, time to sink my fingers into the flesh of life and get out of the abstract. Time to drop out.

I drove west. Caught the ferry to the Olympic Peninsula west of Seattle, headed past the clear-cuts to the water drenched logging town of Forks. A small town soaking in the middle of the rain forest filled with mud, rain, logging trucks and loggers. Men with pin-striped work shirts tattered and diesel soaked, shin-high sawed off jeans ragged with wear held up by Loggers World suspenders, and big, stout cork soled logger boots. Bearded brutes who chewed snooze and said "fuck" at least three times to a sentence. They drove enormous four-wheel drive pickup trucks that looked as if they'd spent little time on paved roads. Mud slung and dented, these steroidal-geared machines were filled with enormous chain saws, gas cans, general wet crap and empty cheap beer cans.

The men were tough looking with a red neck rawness and grit that had a romantic appeal at first glance. It couldn't have been further from the gender neutral/intellectual crowd I was leaving and that's what appealed to me. These were working people, Woody Guthrie's and Bob Dylan's people. I was looking for the "stuff of life" and it seemed like a good place to start.

I felt like I spoke a foreign language when asking around a cafe if there was any work in the area. My tall skinny muscle free frame, white clean hands and long ponytail set me apart like a zit on a prom queen's chin. I tried to act as if I had a pretty good fix on this sort of life and dropped my voice quiet and low trying to assume a Charles Bronson-like mysterious tone, but the naiveté wept from my pores and it was obvious I was green as fresh tossed salad. I went from one booth to the next and was dismissed each time before I finished asking.

Then on the way out an older fellow with carbonated eyes and 3.2 sweat told me I could either set chokers for Hoko-Rainier or go cut cedar bolts out at Lake Ozette. I got the feeling he knew what it was to be out of work but mostly he could relate to my anxious self-doubt.

I had heard setting chokers was about as dangerous as dodging cars on the freeway in the dark with horrible stories of cables and logs and soft body tissue being pinned and crushed, so I headed to Lake Ozette to load cedar bolts on trucks at $4 an hour. I pitched my tent on the edge of town and went to work right away.

Unlike the mind expanding intellectual efforts of college life, loading trucks from five in the morning till five in the evening required absolutely no mental cognition whatsoever. What it did require I had little of: brute strength and an inactive mind.

Endless piles of two-foot long split chunks of cedar called bolts, easily five or six times bigger than an average chunk of firewood, had to be thrown up on the back of huge flatbed trucks and stacked in steel framed ricks headed for the shake mill. High in the mountains, deep in the middle of 1000-acre clear-cuts, cedar bolts were being airlifted out by helicopter to preserve the fragile tiny replanted seedlings, then dropped at the edge of old logging roads where a couple of us lackeys struggled them aboard an assortment of ancient mufflerless relics.

The work was grueling and for the first weeks when the trucks brought me back down the mountain, I would slow tail it to my tent where my hammered body would crash out exhausted until my alarm clattered off early the next morning. I had changed my life. I wasn't sure if it felt good yet or not. My body ached and my muscles were sore. My hands were soft and battered despite the effort to wear gloves. Basically I was a physical wreck trying to live out some romantic notion about a meaningful life.

After several more weeks my body rallied enough that I began to take evening walks. I would stroll into town and along the row of shanty cabins where many of the loggers lived. A cluster of dilapidated living quarters with a row of hard ass jacked up pickup trucks parked out front. Like me it seemed as if every logger had a dog but, unlike Tally, my devoted Golden Retriever (a refugee with a mysterious past from a dark urine soaked cage at the SPCA), these were a scrappy pack of hair trigger curs that loved to pick fights, eat garbage and intimidate. It was hard to stay out of their way when walking into town as the hassled pack was always ready to fuck or fight or both. I felt sorry for Tally as he

9

was a big wimp like me. Occasionally I leaned my head into an open door of a cabin where smoke, beer cans and playing cards mixed with loud voices and heavy metal music in a world of serious machismo. I never learned these skills of masculine play and it's always bothered me. Men in bars, men talking their trash to each other, organized sports, Hemingway bonding, pissing contests, whistling at chicks.

I failed all these classes. I had no nouns or verbs for this language, only the gritty sweat of unease and screaming awkward silences. I saw myself as an hors d'oeuvre, easy to consume and easier to forget. Tally and I had a hard time fitting in. In spite of this I was drawn to the woods, the rivers and the remote wild ocean beaches.

My college trained flabby musculature slowly rallied and I began to explore deep into the rain forest and along wild beaches with my dog. Living my fantasy of pioneer explorer, I wandered off the trail and away from the human process—a romantic version of the beginning days of Jack London's Buck as he heard the calls of his distant ancestors.

The dirt under my nails and the feel of my body changing into something I could relate to was exhilarating. Often on weekends we would walk for hours into the bramble and wet forest. Trying to find the path less traveled or just a path, hoping to be rewarded with a secret discovery of an unknown meadow, is hard grueling work with few remunerations. Conclusion being there is a lot of wet salal, mud and hardhack in a rain forest with no panoramic views or just rewards, only the shivering wet fear of not remembering how to get back to camp.

After studying a topographical map and seeing that five miles of the Ozette River not only had no road paralleling its banks, but no trail, I realized this was what I was looking for. I planned to kayak the river to the ocean, marveling at the idea of paddling from the cool dark rain forest out into the open light and out into the surf. My mediocre experience river kayaking and a plan for getting my boat and paddle back to my tent seemed irrelevant at the onset. I would travel as Lewis and Clark through uncharted waters into the dense wild forest.

I left the next Saturday morning. I launched at the lake, with only half a sandwich in my pocket and a jackknife, and paddled through the tail out where the calm lake dropped immediately into the swift waters of the river and the darkness of the looming Olympic rain forest. I was pumped. I dodged branches that hung low over the water that threatened to slap at me with brutal disregard.

My thoughts were distracted by a memory of galloping a pony across a lawn and being rudely piano-wired by a clothesline into an aching heap. The smell of fresh cut grass and the feel of the dull knife of the rope across my face, that stubbornly insisted I pay a toll, were still with me. Ripped from the bare back of the speeding equine, I was hammered to the hard ground startled, stinging, my nose swollen and grass in my mouth. It felt like a scolding adult with a painful lesson I didn't forget.

The river was a tannic, diner coffee black color rendered from the centuries of decomposing giant cedars. The forest was dark and the undergrowth looked impenetrable along the river. Hemlocks dangled their gentle, perfect needles that looked for light in the cool dampness of the 200-foot high green canopy. Root beer foam swam in endless dizzying circles in the eddies and I, without a lot of choice, moved further in, further away.

Tally ran hell-bent along the river edge, a marvelous runner, both of us adrenalized by a thrilling anxiety. Loving it and wanting it to be finished before anything went wrong. Horribly wrong. Several times he swam the 60 or 80 feet of brown currents to more easily pass massive thick bramble and fallen trees.

Trees that fall out over the river and rake the currents with re-bar stiff branches are called sweepers, and when logs and general river debris clog up against them, they become the dreaded log-jam. Both can be a quick death if caught in their snare. The vision of being sucked down by the giant hydraulic of the river into the depths of tangled underwater logs and pinned between branch and current and never found raced around my head as I paddled past these nightmares. It's good for a high adrenal focal level not easy to achieve in your average daily life. I sat up in my seat and leaned forward for maximum control.

The snarls of logs became worse and I realized I needed to keep exit strategies close at hand. As I maneuvered around a bend, terror struck as the water disappeared under a sweeper crossing the entire span of the Ozette River. A giant fallen Douglas fir lay raking the water with iron strong branches quivering under the strength of the current. Branches jutted out in every direction, five inches in diameter and hard as welded steel. The trunk was some 20 inches above the surface of the hungry black water, enough room for the kayak, but not me.

I knew that in my newly found pioneering spirit not all pioneers always made it home, a scenario I wasn't ready for. Adrenaline sprayed thru me like a punctured high-pressure hose spewing the hot oil of dread into my panicky brain.

The horizontal tree trunk hit me in the chest with a linebacker's blunt thud. My hands struggled to grab on anything as the force of the river pulled and pushed the kayak with half of me in it. It took my complete and terrified strength to hold on as the river slowly and forcefully stripped loose the spray skirt, and then the boat, like the skinning of a hide from an animal carcass. The boat immediately disappeared in the current beneath me and I pulled myself, trembling, up onto the trunk soaking wet and stunned.

I stood shaking, trying to fathom what had happened, while gripping the hard maze of branches. Then, as if in my own defense, a yell erupted from somewhere deep inside my primal self. A yell of victory, a release of terror and a warning for the deep dark forest and this menacing river to back up for a second while I figured things out. I wasn't gone yet but the sound was swallowed in the arbor acoustics above and was painfully unheard making me realize how big and strong I wasn't.

The bramble along the river was a morass of tightly woven branches making it nearly impossible to follow its shore, but eventually I found the kayak floating full of water in an eddy. The paddle bobbed another 100 yards beyond. Tally showed up wet and shaking. I reassembled my gear along with my fragile soaked confidence and decided I had no choice but to continue.

I would continue down the river but with a hair-trigger attitude for quitting. It was now an adventure to finish, not necessarily enjoy. The dark looming canopy of the cedar and fir forest had a depressing effect as I struggled between the "what if?" tapes in my head and the need to be present for my next challenge.

Tally, being on the opposite bank, did not disturb the five or six elk that stared at me bashful eyed as I passed. My confidence and enjoyment toyed with returning. Further on, bend after bend in the river, I could see breaks in the trees and then there was the call of a seagull. The ecology was rapidly changing to the salt and windblown shores of the Pacific Ocean. Around a bend the light shown bright, trees passed to my stern, and to my bow the crash of waves on a long beach.

My dream of transcending from fresh to salt water in the wild was at its climax. The river's brown tea mixed with the soda water of the ocean in small waves that grew rapidly as the current swept me out. I was drinking in all the changes, the gulls, the salt air, the sounds, the wide openness, my eyes squinting at the brightness. I glanced back at Tally who ran back and forth on the beach as he looked for the way to catch up. Of the hundreds of miles of the continental United States that border oceans, this was the only strip not annexed by road, a mere 50 mile area. It is a wild shoreline.

I was taking large breakers over the bow and realized I needed to pull out of my exultation and get to shore. The ebbing river and the large swells were working out their power play and I was caught in the middle. With the next swell that broke over my bow, I struggled to spin the boat and surf toward shore. Shore was a distance now of a half mile and increasing rapidly by the second.

Tally looked very small, and panic hit my veins as the small kayak broached, and the descending swell rolled me over like a bottle. I tried momentarily to right myself, but the panic and the imagery of being sucked under and out to sea made it a short try before I tugged the spray skirt free and went for the surface. The icy water sucked the air out of my lungs and my ears screamed with real panic.

I knew the current was stronger than anything I could swim against. Despite this fact, my response was to fight the powerful flow of the river. Free from the boat I swam like a crazy man. Arms flailing and legs churning water, I could feel my heavy clothes and the spray skirt pulling against me. Microseconds passed and through the froth I could see the increasing distance to shore.

Suddenly my knee hit a soft blunt object that in my panic I assumed was probably a large animal, a shark no doubt lurking in the shallows at the river's mouth. Then my other leg hit it and in the cross currents I attempted to right myself and found soft sand only a few feet below. I stood up, waves crashing, heart pounding like a hummingbird.

Slowly, through gasps of relief and reclaimed oxygen, I realized the Ozette River had a delta. Sediments from time immemorial, washed by the tannic current and cleaned by the churn of the sea, settled at her mouth in a wide low sand flat. I stood knee deep in the water, whipped, beaten and humbled to my smallest self-perception. I slogged to shore, feeling undeserving of my luck, yet truly blessed for it.

I sat on the beach in a shivering wet heap, Tally licking my face and jumping around as if to say, "What next? This is fun!" I was exhausted. I sat head between my knees and from the same place, deep inside where my primal yell had come from, came humbling sadness and relief. There on the sand on that remote beach, where the Ozette River and the Pacific Ocean perform their disturbed yet magnificent acquaintance ritual, I cried my own river. I cried the tears of fear and sadness from my whole life, all 20 years accumulation.

-•-

In the following weeks I felt something shift inside me. My trip down the Ozette River had put a little salt in my veins but not without a degree of humiliation and respect. Nature was a big thing. It was strong and moved when, where and how it wanted. It paid to respect it. Being enthusiastic and having romantic notions didn't count. Ultimately it controlled me. Perhaps I had been jaded or misled by the world of chain saws and logger mega harvests where man seemed to so harshly conquer and control the forests and rivers and mountainsides.

I found myself in a repeating daydream with a vision of the kayak being sucked off my waist as I struggled with adrenal terror up on to the sweeper that crossed the river. Without admitting it, I knew I had come close to having a short life with a violent end. I imagined what it would be like to drown in that tea brown current sucking me under—the terror, the struggle, the sadness and the overwhelming feeling of no breath as my lungs exploded and life drained from my forever missing body. One instant—young hopeful and strong. The next—limp and lost, left to be churned into micronutrient by the immense power of the river as the cycle of nature disposes of the careless and weak.

It felt like luck had finally given me a break when I convinced Lou to take me on as a cedar bolt cutter. He was a short little Makah Indian who had worked in the forest all his life in all aspects of the industry and was working a claim he'd won in a bid which was asserted to have pretty good wood. Lou was a pleasant fellow, who seemed honest and forthright, and I was excited to get in on some real money and work that wasn't as boringly repetitive as loading trucks hour after hour. He told me he didn't drink as he'd found God. He was also not used to working with anyone but would give it a try for a week and see if he thought he was improving his earnings.

The following morning at 5:30 Lou picked me up with my dog, and he and his ten-year-old son and I bounced and lurched our way up the mountain toward his claim, exchanging pleasantries. He kept repeating that he'd never taken anyone on before and gave the impression he was having a hard time trusting the idea. We spilled thermos cups of hot coffee over our hands and laps as we dodged outbound logging trucks and potholes. Every so often the bottom of that old Ford Falcon would scrape a rock and it felt like someone was dragging a piece of cold rebar right across my butt.

Eventually we came to a spot on the mountainside that was Lou's designated lot and we piled out and went to work. We were several miles up off the shoreline in an enormous clear-cut of jumbled stumps and wood trash so immense it was nearly impossible to traverse on foot. It was an astounding sight more akin to the aftermath of carpet-bombing in a major offensive against the mountainside simultaneously with a catastrophic earthquake. Trees, stumps and large wood refuse littered the hillsides in giant proportions.

We were excavating old cedar logs that had been left or discarded by crews 40 years before because they didn't have value or had fallen too precariously into a ravine to yank out with primitive logging equipment of the day. Loggers affectionately known as "cedar rats" were now reclaiming old growth logs, the size of buses, left to rot but due to the resistant qualities of old growth cedar, a slow process. We used super human strength to dog our enormous chain saws, often with six-foot bars, along with sledges, gas cans, bar oil jugs and wedges down, over, around and under the slash piles looking for these giant grandmother cedar trees.

16

The work was grueling and the rain seemed to seldom stop. It hammered your body struggling beneath your torn rain gear and it hammered your attitude. Footing was slippery and muscles whined. We cut large chunks into 24-inch lengths and split out bolts with froes, wedges and malls that we stacked in bundles for the helicopter ride from the ravines to the logging road where my former miserable coworkers schlepped them aboard flatbed trucks.

Lou mapped our day's work and headed down a draw with his saw that was easily taller than himself. I worked 100 yards away on another log, splitting and stacking. I could hear Lou's sharp saw grind and growl its way through the enormous slabs below me. Lou kept his saws razor sharp, which you could always tell by the sound of the motor as it ground through the thick wood. We'd worked several hours when I heard Lou's saw stop in a muffled choke. The world seemed so silent for an instant.

Then there was a curdling scream from Lou's young son and Lou telling him in a panicky voice to be still. They were rushing up through the wet salal, the boy whimpering sobs and Lou clutching his left hand with his right. It was entirely covered with blood and looked deformed, missing its fingers.

His voice was trying very hard, with little success, to tell me he'd swatted the saw away from his face with his left hand. "I hit a pecker pole with the end of my saw and that son-of-a-bitch rode up and came straight for me, right for my face." Lou stumbled in the mud and collapsed on the ground. He looked up at me with struggling eyes, one hand clutching the remains of the other, and then he fell forward on to the wet ground. His face was ashen, his cheek and eye deep in the mud. His boy screamed.

It was a horror film and we were all main actors. His boy was yelling at him and crying and I was trying to get a grip on what to do. Lou lay in the mud, rain pouring down. His left hand was missing much meat and three or four fingers and was bleeding at an alarming rate, my memory taking pictures I wouldn't soon forget of the blood pumping into the tan muddy puddles.

Rain fell with a careless disregard. Time became warped and actions were laced with panic and terror as I struggled to use any logic. I picked up Lou's good arm and dragged his limp, wet and bleeding body through the mud and brush to the car. His boy was now screaming. Beneath my efforts I could feel my body shaking with terror. "Is Daddy dead? Is Daddy dead?"

I managed to get Lou in the front seat lying down. I yelled at the boy to get in the back seat and shut the fuck up. I found a t-shirt, tore it into strips, tied a strip tightly around his mangled wrist, rolled him on his side and tied his bloody hand up high to the remains of the missing dome light in the middle of the car's ceiling. I put his head in my lap and began to drive down the mountain.

I had no idea where to go or what I was doing so when the boy starting his taunting cry again, "Is Daddy gonna die?", I jabbed my foot into the brake pedal, wheeled in my seat, grabbed him by the chest, pulled him up close and yelled into his tear streaked, terrorized face some three inches away, "I don't know what's gonna happen to your dad, now shut the fuck up." and shoved his frightened, whimpering little body back down into a crumpled heap. I startled myself. I was unraveling and everything seemed chaotic.

Somehow parts of the chaos seemed familiar. I was home and my father was scaring my mother and us kids. The tension was unbearable and I was looking at my mother and big brother to fix it and they couldn't. I was the little boy in the back seat and I had just become the overwhelmingly scary person who offered no sympathy, the one I prayed I would never ever be. We all were immobilized by fear, swimming in clay and drowning one by one. I knew how I'd made the boy feel and remembered with pity myself in such despair. I remember vowing that I would never be that way, that I would be a kind and understanding person regardless. But between the potholes and splashing mud, an apology came hard. " Look," I said, "I'm really trying my best here and I don't know what the fuck I'm doing. Your dad will be okay." My voice sort of went up at the end as if I was asking instead of telling. I concentrated on driving; the boy in the back seat sniffled and whimpered quietly. It was a lousy apology.

Blood was everywhere, but was slowly beginning to stop. Lou was semi-conscious and groaning and asking hard questions. "How bad is it? Will they be able to fix it so I can work?"

I think he knew the answer but I tried to reassure him he'd be okay. Mythical hope. He said we had to go to Port Angeles in order for his medical insurance to work. We were still on the mountain road banging our way to Ozette; Port Angeles was another five hours. Eventually we hit better road and I pushed the pedal to the floor when I could as we zigzagged the long muddy ride toward Port Angeles.

Lou wanted to sit up and he untangled his wrist from the overhead light with the missing lens cover. He wrapped the rest of the t-shirt around his hand and laid it in his lap like a basket of fragile chicken eggs. His face was gray and vacant when he told me to stop the car and get the six-pack of Rainier beer out of the trunk. We drove on, Lou drinking liter size bottles of Vitamin R and staring off into space, no doubt realizing his life had changed for good, the boy sound asleep with tear stained cheeks in the back seat, and me concentrating on ambulance speed driving the roads to Port Angeles General Hospital.

Lou swung his head like an old drunken draft horse in my direction and said, "I've worked alone in the woods all my adult life and never taken on a partner. What would have happened if you weren't there?" He paused and finished with a long gulp of sudsy cheap beer trying to erase the obvious answer.

We arrived after dark. A flurry of nurses and white coats scurried Lou into the bright stainless and Formica world of the ER. He was by now dehydrated, drunk and a filthy bloody mess, nothing these logging town doctors hadn't seen, but he was going to live. His wife showed up and my job was over. I was unbelievably exhausted. I crawled into the back seat of Lou's car in the parking lot and slept where that young boy had been so terrified and alone. I was reminded of his tears and my own disappointing response as I fell asleep.

The next morning I hitchhiked back to Lake Ozette to my little camp and hung out for a few days in a semi-distracted state of emotional paralysis. Eventually I decided the life of a cedar rat wasn't for me. The "stuff of life" was here all right but it seemed a little harsh. It was hard for me to continue to romanticize the clear-cuts and the oil skimmed mud, the groaning diesels and the lack of questioning of their impact on the human spirit, not to mention the brutality when flesh and machine tangled.

I piled my wet and moldy belongings in my van and headed back to Seattle.

Chapter 2

Little Men

Hughie and I spent hours in the upper branches of an old Gravenstein apple tree just outside the kitchen window of our family home. It was a place of refuge eight feet from the ground mostly hidden by limbs and leaves. In our remote little hiding spot we'd talk over the world as five and eight year old boys know it.

My brother was my best friend. We needed to be, we wanted to be, it was easy to be. As we climbed the branches hand over hand and left the world below we freed ourselves from the rigors of school and parents, their world of chaos and rules and entered the lofty world of the fantastic. We played our game of "little men."

We invented miniature tree forts, carefully sewed into the branches of the tree, for our imaginary world where little elf-like men several inches tall would live. It was all a secret world that only we were privileged to know—made of little platforms, whittled and carved, and rope swings made from scraps of string and cut to length so these little people could swing from branch to platform to escape the evils of their scary world. Rose thorns plucked from the stems of roses, collected and carried in dirty pockets up the trunk and pressed point first into the cadmium of apple bark with dirty fingers, produced the perfect size steps. Steps that wandered like zippers by the yard from platform to rope swing to hiding spots throughout the upper branches.

Hours would pass peacefully with the rich undertones of connection. The subject invariably turned toward fantasizing our futures and always about the farms we would own. Our farms were the ultimate destination for both of us. For some reason Hugh, the older brother, always insisted that he'd be the animal farmer and I'd be the truck farmer. I was always a little jealous of this aspect of the planning but was willing to accept my plight if I too could be a farmer. We'd talk for hours of the barns and the fields and crops we'd grow. There would be streams flowing full of trout, ponds full of perch and somehow it would all just be there and it would be ours. For years to follow, the image of rolling green hills and life outdoors tending animals was wonderful music that never stopped its wondrous melody in our minds.

I was born in Boston, Massachusetts, August 21, 1951, smack in the middle of the baby boom generation idolized merely for its sheer numbers and opportunities. An American post-war generation privileged into a new level of health, wealth and privilege unknown in the modern world.

America made history as it entered the nuclear age. 1951, the year I was born, was the year President Harry Truman authorized the first of what would begin a long history of some 900 nuclear tests in the desert outside Las Vegas, Nevada, the city of bright light, young and naïve, famous for roulette tables. Frank Sinatra advertised viewing of these kiloton extravaganzas from the verandas of the luxury hotels, initially oblivious to the health concerns.

Simultaneously, leading nations of the world began an organization headquartered in New York City that strove to improve and protect international security, economic health and human rights known as the United Nations. America was beginning to burst its seams in a multitude of contradictory directions. A loaf of bread and a gallon of gasoline hovered at just under 20 cents, "Rock and Roll" was a coined phrase, "I Love Lucy" was the number one TV show and the media began to find its legs in America's home culture. The first oral contraceptives and the first coast to coast phone calls were offered to the public and the American middle class ate it up.

My parents, like so many at that time, were understandably

caught up in the hope of the American dream, riding the wave of prosperity away from their youthful memories of the Great Depression. Young, attractive and well educated, with hearts and minds full of desire and adventure, they left Boston when I was three weeks old in an old woody station wagon with my older brother, Hughie, and me in the back seat. My father's medical career and training led us south through Georgia, Kansas, and several years later to Missouri where my sister Anna came into the world.

Now with three kids, several dogs and a horse, we were loaded up again and headed for more of my father's training in Ann Arbor, Michigan. We rented an old farmhouse across the road from a large dairy farm where my first real memories manifest. The house we lived in had a sagging front porch and banging screen doors, surrounded by pastures of exhausted looking black and white cows. Hughie and I spent days exploring the farm, climbing trees and running through cow patty corrals. Curiosity had us pestering every bird nest and digging up all the muskrat dens.

My father was finishing his residency as a thoracic surgeon and went to work every morning early and arrived home after the three of us kids were in bed, a habit that was basically repeated for the 18 years I lived at home. Young and bright, his brain was a ravenous creature with a photographic memory that fed on learning. From sports statistics to world history to the cutting edge of cardiac medicine, his Harvard trained mind could gobble and retain scores, historical dates and events, names and information with the sharpness of one of his scalpels.

Unfortunately he had little tolerance for those who didn't possess these qualities and didn't mind intimidating those who struggled with the basics, like his children. He could have argued his way out of the Inquisition and made his accusers ashamed of themselves. Brimming with arrogance, he was the Rasputin of conceit and seemed baffled by those who didn't see it obvious to worship his every opinion.

On weekends there were parties. These hyper-charged get-togethers steam rolled through a Saturday night sloshing booze, sloppy slurs and sloppy hands. Young doctors whose promising careers stretched out in front of them, working hard and playing harder, all the while developing their iron shelled egos. Doctors' wives in the 50's struggled between their roles as mothers and holding their husbands' interest as attractive counterparts. It was a time made for men and their careers while wives scurried to fill the voids, patch the misunderstandings, and come out with perfect hair, a pleasant smile, well-behaved kids and a trim waist. A difficult scenario with often tragic effects.

As a little boy, these parties were frightening. It was the loud voices and raucous laughter or some woozy lost partier looking for a bathroom and stumbling into our bedroom late at night, unaware of their bumbling footsteps or Novocain lips expressing apology, or worse, affection.

After a year in Michigan we packed up the station wagon and headed west in the dead of winter for Seattle where my father had been offered a job at a prestigious clinic and he would be able to pursue his own research in heart medicine. My parents' adventurous spirit jumped on the opportunity and we sped through Midwest snowy blizzards and arrived in the rainy town nestled between inland sea and craggy mountains; its only claim to fame in 1955 was the Smith Tower as the tallest building west of the Mississippi River.

Seattle was a boondocks town whose future was as bright as the sun on a clear day after a long rain. We moved to the suburbs on a small island connected to Seattle by a mile-long floating bridge. Mercer Island, where we began our lives in the great Northwest, had been a farm community with summer homes dotted along the shores of Lake Washington.

By 1957 my parents made a down payment on a Sears designed Craftsman house on the north end of the island on a large waterfront lot. Cuba was experiencing a revolution but America was prospering and our family was one of the lucky ones. The Space Race had begun and by my first year of elementary school the Russians had launched Sputnik, an ICBM propelled satellite that orbited some 600 miles above earth, every 96 hours. As it passed overhead, it reminded us over and over we were not first. America's only response that year was the invention of Tang, a chemically sweet orange drink that astronauts would one day take with them into space as their breakfast beverage. It was a slow start for a nation that wanted to be a leading world power.

My parents were happier than they'd ever been. Three beautiful children, good school districts, a promising job and the untamed Northwest filled with opportunities to hunt, fish, ski, and sail its beautiful inland waters. They were young and the Puget Sound region needed exploring. Interest rates were about 3%, land was cheap, crime was low, medicine knew little of malpractice, and youth of the lucky and the fortunate knew no bounds.

Life was promising. What could go wrong? We were well-bred and well-fed, we had good manners, good haircuts and smiled at the appropriate times. My parents had high ideals for their children and would offer them a clear path for success.

Chapter 3

School

My entire life in school was a continuing series of train wrecks that I would barely survive. It injured and scarred me for the rest of my life.

My mother dressed me in crisp new corduroy pants, a button-down shirt and new leather shoes with sharkskin reinforced toes. I had a lunch pail with a jam sandwich, Oreo cookies and Kool-Aid. I could have jumped from the pages of *Life* magazine as your quintessential American boy full of hope, a good haircut and good fortune as I headed for the school bus.

In 1st grade there were six Jim's so the names were handed out as Jim, James, Jamie, Jimmy, Jim W. and Jimmy Z. I was Jimmy. It was a name I'd tried to graduate from to the older sounding Jim but 1st grade wasn't about advancement for me. I was impish, skinny and not tracking the flow during class. I fell in love with Gigi the first day and I did enjoy tracking her flow. She was cute, animated and the fastest runner at recess. She could answer all the questions in class and was in the best reading group of which there were four.

There was a succession from these superlative gifted chosen brainiacs to the bottom group—those of us disgraced and miserable in group 2 or 3 who couldn't even memorize the few words that showed up repeatedly page after page. Little did I realize these days set up patterns that would continue throughout the rest of my life.

It was the beginning of a long list in school of such humiliations, as the school smart and those not-so-smart were separated.

It was a cruel pecking order whose victims were scorned and cast in their embarrassing roles as "losers" at an early age on the ladder of life.

I wanted to please my teacher but the dots would not connect and there wasn't a lot to do but suffer through.

"Dick." Turn page. My fingers fiddled with my corduroys as I struggled along.

"Dick runs." Turn page.

"Dick runs fast." Turn page. I squirm in my seat when Mrs. Harris corrects me with a gentle voice. Eventually this group of lost illiterates moved to the hallway as the giggles and eye-rolling comments from the other kids proved to be too much.

We sat out there in our little semi-circle of fiberglass bucket chairs next to the coat rack in the long looming corridor, stammering in whispered voices, chins on our chests, while chaos erupted back in the classroom. We acted like we couldn't hear, but kids were frolicking like unleashed hounds in the absence of the teacher and not being with them added to my frustration. I wanted to blend into the herd.

My reading group had Kelly C., a bully who definitely was much older than every other kid in class and ended up prematurely tattooed and in Juvenile Hall by the age of 14 when he was in the 6th grade; Jeffery who was legally blind; and me, sweet and innocent with hemorrhaging self confidence. I think we all passed 1st grade so that Mrs. Harris wouldn't have to repeat her poorly paid time in the hallway with us. My report card said, "Satisfactory work progress, although finds work difficult." Gigi's report card was passed around the school bus with gleaming perfect scores. We never spoke a word the entire year.

2nd grade was more of the same. Gigi wasn't there but Theresa was and she was an excellent artist with silky, white blond hair that was always clean and swishy. I stared at the back of her head during class and worked on my art skills so she might notice me.

Reading group remained a torture. The humiliation continued, and when the teacher called us to the hallway a wave of nervous dread washed over me with a crippling anxiety.

Our little group was a hopeless cluster of nice guys finishing last. I didn't want to be a part of them. They were the incompetent, the butt of jokes, the losers, the unpopular. We had bad carburetors or bad fuel, bad tires or we couldn't see, and we chugged and sputtered, stopped and started, with very little progress. Life was trying to cull us from the herd, but no one wanted to state the obvious and put us out of our misery.

One evening the following summer my mother read me a story as I lay tucked in bed. Her soft voice seemed to hold me in a warm and loving place. I loved being read to at bedtime, my mind creating vivid images in a safe blanket of nurturing warmth. But that night she turned the book toward me and asked me to read to her. I could tell it was a test. Much lay in my performance and I squirmed in my pajamas at the request.

I looked at the book. My eyes glared at the words hoping they might finally make sense, and as panic set in my ears heard the rushing sounds of the wind in leaves of aspen trees growing louder and louder and then my eyes rolled off the page. My mother anxiously encouraged me but to no avail. She was incredulous and began to find less difficult books and coaxed me to read a little. I knew this was important to her and I knew I couldn't do it. The nervous dread was an uncomfortable probe that jabbed and poked at my intestines like a hot nail as I squirmed, knowing I was disappointing my mother like I had my teachers.

I was a calf being cut from the herd and tied bawling to a fence, waiting to be branded, while my mother and father tried to wrap their heads around what had made me so insubordinate as to not apply myself to school and learn the basics. It was not only inconceivable, it wouldn't be tolerated.

My parents in their swollen indignity called my teacher and, after a tersely direct conversation I overheard from the next room, my mother insisted I be held back. I was mortified. My parents flunked me, not my teacher.

2nd grade the second time wasn't much easier and now, under the watchful eye of my continually disappointed parents, I began what was to follow me for years: tutoring, summer schools and special classes after school. Good intentions that only seemed to pound in the fact that I wasn't teachable.

While the entire population of kids was let loose like wild horses stampeding out the front door of the school at 3:30 in the afternoon to romp and play in the wilds of our suburban neighborhood, my life took another direction. My mother's station wagon was waiting when school was let out and I was whisked away to Mrs. Besieu's school for the learning disabled. I sat in colorless rooms sounding out vowels and making phonic noises, like a bird recovering from nasal surgery, all the while my mind drifting off in different directions. I was wondering why and how Mrs. Biseau had purple-blue hair, what my friends were doing, wondering if dust made a sound when it fell, wondered what girls looked like naked. I trudged through the afternoons pleasantly sweet but increasingly lost.

We'd drive home after several hours of fruitless coaching, my progress as gloomy and dark as the wintry Northwest afternoon. Mrs. Besieu was nice but ineffective. My parents became gravely concerned. I wasn't up to par with other kids my age and was rapidly slipping backwards despite all their efforts. In our home scholastic and eventually athletic achievement was the passport to acknowledgement and recognition or, in more simple terms, it's what you needed to do to be loveable and important.

Many a night I sat squirming on my chair at the dinner table, struggling to give a reason for my failures in school with the tourniquet tightening around my stomach as I gave testimony from my lousy list of inadequate excuses. "I try. I promise I'm trying," the tears rolling down my cheeks. "I don't know why I can't do what everyone else is doing." I began to throw up after meals as the tension was overwhelming. They were convinced I was not trying hard enough. I would glance at Hughie for support but it was a world with no hope. Anna sat staring at her plate, slow motion tension for all.

My self-esteem draining like an open sore, I felt a failure not worth my parents' love. I couldn't do school and my self-worth was hanging in balance. I used to think, "If I could only get good grades, they would smile and laugh and hold me tight. Then I would be okay."

In the 4th grade my desk was front and center in a large class for optimal attention, an arrangement made by my father. Toward the end of the year Mrs. Dorlack, my young, serious and ever vigilant teacher, had been on recess duty and had seen some bad acting between a few rough boys and in a very distraught effort endeavored to show the entire class what she had seen. One boy had taken the arm of another and forced it behind his back.

To illustrate this, she grabbed me from my desk in the front of the room, her eyes knitted in concentration, and using herself as the victim had me hold her arm behind her back to illustrate her point. When to her disbelief the bully forced the victim's arm skyward, I thought as part of the reenactment I was supposed to do the same. I shoved hard. There was a small audible crack, a pause, and a silence and Mrs. Dorlack ran wincing from the room holding her distressed arm as tears ran from her reddening eyes. And there I was standing up in front of the class, all eyes upon me, feeling terrified.

Someone shouted out across the class, "Man, you're gonna get it." A verbal spear thrust to my gut and the class erupted with hoots and hollers of condemnation. I would never be popular. They really hated me now. They pecked and pecked. I sat back down at my desk with my head in my arms, crying, when the classroom door swung open and the principal, Mr. Wiley, marched in red-faced. His tie thrown over his shoulder and with his belly bulging over his belt, he grabbed my little one piece desk by the back of the chair and whisked it and me in it across the floor, out the door and down the hall to his office. I was mortified. Tears smeared my face.

There in front of the main admittance office, my desk and I were to reside for the remaining several weeks where my assignments were delivered. Day after day I sat, humiliated like a bad dog, eating my gruel and relenting to the thick harness that my life had tightened around me.

In the 60's, at 6:00 every evening Chet Huntley and David Brinkley delivered the evening news through our modern black and white Motorola TV. My father was usually absent as we all stared at the bright illumine, grinding down our daily bread. They gave their "hard as rock" delivery with a seriousness designed to cheer up no one. Hair greased back and scowling, they peered into the camera and volleyed their humorless stories like CIA agents. "Chet? Yes, David. Back to you, David." We watched back with serious knitted brows.

My mother hated the ads and would lunge from the table to turn down the volume whenever there was a break. We three kids drooled food in a TV-mesmerized trance as we made an effort to lip read the lady in the pretty smock talking about Bayer Aspirin and the relief she experienced in her miraculous recovery from a headache. Suddenly in the silence the ad would be over and Chet would be lip-syncing dead air and my mother would lunge back for the volume knob and immediately ask what he was talking about. She was desperate for adult interaction and we were desperate to be entertained. We didn't do much to help each other.

It was a time when a young, handsome college schoolmate of my father's ran and won the presidency of the United States. My parents were ecstatic. John Kennedy had a refreshing charismatic quality and they hung on every word of his televised speeches. The first troops were sent to Vietnam to help the French fight the Viet Cong. The "Pill" was changing the concept of sex, and the youth of the country began questioning the basic tenets of traditional social values which in part opened Pandora's box into political questioning. A tsunami was forming that put the "Ozzie and Harriet" American dream story into question. Hughie and I were loaded in the cannon of youth dissent and, like millions more, exploded into exciting and difficult times untethered by parental respect.

My father's career too was changing. He was moving from the confines of research to the more publicly rewarded world of open heart surgery and notoriety. The hard work was rewarded with weekend parties, usually with other doctors and their wives, but always with plenty of drinks and the volume turned up on excess.

As children, we filtered around the edges in our Bermuda shorts, Vitalis smeared hair and button-down shirts. We were the progeny and the medallions of lucky good parenting and were expected to be obedient and cute with a smile. My mother was the marionette conductor who tried to keep our family organized and within reach, but as the 60's unfolded it was a time of increasing chaos—more like a full wet paper bag of marbles that eventually splits open and scatters in fast moving obtuse directions out of control.

In the 5th grade I was sent to a special private school that required a long ride in a taxi twice a day. There was a uniform and a church service before classes. My smaller class was filled with other "special" kids needing extra attention and it all felt careful and sort of filled with Pablum soft gloves which was like living in a nauseating fairytale, easier but unreal. I was now the "special" kid in the family and the "special" attention was not good for my standing with my friends and siblings.

I was marked and getting more attention than I wanted. The tension was unbearable and my vomiting was now a daily activity. Sometimes in secret, and sometimes I'd make an exaggerated display to get out of going to school if I knew there was going to be a test or some other humiliating experience. Throwing up became a common maneuver and I was all too familiar with the linoleum floor and the commode. Either way, I was becoming increasingly frail, small and skinny, with a little bloated stomach that was as volatile as January weather.

I got a lot of attention for being sick; not a lot of it was very positive. My mother was very caring but my sickness, with no real diagnosis, was pushing on her patience. She struggled between her deep love of her child and her pity for my suffering and a fear that it might be a ploy. The doctors couldn't find anything. It was the age of blind faith in authority and the medical world found nothing wrong with me. In our house, if the medical world found nothing, then nothing was there.

In the 6th grade I discovered a magical relief valve. Mr. Bauer, an exhausted greasy haired version of Ichabod Crane, handed out a pop quiz one day. Adrenalin coursed through me as I hadn't read the chapter because whenever I read anything, after several sentences the words began to blur and my vision would skip off the page. The rustling sound of the aspen leaves became a white noise in my ears and my mind would drift quickly downstream to other subjects. My head became a warehouse full of dusty mattresses and I couldn't think.

The clock was ticking loudly over the door in the room of silent students. With one hand on my brow and the other clutching a sweaty pencil, I stared at the page bargaining with the gods for relief. I had been through this a hundred times before. The outcome was predictable. The leaves rustling in my ears were deafening.

I glanced out at the class, who were all diligently giving it their best, and there on the desk across from me Vaughn Alexander's test paper was in clear view. There were the answers and Vaughn was pretty smart. My quick eye memorized the patterns of dots in the multiple choice maze and transferred them nonchalantly to my own test page. It was easy. I glanced over again and again. It was exhilarating. The bell rang and we all ran for the playground.

I felt light and full of excitement. I'd dodged the bullets of humiliation perhaps and avoided the snapping jaws of parental condemnation. I played joyfully. I had found a way to look and feel normal. Maybe I could at least fade into an average obscurity.

The tests came back the next day and I gloated over the B+ written at the top of the page in red ink. There was an exclamation point behind it. I wanted to pin this paper to my chest and wear it to recess and home to show my mother but I knew I couldn't make it obvious. I was beaming. I felt relief I didn't realize possible.

I felt sort of normal and even while immersed in my own deception, I told myself that I was smart like everyone else. That was a haunting concept and the truth bobbed to the surface of my conscience and I struggled with it for years to come. But for the time being I was in scholastic heaven. At that point my entire focus in school changed and I began inventing creative ways of cheating. Seating arrangements and particular students became vital to this strategy. Cheating made the world take less interest in me and my stomach generally liked this.

In my creative desire to become more adept at my new skill, I developed new, more involved and riskier behaviors. I volunteered to be on window duty on Fridays which basically meant I was supposed to close and lock the windows. This was one of those menial tasks handed to teach responsibility to those who were looking to get on the teacher's good side. I routinely raised my hand and would leave one window latch slightly ajar so that Saturday morning I could return to the empty school, slither through the open window, open the teacher's desk and alter the little green shiny-sided grade book that held the scores of my classmates and me. In moments of a new found anger, I even took the liberty of lowering the grades of a few who never struggled and always got A's. It was all too easy sitting there deciding how successful to make myself, to make my life with a few strokes of an eraser and a pencil.

This plan was almost thwarted by a weekend janitor who pushed a dust broom down the main hall right past the classroom and just missed seeing me through the window in the doorway. I dropped and hid under the teacher's desk, praying he hadn't heard a noise and would glare through the window and investigate, see the opened window where I had entered the classroom and then find me hunched in a crying sweat with the tampered grade book in hand. But I snuck out and ran, guilt and dread propelling my speedy feet.

Then one Friday afternoon as the class was taking another history test and I was stealing glances with audacious disregard at Vaughn's test paper, Mr. Bauer slammed a yardstick down on his desk with a thunderous clap and yelled in a voice that had every 6th grader in the room terrified, "Cheater!" He was glaring at me with a falcon's eye and a high blood pressure reddened face. His right arm shot out and he pointed at me with a long, stiff boney finger repeating, "Cheater, cheater, cheater!" as he marched with pounding feet over to my desk. He grabbed me by the shoulder and scurried me down the hall to the principal's office, a fury of lectures and spittle spewing from his angry mouth.

By now I was crying and flailing about, but his grip was menacingly strong and I knew I was the next meal for him and the villainous principal and for that matter, my parents. I was trying to escape and wanted to run. I squirmed and fought to get away. I wanted to run into the woods and live alone in one of the forts Hughie and I had made and never think about this moment again. I died a little death as they yelled questions and threats. They whispered to each other and then they yelled at me again. Then they called my parents. Recess had started and lots of kids rushed to the office and were staring through the hallway window at the grueling dismemberment of my life while I was being torn limb from limb, blood and spirit splattering on the walls.

When I got home, I was sent to my room. I cried. I promised. I pleaded. I was punished. I said I was sorry, but down deep inside I knew I would not quit. The benefits were too good and I liked feeling normal more than I hated their punishments.

The conflict within was tortuous but the pressure of scholastic survival in our family always led me back to cheating. I just needed to get better at it and that I did. The goal was to get a B average which kept me out of sight from the power people. I wanted to be forgettable, out of the spotlight. First offense was bad enough. I didn't want to guess what would happen if I got caught again.

November 21, 1963, my father left on one of his numerous medical trips, this time to Dallas, Texas, otherwise a forgettable event. I was sitting at my desk in Mr. Bauer's class when Debbie Larsen, the studious office monitor from our class, entered and announced in a loud interruptive voice, "Mr. Bauer, President Kennedy has been shot in Dallas, Texas." She proceeded to burst into tears and stood sobbing as Mr. Bauer hurried past her to the office. It was true, our president was dead, the gunman at large.

With the absence of the teacher, the class erupted into a crazed mob of giddy conspirators firing comments out into the room like fireworks. "My parents hated him," one said. "It was probably the Russians," said another. "You know my uncle says the world's gonna end." But for me a secret, dreaded thought crowded out the banter as I became fixated on the fact that my father was in Dallas. Did he kill the president? I thought he liked him. I knew he was capable. I had seen him angry enough to kill someone, I think. I sat silently with my secret fears.

We were let out of school early and I ran down the trail through the woods to our home to find my mother standing at the kitchen sink crying. She had just gotten off the phone with my father and the two of them were devastated. This was America's version of royalty and for my parents and many others, John Kennedy's articulate visions of hope and leadership were unprecedented. Both my mother and father had known John and Jackie years before and their loss felt personal. For several weeks there was quiet gloom around the house, like the family dog had died, and my parents spoke little.

I continued my devious ways of passing tests but it was a tight rope with continued tension. The stomach aches continued and by the 7th grade I was missing a lot of school and vomiting two or three times a day. Perhaps the pressures of my dishonest lifestyle pushed down into my guts or just unlucky chemistry. I was in pain most of the time, generally after eating, and I spent many an hour in the fetal position on the floor beside the toilet. My sister Anna, younger by three years, and I were the same size—she a robust young girl and me a skinny, shivering little boy all ribs, elbows and kneecaps.

My mother began to worry in a big way. She could tell it wasn't me just wanting to miss school, or that I suffered from a normal flu, and took me to different hospitals and different specialists. So between school and the tutoring after school, I spent time going to doctors trying to figure out why I was doubled over and vomiting so much. Life wasn't fun. I was serving a life sentence in a prison of unhappiness and it looked like there was no chance for parole.

Doctors with latex-gloved fingers, gooped with cold lubricant jellies, took turns probing my rectum or pushing on my aching stomach feeling for answers. If that humiliation wasn't enough, the notorious open-back gowns were. At 13, I was becoming increasingly self-conscious about my looks and much of my pubescence was spent walking the corridors of hospitals hunched over in a painful grimace trying to cover my butt with a robe that always felt three sizes too small.

I was given chalky liquids that tasted like nightmare milkshakes as doctors with rubber moon gloves pushed the most tender, painful parts of my bowels on chilly tables under giant scopes with terrifying x-ray power. Then there were the pillowcase size bags of barium liquid hanging from a pole at the foot of the exam table. From this bag was a hose that was inserted up the business end of my lower G.I. Then some ghoulish nurse, with a brain missing its empathy factor, would squeeze that pillow bag and force that chalky barium up a wrong way street of my large intestine. With an inflamed gut, this had me flopping about like a trout on a dock begging for mercy. "Just a little more, a little more," the doctor would say, as I felt like ten weeks of bowel movements were about to come out my tear ducts as they gushed past the big, red Do Not Enter sign on my sphincter.

When the doctor would finally say that's enough, I was to slide from the cold metallic table and run down the hall to a toilet, barium spewing from my rear, open wet gown flapping as my exposed red butt passed the young, cute, bashful-eyed candy stripers and warm-bosomed grandmother nurses. Life was a humiliating bad dream that wouldn't end.

It took a year of head-scratching doctors to come up with basically nothing and my parents once again began to believe it was a ploy on my part to skip school. That part wasn't all incorrect but there was something wrong as I was definitely in a lot of pain.

"Come on Jimmy!" my mother would plea with me to stop complaining, suggesting I needed to get a little tougher and learn to cope. I hung my head over the toilet like the last moments of the persecuted, waiting for the guillotine. "Now get up and get ready for school."

She was mostly speaking from a point of desperation as her belief system wanted to trust the world of medicine; if they were unable to find something, there must be nothing there. But the part of a child who knows the truth about their parent could tell she was scared, and she was stuck in a world and time where mother's intuition wasn't worth an argument. She mouthed the words she'd been told by the confident world of Western medicine. I headed off to school, hunched over with an ache in my stomach and a subconscious fear that my ruse of scholastic success was based on a weak-kneed survival plan. But it was the best I could do.

About one month before summer in 7th grade, I lay in bed complaining and pleading with my mother not to send me to school. After eating breakfast, I ran to the toilet and hurled my scrambled eggs into the toilet bowl once again. Something snapped in my mother, and we loaded into the car and headed to my father's clinic.

I got the routine exam but this time, as the doctor came into the room staring at his clipboard mumbling medical jargon to himself, he stopped, looked over his half glasses and said, "This boy has acute appendicitis; we need to operate at once."

A fairly simple answer after all the months of questioning. Part of me was filled with dread and part of me was excited. Missing more school was great and being in bed and being able to watch TV all day sounded good but the idea of being cut open and cutting something out of me sounded terrifying.

I was shuttled into the inner catacombs of the hospital, stuck with IV's, draped in white and faded green sheets, and before late afternoon I was watching the dreary overhead lights in the hallways drift by my gurney in a stressless, drug induced haze. All went black, void of landscape and memory. Anesthesia relieved all questions, all time, all light and I slipped backwards down the throat of the clock with no numbers. Some undistinguishable time later my mind woke but my eyes remained shut. There was talking in the room from a number of concerned sounding people including my mother and father. I peered out from the bottom of a deep well.

"Who should tell him?" one said. My eyes winced opened. The room was filled with doctors. Something was wrong. Too much attention. "I will," a doctor said, stepping forward. My mother rushed to my side when she saw me wake and held my hand. Someone spoke. "Jimmy, we opened you up and it wasn't your appendices."

The sensations from my waist reached my sobering brain, and it felt like I'd been sliced in two and sewn back together. I turned my head and vomited into someone's hands trying to get a kidney pan under my mouth. "You have a disease called Crohn's Disease that infects your terminus ileum. . ." My mind sped away to the sound of rustling aspen leaves in my ears. It sounded like trouble.

Here are all these people, including my father. My father generally meant trouble, discipline or something serious. Was I going to die? I'm in trouble again. My mother holding on to me with anxious hands. "Terminus ileum" I heard one say again, "deep tissue infection means bed rest." My eyes struggled to open, wincing at the light, words were coming in fragments. Drugs to keep you comfortable, rest, watch TV. Their faces were the give-away.

They were all feigning cheeriness, talking gently to the little sick boy in bed but their expressions and knitted brows said volumes about how concerning my situation was. I lay there motionless, frightened. I had woken up in the wrong bad dream. Then all the white coats filed out, speaking in muffled tones pregnant with innuendo and concern.

I lay there for weeks, living off intravenous fluids with a steady drip of morphine, barely conscious enough to operate the TV clicker. I passed the hours peeing and being pleasant to the nurses and visitors, most of them friends of my father.

Occasionally I was wheeled down the hall to a room of young, opaquely green-gray looking people with horrible looking bandages and medical anomalies. They frightened me and I didn't like being included with such sick kids. Some days there were new kids pushing their own IV poles and some days kids were missing which led to the question whether they were dead or had gone home. We were a glut of young people with terrifically serious medical conditions in common, not much else. Some looked like lifers, some weren't any happier than I to be there. Medicine fighting to reverse what nature does so naturally, culling the weak.

I remember two nurses in particular. Miss Ing was a tiny Asian woman whom I couldn't understand due to her thick accent, so I always just smiled, nodded and said "yes" when she was in the room which worked quite well. When she left she'd always turn and say "Bseenya", whatever that meant, probably something in Japanese. The other woman came in three or four times in blue surgical scrubs. She was young and pretty and her name was Rhonda. Her blue eyes looked at me with a curious nervous intensity. I didn't know who she was but she seemed to know me. Her adoring friendliness had an eerie subliminal awkwardness to it. She said she was a friend of my father.

After six weeks on IV, the needle in my arm was removed and my skinny little vitaminless body needed to eat real food. They figured between rest and the handfuls of steroids I was ingesting, I was ready for a low residue diet. That meant Jell-O, weak tea and canned asparagus tips, warmed and colorless dissolving in my mouth like forced medicine kicking at my gag reflexes as it slithered down my throat.

Somewhere in the paper work of the industrial kitchen that served the canned goods and death slop that the American hospitals seem to deem as nutritious, I was brought a tray of canned peaches and iceberg lettuce. This was the perfect high roughage diet for some overweight customer down the hall, but not in my intestinal track that was a barbecue of cooling embers. It reacted as a dose of gasoline. Moments after cleaning my plate I was on the floor groping for the clicker that called the nurse, my stitches bleeding, my stomach convulsing, vomiting on the antiseptically cleaned linoleum.

I spent several more weeks on IV's, under the concerned eyes of the medical staff, before I was released and sent home. I left the hospital in a wheelchair looking like a thin bag of wet kindling.

Things around the house were different. My mother had momentarily taken up smoking, a perverse comfort. She and my father sat on the deck biting the filter tips talking over my prognosis. My brother and sister looked at me like I was made of crackly antiqued glass ready to shatter, resentment seething between the lines of their caring comments. My dad wasn't around much. He was developing a state of the art surgical team that justified his long hours away from home, 12 to 14 a day. I thought all fathers worked this hard and just accepted it at the time.

This left parenting to my mother whose love was obvious despite her inner conflict between her rigid parochial upbringing in New England and a free spirit that had escaped to the West coast. Her cooking didn't help my recovery as she seemed to always find food a distraction to her time spent involved in the world. Food was a nuisance that she shoveled in front of us as needed, a fast and furious event she was always willing to finish so she could get to the more important parts of her day. That summer I literally survived on canned asparagus tips, Jell-O, white rice and tea. Anything else sent my stomach rolling and thundering into a groaning cramped day in bed.

By the end of summer, I was ordered to stay in bed until 10:00 in the morning to rest. My diet had expanded to milk shakes made of a blender full of raw eggs, sugar, milk and a splash of vanilla. This was to help swallow the handful of steroids and antibiotics that were to cool off the infection that lay restless in my intestines and also to help put weight on my prison camp looking scatter of flesh and bones that rendered me shivering and slightly bluish in color. As young ill children often are, I was sweet and appreciative in my world of adult care and concern. There were those unanswerable, nondiscussed questions of "why me?" and "am I going to die?" and "why can't I just be normal?" that created an empathetic bond among those who nursed me toward health.

I spent hours in my bedroom. Beautiful hardcover books were stacked high on either side of my bed as gifts from well-meaning people, but they stared at me like a thousand menacing Indian warriors atop swift horses, high on the ridge of the box canyon I was trapped in, their spears and arrows ready to remind me they were the enemy. We didn't speak a common language. Sooner or later I would have to deal with them, or could I escape through life without being able to read? Knowing this made the moth in my stomach flutter and restlessly clang.

A friend of the family dropped by one day and told me she had a gift for me and to look in her car in the box in the back. I figured it was more books or a plastic model airplane which I had assembled plenty of in my long hours.

I was shocked and delighted when I opened the box to find a baby raccoon. It was love at first sight and Dolly and I became inseparable buddies for the next year. She followed me everywhere and I spent endless hours watching her antics, her clever hands that were both gentle and fierce. She rested on my shoulders as I pedaled my bike and slept beside me in bed, all the while chattering and rolling her R's.

Those months following my surgery were much the happier with my little half wild friend. Later in the fall, when the air became sharp and the leaves clattered in the wind across the driveway, Dolly disappeared and as I wiped the tears from my eyes my mother told me she'd probably found a mate. Who knows? That little animal opened up a big part of my heart and awakened my desire to be closer to natural things.

I passed the 7th grade despite missing the last month of school. By the time school started the next fall I had left death's door and was feeling better. I wasn't feeling sidelined and distracted as much by abdominal pains and 8th grade was a sort of emotionally good time when I was at school. There was a skinny young girl in my class who I thought was the cutest thing since new-born puppies. Becky and I became best friends in a brotherly sisterly sort of way. We spent most of our extra time together and stole as many hours as possible on the phone at night.

At our house everything was controlled right down to the telephone. With a single line and no "call waiting", I was relegated to two minutes for my phone calls and only for schoolwork; this because my father was always potentially getting a life and death phone call. And when he wasn't home my mother was perpetually wondering where my father was so she needed the line to be free.

Becky and I devised a method where I'd pretend we were doing important homework and if I mentioned Nikita Krushchev's name it was our code that someone had entered the room. "So I hear there's a party this weekend at Ellen's. Yah wanna go?... Krushchev." Hysterical laughter on the other end of the phone and a dead silence at my end, waiting for curious ears to leave the room.

Built in the late 60's, our house was a two story shoebox with cheap paper thin walls and heater ducts that broadcast noise like an intercom system throughout the house to a family of discontented curious spies. I learned this one evening when I was in my room playing with Dolly and I heard my father's voice on the phone. It wasn't the normal tone of authority and medical discussions. It had a different tone than I was used to and it caught my ear. He was upstairs, in what he thought was the privacy of his bedroom, sitting on the edge of his bed talking softly into the phone. Little did he realize that 16 inches below his head, on the floor, was the heater vent and it broadcast his conversation throughout the downstairs through the vents that were in our ceilings.

His conversation left me shocked, feeling betrayed and seriously angry. It was an anger that lasted for many years and swept up a lot of rage and other short-fused emotions with it, an anger that permeated my relationship with my father for many years. He was talking to a woman in a charming manner with silly jokes and coy flirtatious innuendos that made the hairs bristle on my skinny little neck. I'd never heard him talk to my mother that way. She had been encouraged to attend a PTA meeting alone as he was just too tired. The conversation was planning a rendezvous on his next medical meeting. His voice was whispered and secretive. Cutting corners on building expenses for our cheap house had just cost him much more than a little insulated sound proofing might ever have cost.

My life became an angered distraction. How could he? How could he lie to my mother, to all of us? I would never respect him again. Did my mother know? What was I supposed to do with such information? He'd been so harsh with me about my grades and how I conducted myself in school. Now it felt like a war, I was so angry. I heard him call her Rhonda. She was the pretty scrub nurse who'd given me the eerie uncomfortable feelings when I was in the hospital.

I felt a fury, an angry beast ripping at my body not knowing how to get out. He was lying to me, my mother, our whole family and acting the virtues of authoritative importance. I couldn't look at him, I was so upset. It wasn't hard as he wasn't home much anyway which led my overly exaggerative mind to create sadly depressing scenerios as to where he was. I carried the secret and a lot of the garbage that came with it for many years.

I heard other conversations. He was home less and less. I copied down the mileage on his car and kept track of how far he'd driven. I watched my mother and wondered what I would say. I read a lot into her seemingly full court press toward my father in an effort to look more attractive or to appear younger. She was continually distracted by her intuitive fear of him losing interest.

Whenever he announced he was to go to a medical meeting where he would be away for a few days, I always felt like shouting for him not to come home, but I remained silent until one evening my sadness and rage seemed too much and I ventured a conversation about it with Hughie in the confines of his bedroom.

We had learned to silently stand on a chair and tape a piece of cardboard over the heater vent. He'd been tracking the same information and the relief of sharing our burdens brought us together in a great way. I was 14 and he 17. After a long heated conversation, we decided we were going to kill this woman named Rhonda if she didn't comply with our letters of demands and disappear from the Northwest without our father knowing where she was. We each were experienced enough with a shotgun and it seemed like a reasonable response to protect my mother and our family.

We typed up dozens of versions of our ultimatums on an old typewriter and vented much anger through those keys. Hughie, with his driver's license, had followed my father and knew where she lived. We stuck a final draft in an envelope and would deliver it as soon as we could borrow a car. I returned to my room trying to feel good about what we were going to do. If nothing else, it felt good to have someone else in on this secret we each had carried like a ton of bricks.

The next night we met again and after the cardboard was in place over the heater duct we talked and realized our conviction of shooting this woman had drained away somewhat with the writing of the letter and talking about it. Hugh took the envelope from its hidden spot, lit it with a match and dropped the flaming death sentence into his little metal waste can. Moments later a voice yelled down the stairwell. "You boys smell smoke down there? What on earth are you up to?" A pause and Hugh's grinning calming voice, " Nothing, Mum, we're just doing a science experiment." "Okay, just be careful."

We had decided not to hurt or kill the woman we saw as ruining our family. The secrets continued, but at least there was comfort in the misery while we watched our deceived mother hold down the family that was steeped in lies, silence and alcohol. My father was in the power years of his drinking career and his rage and miscalculation of the world around him was in full swing.

This lasted about a year and then Hughie left for college. His presence was sorely missed. Since we were children the world always worked better for me with Hughie around. I felt lost and alone and trapped by this horrible situation.

Shortly after getting my driver's license, instead of enjoying the freedom of wheels and escape, I found myself wanting to purposely crash the car. Drive off the road into a tree and break my left arm if that were possible. Being right-handed, breaking my left arm seemed like a good way to sustain injury and get a little sympathy at home and at school and thus have a normal family like everyone else. I thought my parents might come together if I could distract them with a crisis. It was perverse but felt awkwardly right.

I envisioned them rushing to my hospital bed and, realizing what was important, stop the tragic familial bloodletting and we could be a family again. I had the tree picked out, a large maple tree about a quarter mile from the house. Instead of stopping at the stop sign, I'd fly right across the street and slam into it. But I just could never figure out how to crash and not either kill myself or break more than my left arm. Eventually I abandoned the idea as too risky.

When at home I retreated to my room away from the tensions elsewhere in the house, and there I became reclusive wiling away the hours carving, listening to music, waiting for the day I would leave for good. One day there was a quiet knock on my bedroom door and my mother walked in red faced, her eyes staring through flooded sockets, and burst into tears. "Do you think your father's having an affair?" She was sobbing while trying to hold her last tattered shreds of dignity together. It was hard to see my tall, composed mother so upset.

It felt like a time to purge my secrets and I sputtered out everything I'd been holding in for the last several years. She sobbed and asked me what she should do. She lay like broken glass on my bed convinced her marriage was over, her life was scorned by this failure, and she would never be able to show her face on either coast again. I felt sorry for her and we talked all afternoon. She was full of questions and desperation. I felt like I was supposed to know the answers but, like school with reading, I had no idea what way was up.

My anger at my father was obvious, as it was hard to see her so pathetic and emotionally beaten. She was angry, sad and desperate and for weeks this conversation seemed to become a daily event. She'd burst into my room in tears and would worry and wonder what she should do. My natural instinct was to try and help her and it helped me be angry at my father, who was never a presence at these discussions, but needless to say it went way too far.

At the age of 16, I became totally immersed in their relationship and thus neglected my own life. I felt responsible, my mother had come to me, and I was under the naive impression I somehow was important in solving their problem marriage.

It was the age of valium and a time when if a family had a house and a car and you were beautiful, then there were no problems. We were to act as if nothing was going on, dress well, smile and act cheerful.

I drove my mother to a psychiatrist once a week as the load of valium she was ingesting rendered her too numb to navigate. I would wait in the station wagon, the rain splashing off the windshield, listening to rock and roll through a three inch speaker. These clandestine trips were never to be discussed along with dozens of other emotional war injuries. They were silently filed away in the closets of messy rooms with locked doors, never to be mentioned again.

Chapter 4

The Summer of Lost Innocence

Summers were my salvation. It was the summer between my sophomore and junior years when a neighbor, who was a bush pilot, helped me find work on a farm. It was in the woods of British Columbia on a homestead miles from the end of the nearest road. It was the summer I almost killed myself, not intentionally but near dead none-the-less .

I was working for Bunch and Oscar, two older folks who'd grown up on homesteads far from humanity and were the most diversely capable as well as the two most antisocial people I'd ever met. They were in a silent war with each other clinging to religious duty and a waning desire for companionship. Despite all, I was relieved to be away from home and learning more about a life I had only fantasized about with Hughie.

The farm was the most beautiful place I'd ever seen. The neighbor had flown there in his tiny seaplane. Tucked up on a wide bench with a view of the Euchiniko River, their modest log house with sod roof, rail fences and log barns was the stuff of my fantasies since I was very young. All heavy work was done on horseback or with draft horses and days were unencumbered by any noise from combustion engines or the low hum of electrical appliances. Other than the couple's lousy company, I had never been in a place I so adored. I spent long summer evenings walking the river banks, fly fishing for fat trout and enjoying the wildlife and pristine beauty.

This was in extreme contrast to my life back home where life around the house was a clustered broken tangle and at school where I was playing football in front of cute coeds or pumping up school spirit to hyper proportion. Academia was a nightmare I was momentarily able to avoid. It was a freedom I reveled in. I felt like Piglet in *Winnie the Pooh*, rolling in the mud after a bath. Spread it everywhere. I couldn't get enough. It was such a relief to be happy.

I loved these remote woods but always secretly longed for a beautiful girl to bound out of the trees onto the trail and desire all this beauty that so intoxicated me. She would want me badly, take me into the shade of a large hemlock and ravage me in the soft pine needles below. There were lots of lonely hours in the woods that summer I was 16.

The aspen leaves rippled tranquilly, the river gurgled and I imagined that I was the only person to ever stand on the ground beneath my feet. On one such evening I came across a young fledgling crow sitting on a pine branch about waist high. I calmly walked up to it, put my finger under his chest, and he stepped confidently onto my hand.

Oddly this little soul had no parents creating a ruckus, so I walked back to my cabin with this little black fuzzball bobbling along on my finger. I jammed a stick in one corner of the log walls which became his new home. His name became CW Moss named for Bonnie and Clyde's sidekick and in the following weeks he was my only friend. I walked the game trails along the river after work as CW flew from limb to limb, squawking and dive-bombing my hat, which was total entertainment in the vacuum of Bunch and Oscar's silent anti-social behavior.

One morning after an early breakfast of moose meat and pancakes, the three of us, after minimal discussion, headed out the door in three different directions. I was to go up river a mile or so until I found a pine thicket suitable for fence rails, cut and peel as many as I could all day, and be home for dinner at six. Oscar would come up with the team later in the week and skid them home.

I grabbed a sharp double-bladed ax, a peeling spud and a bag of lunch and headed out. CW was in close pursuit making everything entertainment as we wandered up river on that hot August morning. A mile or so up river I turned up a creek bed and walked until the pines looked to be the right size. The morning passed as I felled dozens of small poles, limbing, peeling and stacking them. CW squawked and flew about and the sweat dripped from my nose. What happened next is a blurry memory.

There was a noise in the thicket not too far away. It could have been a moose, it might have been a bear but it was definitely big enough to give me a start. My body was delivering the ax into the crotch of a downed pole with all my strength when my concentration broke and the gleaming leading tooth of the ax glanced off the wood and drove deep into my right foot.

I sucked air through my teeth as I looked down recoiling as if to distance myself from the incredulous sight. My boot cut clean away fell off exposing the bone and flesh of my now cleft foot. I grabbed my ankle with both hands and my thoughts shot into warp speed ricocheting from their tranquil hot summer slumber. "Oh, shit!" I thought, "I might not be able to play football this fall. Where am I? Nobody knows where I am." Blood spurted up like a hyperactive drinking fountain when I relaxed my grip for a better look. With one hand I released my belt and wrapped it tightly above my anklebone. "If that was a bear, he'll smell the blood."

A panicky tingling feeling made me nauseous. I was so vulnerable. A lot had happened in a short time. With my jackknife and trembling hands, I now began to cut my pants off to make tourniquets and bandages. My sloppy terrified hands slipped and drove the jackknife blade into my left leg above my knee about an inch deep. I felt like I was unraveling. I stared at my hands, shaking uncontrollably.

My eyes blinking repeatedly with disbelief, I knew I was now in it deep and needed to really focus. Sweat dripped from my face, as flies and mosquitoes buzzed at the opportunity for a free meal of fresh blood. I wrapped my foot with tight strips of denim and tried with all my might to concentrate. "Jesus Christ, I don't want to die. Screw football. I want my Mom. I want to go home."

I realized I was stuck hundreds of lost miles from anywhere. Nobody knew where I was. I hung my head and let my tears mix with the sweat, blood and dust beneath me. I realized it could be weeks before anyone would ever find me. For that matter, Bunch and Oscar in their demented silence may not even notice I was missing.

I wrapped my t-shirt around the blade end of the spud, a tool used to debark trees that looked like a flattened shovel and was about armpit height, that I would use for a crutch. I stood up, attempted to take a step and crumbled forward somersaulting and banging my injured foot hard on the ground. Pain screamed up my leg. I hadn't realized that my foot was functionless below the knee. It hung like ten pounds of meat.

As I sat assessing my situation and fighting off panic, the bandage, now pulsing from inside, was soaked entirely with blood and began to drip on the ground. With the tendons cut, I would have to crawl the mile or so back to the homestead.

I began to pick my way along through the hot summer afternoon, down the dry creek bed toward the farmhouse. CW was following but I don't remember him squawking, only staring at me with his head cocked in his silly humorous way. Travel was extremely slow. I began feeling tired and began resting in the shade of trees. Sleep seemed an intoxicatingly good idea.

I remembered a story about a man hanging on a rope while climbing a cliff, that he had become very drowsy as his strength waned and the sleep he wanted to indulge in had a delicious feeling of comfort and he knew he needed to fight it to survive. I too realized I would bleed to death if I let myself sleep. My mouth dry and my concentration flagging, the warm arms of sleep began to ever pull me closer as the day wore on. I shook my head to stay awake. The hot afternoon had brought dozens of flies and mosquitoes that dipped their protruding snouts atop my bleeding bandage and my bloody left knee; I felt repulsed to be attached to this bloody mass and my hands were drunk with exhausted effort to shoe them away.

Hours passed with moderate headway. Realizing my increasing fatigue was now my biggest obstacle, I opened the blade of my jackknife. As the waves of drowsiness swept over me, with my knife in my right hand I jabbed the blade tip into the side of my left hand startling myself to a more conscious state.

Time from that point went away. I slid on one hip along the dusty trail dragging the bandaged cut foot, pulling myself with my arms, stopping to jab my hand with my pocket knife to stay awake. It was all a blur. I was dusty and bloody and covered in flies, dehydrated from the hot sun and from the loss of blood, and barely aware that I had made it to a pole corral 100 yards from the log house sometime that evening. I pulled myself up to the second rung to yell but nothing came out of my mouth. My body was weaving as I sucked in a big breath to yell again with all my determination but only a soft muted tone came out. The homestead had a dog named Cocoa, a sweet little deer like dog, that heard my noises and began to bark.

I slumped back to the ground and fell unconscious. I remember Bunch had me in a wheelbarrow and drove it right through the front door and dumped me on the couch. Depleted of life's blood and drifting in and out of consciousness, I only remember bits of our conversation.

Perhaps as a reaction to the fear of this kid dying on her couch or her now hyper state, Bunch felt it important to scold me.

Her anger went on and on about how stupid I was to pull such a "boner". In my flagging ability to comprehend anything, I remember being real confused by her word choice of "boner". "You really pulled a boner," she kept repeating. Up to that point "boner" was a locker room term my buddies and I used to describe something entirely different. In fact this may have been one of the few times in my 16th year of life that I wasn't thinking about a boner. It meant something entirely different to her.

She stoked up the ever-smoldering wood stove and boiled a pan of water, dropping in a sewing needle and thread. "I'm gunna sew you up. There's no way to get you out of here for the foreseeable future and we can't have you bleeding to death. Man, you sure pulled a boner."

She handed me an empty leather knife scabbard and told me to put it between my teeth. The *Book of Mormon* disallowed stimulants or depressants like whiskey or any painkiller, she explained, so I was to bite down and endure. She moved a kerosene lamp closer to her surgical field and drove that needle in ... and out ... And in ... and out ... And in ... and out ... I bit down all right. I bit down so hard I shit my pants. I lay on that couch breathing through my nostrils like an Arabian stallion after a 20 mile gallop. I was bloody, dirty and now lying in a puddle of my own feces. Just before I passed out, I remember Oscar walking into the house asking Bunch who that was on the couch.

Sometime that night Bunch shook me awake and gave me a glass of Kool-Aid. I gulped and sputtered sort of like I wanted to chew it. The sweet liquid put the batteries back in my eyes and I drank and drank and drank. I realized how weak I'd become when I attempted to clean up. I hopped carefully on my good foot, while the other tugged with pain, and threw my tattered and soiled clothes down the hole.

I didn't get off the couch for three days. I was too weak and tired and just lay there napping, taking in all that happened. I ate a lot of moose meat and drank lots of Kool-Aid. Bunch shuffled around the house trying to act crabby, telling me stories. The event had opened her up and she talked continuously for those three days. I think she was proud she saved my life and relieved she didn't have to go dig a hole. CW had followed me home and Bunch fed him scraps from the table, another out of character deed of generosity.

The following couple of weeks I was increasingly able to hop around on homemade crutches. My head was obsessed with existential "what if?" questions. A really big thing had happened to me and I felt my spirit shape shifting as I slowly grasped what I had been through. I questioned for the first time the assumption I was mortal. "Shit, I could have died," I kept repeating to myself. I bounced between feelings of immortality and my extreme luck. Things that had been so important, like football, drifted out of my mind like yesterday's wind and I didn't really care that I wouldn't play anymore. All that stuff of high school and parties just seemed so stupid. The picture was so much bigger now.

A month or so after the accident three hunters came in and agreed to get me out. Saying good-bye to Bunch and Oscar, I rode a horse six or eight miles down river where they had a jeep. My foot throbbed on the back of the horse so I swung my leg up over the saddle for relief. The three stitches Bunch had put in were hardly enough, but they had kept me from bleeding to death.

Despite there being no road, the three hunters had taken the challenge to drive and hack their way into the Euchiniko in their four wheel jeep. CW and I were loaded into the back seat and we rattled and banged and winched our way out to the end of the logging road and from there into Quinnell where I caught a Greyhound bus and headed home. CW was stuffed into the sleeve of my jacket and smuggled home across the Canada/US border.

I never played football again more from lack of desire than anything else. The surgery was successful enough but my spirit had shifted. I was no longer interested in the white sugar buzz of thundering bleachers and the general popularity contest of high school. My spirit had shifted to hundreds of questions about the human existence, about life and its fragility. The accident had given me much more than a six-inch keloid scar on my right foot. To this day when I see a murder of crows I remember CW, the bright light in that summer of changes when I was 16.

Chapter 5

The Last Nine Yards

During my senior year of high school, life was flat, sad and marginally tolerable. I was forever finding everything except my girlfriend pointless. I just wanted to disappear into the woods and live by a stream and be away from parents, school and most adults. The Beatles were cranking out songs about revolution, and the music world was alive and leading the charge for a social rearrangement. Parents seemed stiff and from another world. The U.S. government and generally most of the American culture seemed out of touch with the younger people. Sex, drugs and lifestyles— the 60's were a free-for-all. It was an exciting time.

I discovered marijuana before I discovered drinking. I enjoyed getting stupid sometimes before school and smoked frequently in my bedroom in the evening just to tolerate home life. The steroid and antibiotic cocktails I had been ingesting for the past several years had cooled the infection in my stomach and my genetic coding kicked in. In a 12 month period I grew 12 inches to the lanky height of six feet three inches. My body was healing but my academic problems were still festering.

High school ended. As I rode the school bus to the venue where we were to go through the ceremony, I sat quietly looking out the window. My dishonest means of survival in school were at an end and had worked well enough to keep me from the humiliation of bad grades, but I had learned mostly how to be a cheat and academically I'd learned alarmingly little. I took inventory.

I was 18 years old, headed for the University of Washington and could read on a good day at about a 3rd or 4th grade level. My comprehension was still stuck in the 2nd grade. I stared out at the passing pavement, my eyes glazed in preoccupied self-assessment. Bottom line, I couldn't read worth shit. I'd spent years trying before I caved in to my dishonest ways. I felt worthless.

When Hughie had graduated three years earlier, he'd received some of the school's most prestigious honors and then flew off to Harvard to continue the family legacy in those hallowed brick and ivy buildings. I was going to just be a number somewhere in a long alphabet of names while "Pomp and Circumstance " repeated over and over trying to sound meaningful. This while a few mothers dried their eyes, a few rabble-rousers screamed short bursts of enthusiasm at certain names, and a few uncles and uninterested fathers fought off their tears of boredom while daydreaming about the life they'd reclaim without a teenager in the house.

If it hadn't been for the military draft, I'd have drifted away like goose down in a strong breeze looking for something I could latch on to, but as it was, I was heading off to the U of W to hide in the catacombs of industrial academia until the war ended or I figured out another plan for escape.

Chapter 6

Dolgoi

Alaska

Graduating from high school was a relief, but the war zone at home between my parents had sapped all my enthusiasm for anything. It was so depressing I dragged around like an old duffle. When a family friend mentioned an expedition in the Aleutian Islands and suggested I choose a friend and consider going, I jumped at the chance merely as a way to get out of the house. It also meant a chance to get back to the woods.

The details were vague, but we were to go to a small uninhabited island at the base of the Katmai Peninsula called Dolgoi, miles from anywhere. Several years earlier he and a partner had shipped 100 yearling Black Angus cows to this island. We were going to be flown to the island where we were to make a camp and build corrals for the cows. We were to then round up these cattle and have them waiting for several bulls that were being shipped to the location and presto, the Arctic Cattle Company would be underway.

It all sounded reasonable enough to me, in a Wild West sort of way, and my infatuation with this family friend and his stories and exploits had me following him around like a lonely puppy. I trusted his smooth words and didn't know what questions to ask anyway.

I chose Bob to explore the Arctic with me. Bob and I had met in the art room in high school: normally a class for losers, a class for the easy A, a place to escape and have fun with clay or paper, look at girls, and get credit for as little as possible. Bob was a little different; he was making an effort to teach himself some real ceramics. I liked the fact he was taking it seriously and he and I spent countless hours throwing pots, discussing our depressing lives and smoking dope while discussing politics. Toward the second half of high school he and I had the key to the art room and spent our entire days throwing pots, glazing and firing our little inventions.

Our attitudes were a mixture of angry disillusionment, creativity and despondence. Our lives were held captive by parents and school which was equally depressing for us both. When we graduated, we had the choice of either more school or being caught up by the military draft. Our lives did not feel like they were our own; it was a continuum of depressing possibilities.

Somewhere in this deteriorating time we became kleptomaniacs, a self-righteous attitude in our out-of-control lives. It started out as a way to humor ourselves while wandering through a grocery store with little or no money looking for something to feed our recklessly growing young bodies. Smoking copious quantities of dope added to the need for more sustenance, and as we prowled the aisles one day a candy bar slipped into a pocket unnoticed and then two or three and eventually we weren't carrying money at all.

With our tangled long hair and self-righteous attitudes, we'd march down the aisles of a store slyly shoving wanted items into the pockets of our oversized coveralls, a double use for our art room uniforms. A self-assured sense of angry entitlement. As the year progressed under a smoky cloak of depression and anger, so did our skills as potters and thieves.

Bob was enthusiastic about the Arctic trip and we immediately began to prepare by going to an outdoor equipment store and shoplifting all our personal needs. We began to ask more and more questions as the departure date grew nearer and we began to notice a distinct vagueness in the answers we were given by John, the family friend who was the expedition organizer. We did get two one-way air tickets to Alaska and eventually we were to get our final details by mail in a hotel in Anchorage as John would not be making the trip. This is where we'd meet the third, highly experienced member of our expedition, Chauncey L.

Chauncey showed up looking the part of the intellectual Arctic explorer—large bags of gear, parkas, cameras and a countenance of self-assured assumptions, the first being that Bob and I would be carrying his bags. In our hotel room he explained his long experience in the Arctic, his books and education from Phillips Exeter Academy through his PhD at Princeton. Bob and I stared glassy eyed, reminiscing silently of our near failures to complete the 12th grade. I was glad to have someone experienced, despite his obnoxious air of snobbish sophistication, as I had never been in the Arctic and Bob hadn't been out of the state.

The letter of our directives was of no real substance but we caught the airplane to Cold Bay, an abandoned military outpost at the west end of the Katmai Peninsula, just the same. As we landed, the plane wiggled in sideways in the wind, straightening at the last moment. The wheels chirped and the hull of the plane groaned and lurched as we taxied up to the Quonset hut that was the air terminal. We clustered quickly out of the 50 mile an hour gusting winds into the small building where a man was yelling, and then there was an enormous boom of a large caliber gun inside what seemed to be a kitchen in the back half of the terminal. "That'll keep the fucker out of my kitchen." The five of us, who were passengers, stood holding our bags staring into the kitchen where the cook had just shot a grizzly bear that was marauding his pantry. He had stepped in behind the gigantic furry beast, placed a shotgun to the back of his head and pulled the trigger.

The cook looked over at us with the smoking shotgun in his hand and said, "Welcome to the Bearfoot Inn, formerly known as the Weathered Inn. Judging from the wind you'll be here awhile so grab a chair, I'll be with you in a minute."

Bob and I looked at each other with an incredulous disbelief. "Well, Pilgrim, I guess this is the Arctic," I said with a lousy John Wayne drawl. I went over to the window and stared out to the moonscape tundra that stretched for miles over rolling hills without any vegetation higher than my ankle. No trees or bushes.

Where was the forest? There was only a continuum of soggy muskeg stretching over the wind torn landscape for mile upon mile. It was hard to tell that the wind was blowing 50 miles an hour except to watch the DC9 we came in on stick its head into the strong gale, fire its engine, and wiggle and slide into the sky and pound and bump its way out of sight.

As it disappeared, it seemed to carry my enthusiasm with it. This was such a different world and not a very cheery one. I didn't realize how close to the bottom my spirits hovered and now I began falling backward into a deep depression. It wasn't just the lack of trees and the wind and the expedition with no concrete objectives with the arrogant professor and armed only with a dope-smoking friend who was a good partner in thievery. It was my whole life. My life to that point hadn't given me much inner strength.

The rain joined the wind as we sat at linoleum tables drinking diner coffee passing time telling the long versions of stories that were pretty boring in the short version. Our weather delay would end up being ten days. In those ten days Chauncey, Bob and I drank strong whiskey with the two welders and seven military men who were weathered in with us. This and the hangovers didn't help my gloomy disposition. Chauncey seemed right at home tossing back jiggers of the brown liquid that fueled his stories with a slurry of sloppy adjectives.

Bob and I took long walks across the tundra, bent over in the gale winds, amidst the abandoned rusting Quonset huts left by the military after World War II that housed a thousand soldiers in this lost abandoned landscape. The wind blew and it snowed and rained from every direction the entire time beating away any chance for me to reclaim any happiness. I sunk deeper and deeper into my own gloom.

One day an amphibious de Havilland Beaver dipped out of the clouds and landed. We loaded up our supplies, including a ship to shore radio that was our life line back to the world, and flew up the side of the great Aleutian land bridge toward Dolgoi Island where adventure and 100 cows awaited us. The sea below the airplane was white capped and violent and I was relieved to see a small inlet on our island that had calmer waters for landing.

The pilot yelled over the loud grinding engine that he was not going to turn the engine off after we landed and was only going to stay five minutes to avoid getting stuck in the mud on the beach. We swooped down, skidded over the water and screamed and growled our way 100 feet from shore into shallow water. "Five minutes, boys, five minutes and I'm leaving!!"

The door slid open and Chauncey started firing orders. He jumped into the icy waters fully clothed, grabbed a small camera bag and marched to shore like Christopher Columbus landing on Hispaniola. Looking at the waist deep water and the wind and the cold wet tundra waiting on shore, Bob and I quickly pulled off our boots and pants, and jumped into the water. We ferried the supplies back and forth to shore, our bare legs and bare feet numbing and turning purple while Chauncey strode off across the spongy tundra looking first to the south and then to the west with little regard for Bob and me. The pilot yelled at us to call in on our radio once a week to check in, otherwise "you're on your own."

The door slammed shut, the engines growled and screamed as he headed up into the wind and down the bay and off through the clouds. As we stood on the shore, the wind pelted our bandy shivering legs and as the airplane disappeared off through the clouds, I felt a deep sense of dread.

Chauncey had located the remains of an old cabin we'd been

told about. Missing the door, the one window and most of the roof, we moved in spending the day making it as water and wind proof as we could. Having a project to do helped with my angst, but the weather's violent temper was a hard match. The gray gloom had moved into my skull and brought with it a low level headache and a continuous feeling of musty exhaustion.

We made beds from the deep mossy tundra and spread tarps over them to keep out the wet. That first night we tucked into warm sleeping bags, listening to the wind scream and howl around and through the little 12 by 12 foot shell of a cabin, the plastic flapping recklessly as the sound of rain dripped its not so soulful rhythm into cooking pans and pots on the wet floor.

By morning, Bob's sleeping bag and mine were soaking wet from the leaky roof. Chauncey woke up dry and charged up, full of plans as to how we were going to spread out and cover the island looking for our herd of cattle. He had maps and directions and told us to head out to the west and summit the hill that overlooked the rest of the island. He would cover the vast area in the other direction.

We all packed some food and agreed to meet that evening. My head felt like it was stuffed with an old pillow as Bob and I trudged off across the barren landscape. I tried singing to myself but the strong wind ripped the words from my mouth and diluted them over a million miles of wind blown ocean. We walked all day, with our binoculars scanning the wild hills, and saw little more than a few ptarmigan plus a falcon that flew like a sharp knife cutting a path across the blustery gray sky. When we climbed to the summit of a hill, a rare event happened and only for a brief minute.

The wind had been blowing at about 30 knots from the east with a driving slushy rain before it turned around and blew in from the north with a thick white snow that only lasted for 15 minutes. Then all the engines of weather ceased and the sky turned blue and the wind calmed.

Relief poured from my soggy spirits as we stood high atop the hill and looked to the north across the sea to the large volcanic cone of Mt. Pavlof. The mountain that stands shoulder to shoulder with her seismic sisters on the south end of the Katmai Peninsula looked embarrassed as it stood shamelessly naked, no weather to hide her volcanic shoulders.

We scanned for Chauncey off to the east. He was given away by his parka hood. The orange lined hood, unzipped down the middle and draped back over his shoulders, made him easy to spot. He was only several hundred feet from the cabin - sitting, not moving. The great Arctic explorer wasn't feeling very exploratory.

We slogged in toward dark, wet and tired. Chauncey sat in his dry corner, lantern blazing and sipping whiskey. I had experience at detecting drunkenness which he confirmed in a few sentences. Our leader was swimming in deep booze behind his cleanly shaved Princeton smile. He told us he too had not seen anything in the many miles he'd covered to the east. Bob and I stole a few glances at each other, wondering if we should bust this drunken BS'er, while I uncovered the radio to do a "call in."

I set the large metal box upright and plugged in the battery pack. All the meters were dead. My heart sank and I felt panic. I checked the connections and flipped the on/off switch a number of times before I proclaimed it was dead. Bob jumped across the cabin and stared at the lifeless needles with me. We knew what this might mean and stared at each other with pale vacant faces.

We turned to Chauncey who was taking no interest except to sip from his tin cup of booze. "I was using the batteries to power my electric shaver and they just went dead. Sorry." Chauncey's voice faded away in an embarrassed muffled slur as he took another sip from his cup.

The room was silent less the whistling wind outside. Rain dripped into frying pans and pots in an uneven musical throb. Bob and I looked at each other with a brewing anger and Bob started to cuss, first in a quiet voice that was full of insult then exploding into an anger that burst into a fury of caustic attacks. He stood up over Chauncey who sat on his sleeping bag not reacting. Bob swelled up and screamed insults criticizing him from his pompous over educated bullshit to his lying about how much ground he covered that day.

I sat hunched by the radio, a little nervous about what Bob might do and worrying about how we were ever going to get off the island of Dolgoi. When Bob began to run out of caustic missiles, Chauncey rolled over, stuffed his legs into his dry sleeping bag and fell asleep.

Bob was still angry as we sat in our wet sleeping bags and ate cans of sardines. Trying to sleep in my water logged bed, the moldy pillow of depression that was clouding my ability to react to anything found little relief as Chauncey snored a retaliation to the menacing whining wind and Bob hurled insults telling him to shut the fuck up.

Chauncey was morose, quiet and hung over the next morning. I was depressed and moved like I was in a world of plaster thickening around me. Bob was still angry and as we left early he was still ripping holes in our deposed leader's character. We decided to walk the shoreline for several miles and then head overland to another small hill to locate the herd of cows.

About a half mile from our camp we came across a pile of bleached bones and black hide in the shallows of the tide waters - a field butchered cow. We tried to figure how she'd died, with no conclusions, and walked on. Another quarter mile another skinned out cow on the shore. And another just past it. It was eerie. There were field butchered carcasses all along the beach. Bob and I had been talking about our marooned status but soon shifted to what was happening with the dead cows.

Bob said one of the welders back at Cold Bay, in one of our late night drinking sojourns, had warned him of a fish boat out of a little village called Belkofski. He said that they were a marauding band of tough guys who carried guns and loved to take pot shots from the decks of their purse seiner at any and everything. The boat's name was *The Freedom* and he'd recommended we take cover if they came around.

We walked on making up stories about *The Freedom* and the crew shooting and what we were going to do. We cut up over a hill to a vantage point five or six miles from our camp. Between rain squalls, we glanced back to see the little orange hood on Chauncey's parka just outside the cabin.

Then as we scanned back across the bay there was a boat, a purse seiner idling into the calm waters of the bay. We lay on the rocky ground at the top of the hill and stared through shaky binoculars at the bow of the boat searching for the name. *Freedom* we both said in unison and looked at each other, wondering how much more this trip was going to dish out. We lay close to the ground and watched. The orange hooded parka too was out of sight. 45 minutes later the boat swung a large arc around the bay and headed back out to sea.

When we finally stood up, I noticed a movement across the green landscape about four miles to the east. There were nine cows running up and over the rocky cliffs away from us. They were wary as the wind and had either seen us, the boat or smelled something that told them to run for cover. We deduced that our marauding fisherman friends were in for a visit to pick up some fresh red meat. They probably left when they saw no cows near the beach where they could shoot and butcher easily. We had no reason to stay, but the question remained as to how were we going to get out of here?

For the next six days we talked over plans. Chauncey kept himself well liquored up at night, claiming that someone would come sometime. I was curious where the new bottles were coming from. We had another week of canned goods and then we were out. My depression felt permanent. Bob was locked down in anger and we were stuck on this remote island sleeping in wet bags. We were an unhappy group with splintered objectives, tolerating the weather, eating canned foods and trying not to unravel.

One afternoon, like a ray of warm sun, the unmistakable whine of the de Havilland Beaver broke through the noise of the wind, curled around the hill to the west and landed like the beautiful bird she appeared to be. We immediately grabbed a few wet belongings, stuffed them in our packs and ran to shore wading out waist deep to the plane. The door opened and we piled in wet and happy. The pilot was a little startled, "I hadn't heard from you and was in the neighborhood and thought . . ." "Hey, man, get us the hell out of here," I said with an inkling of cheeriness in my voice.

We landed back in Cold Bay an hour later and timed a flight out and back to Anchorage within an hour of our arrival—better take it before the weather won't allow it. The wind was taking a small rest from its incessant beating of the Arctic landscape and our escape took full advantage of this.

Bob and I parted with Chauncey in the airport trying to pretend we were all going to be friends and would see each other another day on another trip north, but Bob and I were secretly betting the contrary. We walked out of the terminal in Anchorage and walked in damp clothes and wet boots into town. We were flat broke and had only gathered a few of our belongings in our rushed departure but it was good to be back around trees and a little friendly humanity. We camped in a park for a few days, went to the friendly Safeway store and lifted a few items to eat, and a few more for the road.

I knew of a distant cousin in Manley Hot Springs, a microdot-sized town of 27 people, 150 miles north of Fairbanks. We hoped with no real reason to get work there. We hopped on a freight train that led us north to the boom bust town of Fairbanks, deep in the interior. The following morning we hitchhiked west to Nenana, a gold rushed over town stretched out along the Tanana River. One of its few claims for recognition was that it was the finish line for a raft race from Fairbanks to the bridge that crossed the mighty brown currents of the Tanana.

Bob and I struggled through the brush, fighting off swarms of mosquitoes below the bridge and found several rafts abandoned in the bushes. We chose one that was plywood, built over six oil drums, and seemed to be in reasonably good shape. We found three poles with small pieces of plywood screwed into one end that were to be our oars. The idea was to float the river to the landing at Manley Hot Springs and secure enough work to pay for a ticket home. We shoved off with all our strength and rowed our ship out to the center of the river where the cool breezes minimized the mosquitoes.

I was feeling my first glimmers of happiness return as we slipped down the river and into the wilderness of the Alaskan interior. The raft was far too awkward to do any real rowing so we were content with just drifting along watching the river flow.

Bob was still making perverse jokes about Chauncey and he was able to get me to smile for the first time since we left Seattle. I was enjoying feeling the curtain of darkness lift just enough and I realized how sadly depressed I had been feeling.

Our Safeway caper had produced a large box of Minute Rice, raisins and a plethora of candy bars. Our kleptic skills specialized in candy bars. We collected small pieces of wood that drifted by in the river, dried them on board, and once a day lit a small fire on the blade of one oar hung delicately overboard off the stern. The plywood blade was about ½ inch thick and didn't burn too much before the water boiled in the one gallon tin can nestled in next to the heat. Then we'd quickly pour in our instant one minute rice and a handful of raisins, pull the can from the heat, roll the embers into the river before it burned our stern paddle and presto, our food for the day—rice pudding of sorts.

We drifted for three days and nights. It was mid-summer, close to the equinox, and remained light about 20 hours a day with a few hours of semi-dusk, a short time for the owls to fly the quiet shadows before the sun pushed for a brighter spot in the sky. The shore passed hour after hour. Moose stood baffle eyed in the calm waters of the sloughs, submerging their powerful heads to graze the bottom flora. There were few signs of humanity and the river had her long muddy way with our raft. The long days of tranquility did a lot to improve my attitude. Nature was such a healing force for my spirit.

We were drifting lazily on the inside bend of a large sweeping turn when we saw a small painted sign a good half mile away hanging in a tree: Manley Hot Springs. We jumped into action and began rowing furiously toward the opposite shore. The awkward crate shaped raft moved preposterously through the increasing currents as we inched our way over and down the river.

We were a good mile past the sign as we neared the shore on the side of the river that had a tremendous current. We were yelling at each other about how to stop and warning ourselves of the terrifying sweeper trees that reached out over the river from shore. It was impossible to land in between these large imposing obstacles. It all happened very fast.

The raft was close to shore but too far to jump because of the strong deep currents, so we hastily decided to pull on our heavy packs and row directly under a large sweeping pine leaning out over the river. Its jutting branches raked the water. The raft shot beneath the horizontal tree and we took the trunk directly in our chests.

In moments we were dangling over the river, using all our strength to pull ourselves up and all our wits to balance as we walked through the iron armed branches to shore. We were both a little shaken, and a good mile or so from the road that was six miles into a town inhabited by people who weren't expecting us. The mosquitoes swarmed. Maybe they weren't home or had moved. We'd given ourselves few alternatives. We fought the brush and thickets and the mouthfuls of mosquitoes to the landing and then hiked the road into town. We were out of candy bars and our can of rice and raisins hadn't made the trip to shore.

It was about 6 in the morning when I knocked on the door of the little log cabin that said Hetherington outside. A man answered who looked to be clearly six foot eight and at least 350 pounds. He glared down with an eye of disgust at the presence of two disheveled strangers, standing knock-kneed toting heavy packs. I tried to explain who we were and what we'd come for. Two filthy tall skinny guys with long hair, hungry and looking for work. Keeping in mind that rural Alaska in 1970 may as well have been 1946 any place else, the dirty hippie was little more than the butt of demeaning conversation suitable for target practice.

When I mentioned I was a relative of his wife, he acted as if I'd trapped him and yelled into the next room, "Daisy, YOU have some of YOUR relations here." Daisy popped her head around the door with a beaming smile, happy to see us but I could see the conflict in her eyes realizing how hard it would be to placate her husband.

They put us up in a bunkhouse used for firefighters, and Bob and I went to work to give hippies a good name and to earn a little money. We needed air fare as we hadn't figured out how to shoplift it. We cleaned and painted and worked like the possessed. When one job was done, we'd go find the big man in his airplane hanger and ask for more. We were laying it on thick. "Yes, sir. Thank you, sir." And "No problem. We'll get right on it. Should we sweep the shop when we're finished?" At the end of ten days we had won over the little town and despite all the bad jokes about long hair, we felt we'd succeeded. We grabbed a ride on a truck heading for Fairbanks with enough money for tickets to Seattle. Our hosts had been generous beyond their means.

The plane arrived at about midnight and we took a bus to downtown Seattle. Completely broke and without anyone we felt comfortable calling at that late hour, we decided to walk the 12 miles home. It fit into our new attitudes as Alaskan explorers.

It was about 4:30 when I passed by Becky's house, the girl from high school who had given me so much comfort. I said my goodbyes to Bob and thought I might sneak up to her window and wake her as a surprise. It was barely light as I stood in her driveway, realizing her window was directly beneath the room where her father and mother slept. I carefully tossed a single pebble at her window and there was a small sounding "tack" as it bounced off the glass. I waited and no response. I wanted her to look out through sleepy eyes and see me standing there with my pack on, looking like a big swollen hero just in from the Alaskan woods.

I threw another small rock and there was an unbelievably large crash of shattering glass. Before I could run, there were three or four faces in windows looking out through sleepy bewildered eyes to see what the noise was. The condemning eye of her irritated father pinned me there in the middle of the driveway.

Chapter 7

College

College meant I was out of the house but not out of the classroom. In 1970, "in state" students with a minimum grade point average of 2.86 (exactly what I had) were accepted into the University of Washington with no SAT tests and no interviews; it was automatic.

I lived in a concrete dormitory with 1500 other students where we crammed into cafeterias and ate industrial food three times a day, showered, studied or slept in the humming beehive of hundreds. We were a puppy mill of some 30,000 University students.

Dormitory parties were fun in an over the top sort of way, but it was the student marches that warmed up all over campus in 1970 protesting the Vietnam War and took over buildings and the interstate freeway that had my attention and were truly exciting. People were so alive in discussion, questioning the norms of a world that seemed to be heading for disaster. It was all the questions that I liked and probably the anger as well.

I wandered the wet streets and the worn carpets of the dormitory but it all meant little. I was living the big lie, faking my minimal literary capabilities. I was fighting off more depression. Not much made a whole lot of sense.

I'd come home to the dorm from classes with a lack of feeling any kind of relevance or interest that any of it was worthwhile. I'd nap all afternoon and then slog down to the cafeteria, eat paste of different colors, and return to my room and try to keep my brain matter from leaking out onto my desk while I stared out the window at wet pavement in one of the rainiest winters in Seattle history. Still unable to read adequately, my charade of scholastic survival was as depressing as the miles of wet concrete I trudged on back and forth to school.

It was a 101 class in archaeology. A test. I wasn't prepared. I knew nothing of chapters 9 thru 14. I had not prepared for how I was going to cheat my way through, in fact I didn't even know we were going to have an exam. I sat in my chair feeling doomed when I realized I sat next to a very bright person. How lucky could I be? I copied her paper word for word. This was my big mistake.

I waltzed out of the room feeling my hollow confidence, but several days later got a call to come to the professor's office at 3:00. He was a sinister fellow and laid it on thick. He had figured it out and proceeded to scare me nearly into a catatonic state. He threatened to kick me out of the University, certainly from the class with a failing grade and he was going to spread the word throughout the department and on and on. I sat there with no alibi; I knew I'd been wrong, that my entire life had been wrong. I had been bad and used poor judgment, and the words still stung hard. It was difficult not to have a defense, but I had none I could share.

I spiraled downward. I was back in 6th grade, my cheating secret revealed, a deer caught in the headlights, the impact of my life crushing the life from me. Guts spilled and I lay on the side of the road, swollen and bloated, legs twisted. Women and children would turn their heads away when they saw me as they sped by, ravens pecking at my eyes as the torturous hours passed.

I stumbled back to the dorm. After six months at the university I was ready to quit, run away and hide, become a bum somewhere in the woods. Several days later, still in my fog of self-absorption, I walked past a building with a small sign in the window that said Foreign Studies.

I wandered in and asked what it took to go to school abroad. The lady at the desk said, "Right now it'll take a $100 deposit and you can leave next week. We just had a cancellation from a student

going to Avignon in southern France. Would you be interested?"
I didn't know where Avignon was and I didn't care. I ran back to
the dorm, sold my 10-speed bike to a fellow in the dorm for $90,
borrowed $10 and ran back and paid the lady.

Then I called home and told my mother, or tried to pretend I
was asking. I needed to change something. "I leave in 10 days. I've
already made the deposit on the ticket."

My mother acted reluctant but I could tell she was envious.
She and my father had decided to try again. A three legged race
across a lake of thin ice. Who knew if they'd make it. I just knew I
was not going to give a shit or be around if they didn't.

Chapter 8

Mule Sweat

When I arrived on the train platform in Provence's most beautiful walled city, Avignon, I couldn't even utter the words, "Je ne pas parle francais" as I didn't know a word of French. It was spring quarter, the hills were green, the éclairs luscious and the wine divine. My eyes were wide open and I was drinking in the warm wind, the delicious distance from home and flavors of the people.

Classes at the University of Avignon were in French so it was as if I were swimming upstream lost, blindfolded and gasping for air, but I loved the sound of the language. It was like the food: buttery, rich and it made my mouth happy. I couldn't get enough and once the basics were mastered, I wanted to stay up late and gorge myself in conversation and wine. I began to dream in French and glimmers of life began to return to my smile. I learned the language like an infant, entirely through audio retention.

The American students left me bored but the countryside and the people were like finding some ancient roots. I'd bicycle through windrows of Van Gogh's poplars that sheltered wheat fields from Le Mistral, the strong wind that blows across southern France, and hitchhike past the burnt umber cliffs of Cezanne, the wind in my nostrils giving healing to my fractured soul.

One early morning I passed a little bald man on a staircase, he going down and me heading up. I was rushing in to see the hand painted Op Art of a little gallery. I'd bicycled there under the morning sky, orange to the east rising over the fields of grapes promising another day of warmth and beauty. There was a registry in the entryway where I signed my name and noticed the signature just above my own said, "Vous etre plus con de moi." signed Pablo Picasso. There it was, his unmistakable signature. I ducked back out the door to see his little car bumping down the dusty road through the grape fields. He'd written, "You're more fucked up than I am! Pablo Picasso" a humored response to the bizarre art exhibit he'd just seen.

I left the University of Avignon one day mid-sentence, without intention of returning ever. It was in the middle of a bus ride full of American students, slobbering over each other, feeling clever as they sang "100 Bottles of Wine on the Wall" while guzzling some of France's finest. After ten minutes of waiting at a cafe bathroom stop, I told a friend to tell the bus driver that my friend, Tom, and I weren't coming back. We climbed through a little bathroom window into the back alley and ran off down the street, throwing our books into a hedgerow and disappearing into the warm French countryside.

It was the first of many of my efforts to leave college and create a life of more meaning. I had been in school as a response to family pressure and the beckoning call of the draft board, but on that day nothing made more sense than running away, so I did.

I ran like a happy jack-the-rabbit, no place to go but escaping Mr. McGregor and his shotgun full of books. I was a tall skinny unconfident young man, desperately trying to grow a beard and as directionless as a car with no steering gear. Wounded by some family shrapnel, I was desiring adventure but was somewhat baffled as to which way to go. Tom waved good-bye the next day, bound for England with his guitar and a song he'd written for a woman he'd met in a bar and couldn't stop thinking about.

I wandered for several days exhilarated by the image of my escape and wondered what the reaction had been back on the bus. At night I would nurse a cup of soup and a glass of wine in a cafe until closing time and then slip off into the night and sleep in a doorway of an ancient cathedral under piles of collected newspapers. I don't remember having more than pocket change.

Eventually I made my way to the countryside and to Solonge Bouget's farm high on a sun drenched hill in southern France. It was well known she took in travelers who were willing to work, all-be-it for no pay yet some modest food and a place to sleep. Young Jim's farm dream, long submerged under piles of Bermuda shorts, family protocols and draft cards, was still in me way down deep and I missed it when I took the time to daydream about it.

I trudged up the hill in the late afternoon sun to find an older woman sweating profusely as she and her two mules cultivated a stand of grapes. It was a scene from a Baroque painting. In soft pastel afternoon light, these two mules were choking on dust while their flexed wet muscles were carefully pulling the claw fingered cultivator between arbors of lush grapes. The strong woman focused hard as she maneuvered the wooden handles and reins. I stood staring.

Was I seeing my future? Her clothes were worn and patched, her long gray hair pushed up under an oversize hat, and her oversize hands, like polished oak, directed the animals with a strength and gentleness I had not seen hands ever do before. She smiled as if she knew me and began a conversation at a breakneck speed while unhitching the two lathered animals.

My language skills were those of a person who'd skipped out of school and hers a dialect from the North that I only barely understood. She handed me the lines of Baba and Flicka, the two sweat soaked heaving mules who acted as if they didn't understand French or English, and we headed down the hill. She continued to talk on, smiling and laughing, answering her own questions after brief pauses as she realized I had no idea what she was saying.

I feigned competence in my crash course as a mule skinner. I was exhilarated by the animals, the late afternoon sun cooling to the west, the view of the arid rolling hills and this woman with a Zorba like spark for life.

We passed a dried out garden where Solonge stopped and niggled a hat full of potatoes from the soil with thick fingers. "Les pommes de terre sont le coeur de le monde." Potatoes are the heart of the earth, she explained, very important for "philosophy soup". We made our way past chickens and goats to a cluster of tired rock buildings. We put the beasts of burden in the shade and headed to the house, a small stone building that might be mistaken for a barn.

Chickens scattered like dropped marbles as we shuffled through the front door into a simple dark room with a table, a counter and six or eight chairs. Every surface was crowded with bowls of milk with cheese curd dripping into more bowls while thousands of flies buzzed between. There seemed to be more flies in the house than in the barn, all enjoying the delights of this cheese factory.

Solonge laughed as she washed the potatoes. She smiled and laughed continuously as she began her famous philosophy soup. Potatoes from the heart of the earth, garlic to keep the spirit fresh, spinach for strength and on she rambled as she did every night thereafter as a ritual of reverence and thanks to the food and a spoon of soft cheese for decadence and flavor. Everything she added had an importance and a meaning. It was her evening story.

As the evening cooled and the shadows lengthened, the bowls of milk were gathered and moved and workers began to show up to eat. There were the two bare-chested sweaty guys from Czechoslovakia who were continually arguing their politics with extreme intensity. I could never really understand them but they seemed both passionate and idealistic. Their arguing lasted the length of the summer, sort of like an all-sports-all-the-time radio station, except these two guys were into extreme politics all the time.

Gebair would come for dinner often. He was about Solonge's age, a farmer from down the road who showed up often on a little Vespa motorcycle with no brakes. He'd coast into the yard, hooting and yelling, till he side swiped something to come to a halt amongst great laughter. His happy, ruddy face and baseball mitt hands with bratwurst fingers were often the focus of my attention during the evening's conversation which, like the philosophy soup, was rich and diverse.

There was homemade wine and cheese, of course, and after dinner Solonge mixed a little cheap tobacco and a little of the expensive stuff and hand rolled a cigarette. The conversation would slow as we sucked in and exhaled, our eyes at half-mast as we were in the moment of this one luxury at the end of the day. It also sent the flies looking for cracks in windows as we filled the house with musty swirls of smoke.

The conversations were rich all those evenings as we sat in that little room talking in fragments of many languages. We talked of revolution and fascism and the "American business man". Solonge always got a kick out of that phrase and pronounced it like bees nest. "Maybe when I'm finished farming, I'll become a "bees nest man." There was always thunderous laughter after a joke like this.

We were tired from our hard work on Solonge's farm; my muscles were awakening from their academic hibernation and my skin was brown and dusty. I was happy under my dirty crust. We never seemed to get around to bathing, or at least I was missing out on the opportunity as part of my baffled comprehension of Europe's diverse languages. We'd milk 40 goats and the cow, hoe in the dust, work the hot obstinate mules and I don't ever remember seeing more than a glass of water at a time. I got as ripe as a summer compost pile. It never really bothered me until I met Pascal.

One evening as we all sat bleary eyed around that little room a young woman about my age showed up in the doorway. "Bonsoir. Je m'appelle Pascal Bruyelle et je voudrais travailler avec les chevre." Outlined by the doorway of the dark fly filled room stood a young woman who simultaneously stopped and started my 19 year old engines. She was invited in and given the remains of the soup. While she ate, the conversation drifted back to wherever it had left off but my attention was on the girl eating soup.

For several weeks I had spent long afternoons herding the goats uphill behind the farm to eat bunch grass in the ravines and under the olive trees. Chocolate (pronounced Sho-co-la), the handsome buck whose horns stretched clear back to his rear end, was forever on the prowl sniffing the asses of his does checking their estrus for signs of ripeness. He was ever vigilant and continuously in rut for a doe that would stand for him.

Long hair flowing, this was a macho breeding machine whose continuous flex had tireless enthusiasm. He had the pick of his stable, ever confident, ever ready. To that point in life, I felt pretty much his opposite. My horns were long enough but my experience was an ever flagging question. My imagination was not.

Then that evening Pascal shadowed the doorway in her tight little jeans and blue and white striped shirt. I was lacking Chocolate's confidence but not his desire. As she ate, I found myself staring at her, slack jawed and dumb founded. We exchanged glances several times and I, with a hair-trigger smile, was wishing I could say a thousand things but was caught up in an internal wrestling match. My lowly self-consciousness versus the devilish bliss of desire.

I wanted to reach out across the table and hold this woman in my arms as she melted into moans of rapture and happiness. But I feared she wouldn't like me, my beard wasn't manly enough, my muscles skinny and not big enough, and I probably wasn't her type anyway but she was awakening the inner buck in me. She probably had a boyfriend named Jean Paul or Geakim who was the hero of the French national rugby team and looked like the sculpture of David in Florence. And no doubt if I ever showed any interest, her friendly smile would turn to an abrupt disdain and disgust as she rifled insults at my inadequacies. I couldn't take that so I stayed silent and tried to keep my staring from being too obvious.

The room full of workers thinned out and I decided I would head for the barn where I slept in the hayloft and I would dream of what might have been with Pascal if I'd only had the guts. Solonge told her of several options for sleeping and to my total amazement she chose the barn loft with me. We walked in the dark, lit by stars in the cool relief of the day's heat. We lay in the thick piles of hay, several feet apart, staring at the dim shafts of light that glanced across the loft while 40 goats chewed their cuds under the watchful eye of Chocolate, a floor beneath us. There was a long silence.

I was self-absorbed in a scrutiny of how rank I must smell and images of Geakim, the fictional all-nation rugby star, when Pascal said with a musical softness, "Bonsoir, Jimmie Cowboy". My eyes bugged out into the dark room, staring into black looking for light. Jimmie Cowboy was the affectionate nickname the farm workers had given me, named for a cartoon hero character taken from a French newspaper. Did this mean she liked me?

My mind shot off like hyperactive sparklers, but my body lay motionless. The mental gymnastic continued. My mule sweat smell, skinny muscles, awkward hands, performance anxiety and of course the dread of rejection coursed my thoughts. Eventually I could hear the heavy labored breathing of Pascal and I realized I had missed my cue. The train had left the station and I definitely wasn't on board.

The next morning I was exhausted as I sat up alone in my hayloft bunkroom, self-disappointment seeping into my heart like the morning sun through the cracks in the barn, strong and intense. Through the open door I watched as Chocolate led his harem up the side of the hills behind the farm. His long beard flowing beneath him, his horns strong and massive, he dominated his lair and was in charge and he knew it.

I began to hate that goat in the following days as I worked

the farm. Pascal's every smile and laugh made me miserable and I slunk about like a gut shot mallard looking for a place to suffer. She said the hayloft had made her hay fever bad and chose to sleep with the rest of the workers in the bunkhouse. I tried to rally subsequent moves toward her, but generally in my own mind until I was pretty much talked out of any effort by my personal negative haranguing.

When we eventually parted, she handed me a piece of paper with her name and address on it and told me to write. I wished her luck and she stood up on her tiptoes and kissed me on both cheeks. We both turned a few shades of red and she headed down the road toward Switzerland to see friends. I returned to the barn with a heart full of frustration and Chocolate and his harem. That piece of paper with her name and address on it stayed in my wallet for many years until I was married and at that point it was time to let her go.

Chapter 9

Tet Offensive

I knew I'd be drafted if I stayed out of college longer than a quarter, but it was a wonderful time. Working for Solonge forever changed me. It affirmed my love of the farm and working with my hands. It affirmed my dream of a simple place where I could feel safe and laugh and have friends around the table and we could argue and cry, love and lust, and do purposeful work.

-•-

I walked the ragged carpeted hallway back to my dorm room. It was a quiet interlude in the otherwise bustling industrial strength factory of students. "Alice's Restaurant" was drifting down the hallway from a transistor radio. I fumbled with the keys as I looked through my mail. There was a letter from the U.S. government. It had a sinister feel to it. The government was still the hot topic on campus and the butt end of a million bad rumors. The Vietnam War raged and probably accounted for about half the enrollment of the University of Washington's male population.

I tore open the letter and a simple sentence stated that my student deferment (S1) had been upgraded to my now current status of (A1). I was being drafted. It said I needed to report to my local draft board the following Monday at 7 a.m. and be prepared to stay for three days for physical and mental evaluation.

My knees sort of buckled me onto the edge of my bed. "Fuck me!" I wheezed. "There must be a mistake. They can't draft me. I'm in college. I'm, I'm . . ." my thoughts trailed off into fractured thoughts of fear. I saw green jungles and green army fatigues and screaming people and explosions and burns and bullets. "They can't fucking . . ." my voice blew no air and I sat on the bed bleary eyed. The hallways were getting busy with students. Some guy complaining about his psych test stuck his head in the door and yelled "Bastard" and disappeared. Another face.

This time it was Mossy, a goofy kid from Mossy Rock, Washington. He looked distracted as he walked into my little dorm room. "I just got a letter from the induction board and, man, I just got drafted." "Me too, me too . . ." my voice trailed off. The verdict was in and the jury all agreed. Mossy and I were the next two victims in the American nightmare called the Vietnam War.

I called Hughie back at Harvard and before I could tell him, he went off on a rant about the demonstrations on his campus. "We took over the Student Union Building and those fucking cops, man, were so ruthless, they were just beating us with clubs. It was so tense and fucked up. Man, those fucking nightsticks fucking hurt." I interrupt, "Hughie, I got drafted." My voice breaks and I want him to help me.

"What am I going to do?" My heart sank into a hopeless empty place and I began to cry. "I don't want to get shot. I don't want to shoot anybody. Man, I'll die. This whole fucking war is so horrible." By now I'm sobbing. Hughie was suddenly silent. We both knew this was big. Bigger than us both. I knew it was more than he could fix. Big brothers can fix a lot but this one I was on my own.

"I think we're invading Cambodia," Hugh said quietly but with a firm anger in his voice. "It's called the Tet Offensive. Those fuckers aren't telling us we're doing it, but they're drafting 300,000 more kids. There's a war over there but there is a war here now, too. We gotta stop this fucking war."

The following Monday my mother volunteered to drop me off in front of the induction office. The ride was silent, the car was cold and the streets were wet. I went with a lingering case of nervous diarrhea, a toothbrush in my back pocket and a one sentence letter I'd coaxed out of my childhood doctor claiming that Crohn's disease made me a bad candidate for the service.

Some 100 of us sat in chilly fiberglass desks facing a red faced shrill sergeant who bull-horned directions with no uncertainty. "You will be here for three days to undergo physical and psychological testing. You will cooperate to your fullest ability. We can ascertain who is attempting to fail any of these tests, and anyone who does will be fully dealt with. This is the U.S. military and we don't fuck around. So girls, let's get started." I squirmed on my chair as I felt the sluiceway of my bowels getting ready for an evacuation. I raised my hand and asked where the bathroom was. The sergeant snapped back, "Sit down and shut up. You're my property now and you'll shit when and where I tell you."

I looked out across the room, everyone puckered in their seats. 90% of these young men would have given anything to get out of this predicament. Some had been partying since they got their notice and were so exhausted they were having a hard time concentrating; others were so high on experimental chemistry who knows where they were going to land.

A bunch sat like me in sweaty terror looking for any chance to fail, like messing up on the multiple choice questions by blackening all the little boxes. It wasn't hard to figure out ways to screw it up, but trying not to make it look too obvious was hard. The other ten gung-ho guys sat in the front row and pretended they were already in the service. They'd taken it upon themselves to get military haircuts and chirped responses with crisp, "Yes, sir, sir!" and "No, sir, sir!" rehearsed like actors in a ROTC recruitment film.

We all passed the written exam, presuming it was spelling of our first name correctly that graduated us. We moved to the physical exam where we all stripped to our underwear. Shuffling in lines of bashful, scrawny and fat bodies, fit proud physiques, with guys who shit themselves and acted oblivious to seem crazy, guys who carried secret vials in the elastic bands of their underwear to empty into their urine samples. This was the show that many had considered their best escape.

The doctor felt our testicles for hernias and we coughed and whispered insults and comments. "So do you go home and have sex with your wife after doing this all day?" The level of tension thickened as the uniformed military brass barked orders and we were visualizing a long future in meaningless lines with grave consequences. We donned headphones and were told to raise our hands when we heard a beep, which immediately sent 75 arms in random un-succession into the air. Everyone wanted to fail. I think hearing that we should raise our hands was considered the passing of the audio test.

At the end of the first day, still in our underwear, we shuffled into individual interviews where a panel of doctors sat us in cold metal folding chairs and from their overstuffed leather thrones asked a few questions about our medical history. I produced my wrinkled letter from the clutches of my sweaty fist. There was a pause as the young medical doctor read it. He looked up, smiled at me and said, "I don't think the Armed Forces will be needing your services. Thank you for coming." I couldn't believe my ears. The childhood I'd spent in hours of pain, doubled over on the bathroom floor, had found a silver lining. I was free from the draft. I was free from having to go to school. I was free from worry. I was free.

I dressed and walked out into the light of a spring afternoon. The sun poured down and spread its delicious warmth over my face and the wet streets. I felt light on my feet.

Outside the recruiting office an elderly lady had a grocery cart full of flowers. I gave her a $20 bill and she excitedly gave me a full armload of fresh daisies. I crossed the crowded highway, feeling somewhat invincible, and walked the six or seven miles back to the University district and under the wiper blade of each parked car I passed I stuck a fresh flower until my arm load was gone. The world looked different. I was free.

Chapter 10

Living In My Car

My freedom began to shift shape in the following weeks. While relief from the draft and school was still settling in, I hadn't given any real thought to what I was going to do. It had always been a rather lofty and abstract concept. It meant a departure from the "three hots and a cot" that came with school. Survival became pretty basic as my money dwindled.

My decision was to live in my car, live cheap and go when and where I wanted. I first owned a '67 VW passenger bus that seldom ever ran well. I had no experience with mechanics. My parents always had the garage do their work, but I was in no position to afford such luxuries so I managed to just go the route of neglect. Maybe it would just spontaneously stop dripping pools of oil and chugging through intersections if I gave it time and said nice things to it.

The idea had been to spend my last few dollars on the van and give up on paying rent. Neglecting engine work, I then spent countless hours modeling and remodeling the interior into the perfect living quarters. The back seats were all removed and given to friends for dorm furniture. I dismantled wood pallets and fashioned free dunnage found around building sites into food boxes and chests that slid perfectly under the double bed in the back. It was a work of art. Folk functional and a nest of warmth and security.

My dog and I slept well. With the little handmade curtains drawn shut, I could park on any street and look like any other parked car. The infernal rain of the Northwest patted softly on the roof and I was as snug as a chipmunk in a den of leaves, but like that chipmunk I had no commerce, food or gas. Eventually I found it impossible to go anywhere dependably, and the pools of oil and the missing bumpy chugging weren't improving despite all my verbal encouragement.

So I sold my one worldly mechanical possession and bought a much cheaper 1967 VW bug convertible. My plan was to rebuild the engine with the extra money in a friend's garage and have enough left over for a highly desired road trip. I had no experience twisting wrenches, only the desire to learn. The first thing that became obvious, as the piles of greasy parts, oily nuts, bolts and objects of unknown origin grew, is that engines are basically a lot easier to dismantle than to reassemble.

The rebuild was a grossly underestimated project and I struggled many a night reading and rereading manuals while scratching my head with black greasy fingers. A friend with a similar project was in the other half of the garage and, although definitely far more adept at mechanical pursuits, I remember push rods and nameless gizmos scattering as our dogs bounded in to greet us. The invariable question was: "Is this your dealy-thingy or mine?"

But the gods prevailed and after weeks of what seemed to be permanently blackened fingers from grease and grit, that little maroon and black bug shot out a puff of smoke and settled into a quiet rhythmic gurgle. I had completed a valve job on my little '67 VW bug. I was ecstatic and completely surprised.

Within the next few days I'd removed the front passenger and back seats, dismantled more pallets and built a bed that stretched from beneath the glove box to the back window, a remarkable distance of eight feet, giving my lanky six-foot three-inch frame plenty of room to stretch out. Where the passenger seat had been, the bed folded on hinges into a seat complete with small storage box beneath and a sheepskin for comfort above, this in case some beautiful hitchhiker might need a ride. The back seat area had cabinets built beneath the bed for food and storage. It was very small, cozy and warm and on starlit nights I could pull its little convertible top back and sleep beneath the stars. I was thrilled at my invention and without test-driving more than several blocks, I set off across country to work, live and find adventure.

I think I started with $21. That got me to the Yakima Valley in eastern Washington where I picked fall apples in those gorgeous plump orchards. Cool and silent in the morning dew, with only the whisper of Hispanic voices and the muffled tumbling of apples filling big totes, I felt I was where I should be. The afternoon's sun dragged long, showing past Mt. St. Helens and Mt. Adams to the west browning our skin, sending us searching for shade.

I saved $7 a day by not living in the migrant quarters and felt like a Las Vegas high roller when I left with $300 in my pocket a month later along with an enormous gunny sack of Spartan apples to be eaten with the tin of Safeway peanut butter in the back seat.

I headed east with no particular place in mind. Just drive. Fill up the tank and just drive. It was more about movement and time and the feeling I would find whatever I needed if I just kept going. Flatulenting my way across the prairies, a condition brought on by my limited diet, a smile smeared wide on my face, I began feeling more in than out of control.

The country spread out in front of me and I settled back with my three-inch speaker and some good AM radio. As a parting gift I'd promised my mother, back in Seattle, I wouldn't drive past the speed limit of 55 MPH. I loved my Mum and pitied her stuck spot in life so I honored her wish. This safe slow speed may also have had something to do with my mechanical lack of confidence.

In the back of my mind, as the flat landscape drifted past, I envisioned horrible pinging noises, then clanging erupting from the engine with a final booming explosion and my whole world coasting to a halt on the side of the road miles from downtown nowhere. But it never happened. Had I buffaloed this little engine or was it setting me up for real tragedy?

In the early 70's there were no speed limits in many wild Midwestern states. Pickup trucks and Cadillacs would pass me going well over 100 miles an hour, quickly slipping off down the drain of that long straight miraged highway as I sputtered along with my dog and scratchy little radio singing "Freedom's just another word for nothing left to lose." My thoughts drifted aimlessly as the hours passed.

There were some nagging questions of commerce and what I was going to do with my life. I had not given a lot of thought to it while living in my previous world. At that point, my life was all about surviving. Apples and peanut butter, 426 miles to Bismarck. The radio crackled. I passed a farm on the flat Midwestern prairie. Why would you settle out here miles from anyone?

Thinking of my own farm someday, I yearned for the musk of animal paddocks steaming with piles of wet hay and dung, with artistic visions of broken machinery retired to rusting piles in out of the way places. And there were neat rows of vegetables in long lines, extraordinarily plump; the soil was black and moist with richness and there were no weeds—none. I wanted a cabin on the edge, small humble warm and dry. And children, there would be leagues of happy children running, laughing, playing with their dogs and animals, and there would be a beautiful woman with long flowing hair who, with a smile, would take the ache from my back and worry from my thoughts.

I'd spent a good portion of my time in life so far rejecting things: school, parents, government. All my teachers and guides had pushed me in a direction that meant absolutely nothing to me which resulted in me becoming a cheating thief. There were dozens of uncles and grandfathers and cousins right down to my father and older brother who'd attended the ivy covered walls of Harvard University. Well-bred and well-fed for a life that wasn't for me.

I wanted a simple life that had its own richness, full of color and music, children, a garden, friends and neighbors. Was I driving in the right direction? Eventually there were trees in the incessantly flat, barren Midwestern landscape and the ever flattened road began to go up and down with some rolling hills as I noticed I was low on gas, as well as money, peanut butter and apples.

I took a brief job building pallets with a few hobos near a railroad yard and my mouth watered at the bundles of clean pallet wood yet to be assembled, clean new lumber unlike the recycled pallets I'd used to build the cabinets on the inside of my little car. Long highway miles and menial jobs always had me daydreaming about a farm.

Several weeks later in a farmhouse iglooed under three feet of snow, I sat sharing a meal with some generous Midwestern hippies. A gentle looking man named Amilio, who wore a long black ponytail and had understanding eyes, had been listening to the evening's conversation and turned to me, in response to my blather about the ideals of farm life, and said with calm wisdom, "You don't seem so much a traveler as a person who needs a home, a resting spot to do your life. You need to go start your farm. That's where you belong." He smiled with clear gentle eyes.

The words came loud and clear without judgment and all else seemed to quiet as I pondered his direct comment. Delivered with grace, it was as if I needed to hear those words of permission. I withdrew into my thoughts. He was right. It was time to fill my cup with this dream. At least try until I couldn't. I could talk and fantasize or I could dig in and do it. I decided to do it.

Where do I start? How do I start? Which way do I go? I'm living in my car and I want to buy land and build a homestead. That thought was a little scary, a little overwhelming. My parents would never go for the idea and I didn't want to be involved with them on something so important anyway. I'd have to earn the money.

My helter-skelter plan was to work any and every job I could and save the money for a down payment. There wasn't a logical or well thought out plan to any of it, but it was time to begin. My life needed direction and there in that snowy farmhouse in Prior Lake, Minnesota, in the kitchen of friends listening to Bob Dylan's nasal laments about a world needing change, I made the decision.

My thoughts broke loose like a herd of wild brumbies spilling out over the desert thundering hooves of happiness. I would build a cabin and all the fences and barns. I would build by hand, off the grid and bring the revolution to a model of practical living. Grow my own food and live deliberately. It was time to start.

It was now the most important thing in my life. The only reality was I needed money. Lots of money. I was 20 years old and living in my car but my resolve was as big and clear as the Midwestern prairie sky.

Chapter 11

Saving for a Dream

The decision became the theme of who I was and my sights were set on some fantastic vision somewhere in an abstract future. I could sort of taste what I was after. God knows I had thought about it a lot. There were a few vague molecules bifurcating and building into concepts that my 20-year-old brain saw as my best possibility. It felt good to have a goal.

It motivated my every action. It was a lot of talk, but talk was the beginning part of the seed I had planted and wanted to grow. The truth is I wanted this thing, this farm, and I wanted certain qualities of life but I had absolutely no concept of how I was going to pull it off.

I wasn't sure what it would take financially, but that didn't seem to really matter. I only had laborer's skills for wage earning and, with minimum skills, I hovered at the bottom of the wage earner's barrel. Having left the family process and claimed my independence there was no one in the family I could ask for money. It's lucky I didn't know how preposterously difficult it would be or I may have quit before I started.

I just sort of adopted this Puritan ethic that I would endure. Life would be hard, but "hardship and difficulty" had a romantic notion. Maybe Bob Dylan would write a song about how I quietly toiled, the frugal popper, who ate porridge by candle light and counted his pennies. I was looking for the richness of experience to be a few lines of a good poem about struggle. There had been such hollowness in my experience of schooling, coupled with my crippled scholastic capabilities, that I just couldn't go back to academia without feeling like I would experience the final stages of my own spiritual suffocation.

My vision of farming, all-be-it romantic, felt like a way out and through—a move toward light, to feeling happy. I could be honest trying anyway. At first it was hard to give myself permission to want to be a farmer.

The voices of my parents and the world I'd grown up in yammered the endless looped tapes about good schools and career driven education. There was a linear path that I had been coerced and prodded toward, proven by generations of Harvard trained professionals, many of whom were my relatives. I'd been given all the best opportunities and had come to realize that parental acceptance and value came from following these directions. The family system required my cooperation on this point. And as much as I wanted to be thankful for the scholastic gifts of opportunity that came with my DNA, I had to decline. My plans to buy land and farm were a hard charge in the wrong direction and would be more disappointment to my parents. I would have to put distance between myself and the family.

After that night in the little snow-covered house where this moment of clarity came to me, I took inventory of my situation. I had hardly a dollar to my name and a carburetor with a chronic cough. My dog was low on kibbles and it was cold outside.

The sign in the window of the Royal Fork in Prior Lake, Minnesota, in the little strip mall with the frozen snowy parking lot, said: Help Wanted - $1.08 an hour. I worked eight hours cleaning the filth and grease that accumulated around and under the bubbling vats of mystery smorgasbord swill. "Just like homemade" the sign said. Sort of an obesity feed station center for the unaware. I collected my after tax paycheck of $6.58 and left. My shoes did not squeak on the tiled floor as I left but slid away quietly on a permanent sheen of grease. This wasn't going to work.

Next I plowed fields. I met Ben Casey outside a corncrib next to his idling tractor early one morning. A night's frost was having a hard time letting go in the shadows as the temperature hung around freezing. He shouted directions over the battering sound of the cold diesel, short sweet and to the point. "Follow the row down to the end. Turn around and come back on the other side." He'd opened the field up splitting the 100 acre dried soybean stalks into two perfect squares with a clean black furrow that ran the length of the tan dead soybeans litter. "I'll see you this afternoon."

I didn't know the first thing about how to drive a tractor but gave him a vague nod sort of hoping he'd run me through the basics but was too afraid to ask. Life had taught me to just fake it. I hated that feeling. The noise of the engine hid the hesitation in my voice. My masquerade in school of cheating wouldn't do me any good here.

Through trial and error, I jerked and lurched toward the field. Like a giant green and yellow injured insect, the John Deere rocker shaft raised and lowered, banging and bashing about. Moments later Ben's truck reappeared in the driveway and he sauntered over. He yelled above the engine, "3rd gear", and leaning over my feet showed me the correct configuration, jamming the second of two gear shifts in position "and lower the rocker shaft to about here." His hand slid the control down, and down dropped the plow.

I released the clutch and away I went. Inside I was beaming with excitement. The tractor dropped over slightly as its right tires followed the opened ditch of the previous furrow. I turned to watch the ground being sliced by the coulter and laid open and upside down in a long rich earthy row. I was plowing. If I'd have caught the winning touchdown pass or been kissed by the homecoming queen, I wouldn't have felt as good. 15 minutes later, at the end of the row, I lifted the control on the rocker shaft, turned, dropped the controls back down to the same spot and followed the opposite furrow back to where Ben Casey had me begin. Ben was gone. I did this all day on an ever-widening field of moist black earth. I swelled with pride at each turn.

By afternoon I felt like a veteran, the diesel smoke belched and the engine groaned and slabs of cool dark soil flipped neatly over. I was in heaven. I worked for Ben for a week and was paid $4 an hour, which was a dollar over minimum wage. I felt like I had my toe on the first rung. Life felt good. Or at least it felt like progress. He suggested I try Bill's Millwork over in Savage. They could always use a good carpenter.

Bill was at the front desk when I went to apply for a job. He stood smoking cigarettes and cracking lewd jokes in front of his crew and secretary. Bill was short and wiry; his hair looked like a still life sandstorm held in place with shellac. The combed fins along the sides of his head were reminiscent of bulging fish gills. His capped-toothed smile blew cigarette exhaust through wheezing laughter, exposing bad dental work and wads of gum that clicked and snapped as he spoke.

"So you want a job, do yah? Buy me a drink cross the street at the Patch Tavern and you can start tomorrow." He laughed and wheezed and goaded approval from his crew. "Just no foolin' around with my sexretary." They all thought he was hilarious and we headed across the street and I sealed a deal for a $4 an hour carpenter job.

He introduced me to Gary and Jessie. Gary was an affable guy whose wife cranked out the first of their eight kids in high school and, between bad credit and bad birth control, was going to have to work for Bill and endure his bad jokes and bad breath and breathe his second hand smoke the rest of his life. Jessie was big and quiet with enormous hands, out of jail on probation for killing his high school principal with a single punch to the jaw. He said, "I just lost my temper. He was going to expel me again and I didn't want my dad to find out cause I knew he'd beat me. It was an accident." He was bigger and stronger than he realized. As a gesture of friendship he promised to take me ice fishing when the lakes froze hard enough. I settled into a job at Bill's Millwork. They liked me and within a week I got two raises and was flying high at $5 an hour.

Every night after work everyone would pile into the Patch Tavern, or any other convenient drinking hole, and talk about getting laid, deer hunting, ice fishing, getting really drunk or combinations of all four. As the crowd wound down and headed home, I'd say goodbye, jump in my little VW with my patiently waiting dog and drive around the corner and park, crawl into my bunk and dream about all the money I was saving. I was a fiendish money saver with big dreams and what felt like important progress. I would save three out of every four paychecks.

Several months into my job I huddled in a cold phone booth and deposited $4 in quarters to call home, mostly to check on my mother's lingering battle with cancer. My father told me to high tail it home if I wanted to see my mother again as things weren't good. It felt like a setback to have to leave my good start, but I wanted to see my mother again if she was going to die.

I told Bill and the crew and left the next day and drove 56 hours nonstop through two Montana blizzards at 55 promised miles per hour back to Seattle. Despite being tense and tired and irritable, my mother had made a recovery by the time I arrived home. She had been given a six month prognosis at one point and was able to defy medical logic and prediction for the subsequent 27 years, an inexplicable mystery.

Seattle was having a typical wrist slitting winter—dark wet cold and gray. Everything in Seattle is a redundant gray, pavement gray, except when it's wet and then its cold gray dark and wet. I began to start spending my hard earned savings and home was a place where my dreams were usually derailed. So I packed up Tally and left.

We decided to head to the San Juan Islands several hours

north of Seattle where I had friends. It was a beautiful place but I knew work would be hard to find. My sullen mood was largely due to the feeling that if I wasn't moving forward in my dream, I must be slipping away and that left me feeling defeated. I was so confident at first.

I wasn't able to articulate my desires to my parents (from whom I was always desperately seeking approval) as they were too wrapped up in their own struggles. Those hard medical facts forced lots of marital questions into the light which had long been a tangled mess of barbed wire too thorny to make sense.

They were a generation that didn't know how to find meaningful professional help fearing the connotations of mental illness or that their peers would see them as somehow flawed. God forbid. It seemed easier to outwardly appear gorgeous, happy and prosperous, despite the lack of inner calm. Unfortunately while my mother was smiling, the back of her head was caving in. My father's inner personal injuries and pressures from work to rationalizing his infidelities led him into heavy rituals of reconciliation with a bottle of Jim Beam.

I'd saved $800 but it was beginning to slip between my lists of needs and survival costs. My dreams staggered through my thoughts like a poor drunken fool too preposterous to believe but too poignant not to want to. Good intention has nothing to do with a good plan. My self-esteem and progress was a ship tossed helplessly at sea. So I drove north to visit friends in the San Juan Islands and see if I could find work.

Chapter 12

Rabbits, Rednecks and Mud

There were only three cars unloading off the ferry from Anacortes to Friday Harbor in the rain that December afternoon in 1972. The local sheriff was standing by his squad car at the top of the off ramp and waved at the first two cars, raising his chin and smiling.

His eyes were knit in a curious scowl as he inspected my little VW, the long hair inside and my license plate as I drove past. I glanced into the rear view mirror without turning my head to watch his hyper-vigilance and not look too suspicious. I can feel guilty around someone like that even if I were coming from church after volunteering with the needy. He was definitely taking notes and I felt an impending dread.

Buck Gates, the cop, and I would have an aggravating relationship for the next several years. A week later I was pulled over, with flashing lights, in the middle of the sleepy town of Friday Harbor and lectured for three different infractions. First was that mud, splattered up from the hundred or so miles of road that crisscrossed the island, was covering and obscuring my license plate and we all know that deserves at least 20 minutes of public humiliation, lights a flashing.

The second was driving with bare feet. Having just come from the public showers at the port dock, I'd scampered to my car without shoes and, against my better judgment, not only backed out and over the yellow line in an abandoned parking lot (not many people boating in the dead of winter those years), ignored all that my parents and teachers had warned me of in life and recklessly propelled my little VW bug without shoes. As he snapped the pink ticket at me, ripping it from his little book, he told me how this town wouldn't tolerate my type, so either shape up or catch the ferryboat out. A week later I was pulled over for going 28 in a 25.

In the early 70's every cop in Washington State had his nose out of joint because the first successful hijacking high over the Cascade Mountains by D.B. Cooper had taken place and left them clueless. Every longhair and transient was on some level a suspect. Police power didn't like the public display of their inability to catch this clever crook. Besides hippies were always a target for the un-evolved small town cops to show their intolerance and express their anger. But the island had a magic that superseded such pettiness.

The allure was in its gray green rocky coastline, the seaweed streaming a hula rhythm in her currents, and the dark waters that seemed to change and shift with every mood. The thundering rich emerald green firs bowed and nodded and shook their wintry manes as the winter's southwesterly took turns beating in from the Straits.

It was a time when fishing and farming were important industries and everyone was related to someone who spent time doing one or the other, and often both. The Port of Friday Harbor was a lonely place in the early 70's and all but five or six boats in the harbor were fish boats. The onslaught of pleasure boating that eventually would replace these large wooden beasts of ocean labor would reverse those figures in a short 25 years.

The valley farms that swept southerly toward their water views of the Straits of Juan de Fuca and beyond to the ridged chilly peaks of the Olympic Mountains melted my heart. Deer were abundant, but the Belgian Jack rabbits were at epidemic proportion. Like ants or mosquitoes at a picnic, they were everywhere.

Farmers hated the rabbits. Collectively these Lagomorpha consumed gargantuan proportions of grass and, to exacerbate the situation, they dug warrens. This limitless tract housing was continuous and could spread over an acre. They dug everywhere and subsequently ruined field after field of potential grazing land by burrowing and rutting the fields. In an evening on the south side of the island, fields had an hallucinating imagery of brown shifting earth.

The bunnies numbered in the millions. Crawling, hopping, screwing like bunnies, dying, and forever eating and digging. Introduced 75 years earlier by a mink farmer who, apparently disgruntled by his profit margin, released what had been his animals' food source when his business folded. With no real predator, these large meaty animals swept from north to south with free abandon. It was unusual not to hit at least several driving a short distance across the island on a warm summer evening.

Young people put themselves through college, or at least got good drinking money, by netting hundreds of them at night. Driving old trucks or chopped cars known as "bunny buggies" through fields, they netted hundreds of spotlight baffled bunnies. Thrown into wire cages, on the backs of these farmer invented contraptions, they sold for meat at $1 apiece and $2 if they were killed and cleaned.

There were many cheap beers guzzled as spotlights and headlights streamed and flashed across dark island hayfields at three in the morning. But like cutting the green grass on the front lawn, it only seemed to encourage their growth. Money has never been made so easily while having so much fun as the farm kids who drove through fields on an August night, speeding along with cold beer and a salmon net, helping their parents rid the fields of these pests and fattening their own pocketbooks.

But for me, with my disciplined savings plan, they were a free food store. Bunnies along with mollusks on the rocks from the west side of the island were nourishment for many a meal. Stews and chowders were made for almost free, along with spring nettles, which ultimately put more money toward my savings despite the continual ribbing of friends about my road kill stews.

There was so much protein crossing the county roads in little bunny suits, it was always just a matter of time before you or the car in front of you knocked one in the head without destroying the flesh. With a quick swerve to the side of the road, I'd lean out the driver's door and throw the limp carcass behind the front seat, only to cook it for dinner a few hours later. It saved a 22 bullet.

I got pretty good at detecting the age of the animal which had a lot to do with one's ability to ingest it later. An older animal had a rubbery sinew comparable to a Michelin steel belted snow tire. But a young rabbit tasted just like chicken; only difference was there were four legs instead of two. I was glad to have it. It was a helpful means to an end.

That first winter was long wet cold and dark. I slept in the driveway of friends in my VW bug, my arm around the skinny frame of my devoted Golden Lab, Tally. My old friend Danny was surviving the winter in his bus with his dog and was envied for having a job pounding nails regardless if it meant putting up with his boss who seemed to pride himself on the top 50 ways of being a jerk.

Often I'd drive to the end of Cattle Point Road bumping along dodging mud puddles to the end of the park, past the abandoned concrete military building, off into the field overlooking Cattle Pass. This narrow passage between islands ebbed and flowed with enormous hydraulic fervor. Littered with piles of drift logs battered and smoothed by winter storms, it was a wonderful place to watch the hundreds of gulls drift, lift and fall, calling and crying. A bald eagle with one well timed marauding swoop could send an entire rookery of hundreds into a frenzy, like swarming honey bees.

I lay in my bed in my car staring at the ceiling a few feet over my head. The Northwest rain pattered its infernal drizzle on the roof of the Volkswagen. Tally groaned as he woke and looked at me with warm liquid eyes. All he wanted out of life was to be there with me and get fed. Such simple aspirations.

I lay there warm in my sleeping bag wondering what my desires were. What made me content and happy? Wanting a girlfriend came to mind as a priority, but when perusing the idea I felt muddled and confused. I had so little self-esteem for anything, but mostly with women. I could conjure up a million prospects in my mind. A few were cheerleaders from high school, one was a waitress at the diner in town and many were women just walking down the street. The backs of my eyeballs were always fully exploring, yet my expression and words acted disconnected from such notions. I truly wouldn't know what to do. I just wanted it. A frustration that was hard to comes to terms with. But here I lay in my car with my dog.

Dampness from our breathing has skim coated the interior and I remember I may have to jump-start the battery of my little hotel on wheels, as my battery is on a "cannot resuscitate" diagnosis from the garage in town.

This meant that with the door opened wide, my sleepy legs would have to push with every ounce of disc-popping, blood-spurting effort I can come up with, before my morning cup of coffee, and slowly roll the cold metal beast inch by foot across a field, lactic acid screaming in my thighs and my temples threatening to explode. Hopefully I gain a little speed. Faster and faster until I jump into the driver's seat, key on and pop the clutch while forcing my swollen engorged heart back down my throat. This act to be repeated until gas finds spark and ignition is made. Not a very posh calling card when trying to impress those cheerleaders.

So I lay on my back to change channels of thought and wonder what happened to my dream of the farm. Money, like blood, seems ugly but necessary to live my life. The rain dripped on the windows, and in the Northwest has a way of making you feel it may never stop—ever—and you'll get old and die, depressed and covered in a green mold, particularly when you're sleeping in your car in a remote field. Probably not found until some rabbit hunter stumbles across a litter of rusty metal parts and a car battery gleaming in its plastic shell.

Money was sifting through my fingers as the days passed. I had been waking myself early most mornings and heading into town to the Riptide Cafe where I'd troll the booths of men sipping white mugs of thin coffee and plates of runny eggs and hash browns slopped over with a good dose of ketchup. "Scuze me, I'm looking for work if you might know of any." The pause.

Two men look up from their world and there I stand. Tall skinny and disheveled. My long hair pulled back, my jeans dirty and full of holes, lots of battery acid burns on both upper thighs and on the shoulders from carrying dead car batteries. I wore enormous mud-brown colored sweaters and surplus raingear and looked like an unlucky find if you're walking on the beach studying driftwood and kelp. Mostly these guys were not.

I worked one day throwing sheetrock scraps into the backfill of a house under construction. Wet cold and tired, I asked the boss if I could get paid at the end of eight hours and he told me to fuck off as he stood there flexing a 24-ounce framing hammer gripped in his right hand, water dripping off the fronts of our hats. My withered self-esteem smeared a pathetic expression of defeat across my face and I drove away cussing at my steamy windshield.

I needed that subtle body language game. Stand there on the balls of my feet with a sort of swollen body gripped with that subliminal message that I was ready to challenge or fight. Talk with a cocky self-confident smile, testosterone dripping from the corners of my mouth and the look that, when it comes to babes, I'll tell you stories you can't even fantasize about. Your lunch hours will be pure entertainment and, by the way, I tell all. Besides being a linebacker and an all-state wrestler, I have my own tools and one of my girlfriends works at the donut shop so I can bring cases of fresh donuts everyday to work. Free of course. I can start tomorrow. Today I got to go home and skin out the buck I shot out the window of my new Dodge 4x4 with a Hemi and a custom lift kit. Oh, and by the way, pay me anything you want, I just want to be part of the team.

These qualities I did not possess. I rocked back on the heels of my feet and felt they saw through me instantly. The words came out, but the confidence did not. My little Volkswagen didn't have that workhorse image with its bent bumpers and decaying ragtop. One glance inside sent off alarms in the mess of a bed crumpled with clothes, ten tins of peanut butter and a wet smiling dog. My tools were few, but I needed work.

Leonard drove up in a vintage 1948 Ford pickup half-ton one morning while I sat in a booth nursing a thin cup of diner coffee, fantasizing at how good some eggs and hash browns would taste. He walked in all buoyant and full of himself. His hair was blown dry and held in place by a handful of spray products giving the shellacked helmet hair look.

For Leonard most days were good hair days, and he had that look like he and the Mrs. got lucky last night and today he was feeling like a million bucks. He stood in the doorway, with his jacket collar pulled up, one arm up on the doorjamb looking sort of Travolta-esque in a scene out of "Saturday Night Fever."

For a second I thought he might break into verse but instead announced to everyone present. "Anyone looking for work? I need a couple hippies that will work for low pay and don't mind freezing their ass off." He laughed out loud because he found himself so incredibly funny. Simultaneously the heads of all the men I'd been pestering for work turned and stared at me. Spotlight on me,

I raised my hand sheepishly, sort of admitting to this crowd that I was not only a hippie (generally a bad word) but that I needed work and was willing to work for low pay in the cold.

Leonard pivot toed on over and explained that Jackson's Cannery was going through a major do-over, as the salmon season next summer was looking good and they were remodeling. "I need a carpenter full time but I'm only paying $3.10 an hour. It's cold in there in the winter, so dress warmly."

As he turned and glissaded toward the door, my spirit soared with excitement. Confidence was seeping back into my veins. I raised my hand and asked the waitress to bring me a plate of eggs and hash browns. She smiled, winked and said, "Alright. Mr. Big Spender's got a job."

Russ worked at the cannery as well. He was in his late 40's and felt like life had wronged him. As a fisherman he had to work winters to make it through the year and this was an injustice. His heart was on the water, and time good was time fishing and all the work ashore was killing time.

Leonard was right; the cold winter wind blew through that old building that stuck out on the point with water on three sides. A cold wind in the 40 plus degree range, blowing at 20 knots off 46 degree water, penetrates clothes and one's spirit in a large cavernous barn-like building with no insulation and lots of wet concrete. The cold of the maritime Northwest penetrates like no other.

Russ and I worked well together. A large polar bear of a man wrapped in coveralls, Russ spoke very little preferring to chew antacids all day and keep his thoughts to himself.

The hours and the days passed in that cold building where the waves pestered the bulkheads and the wind prowled through, but I was able to put three paychecks in the bank and live off one. My life was progressing once again toward my fantastic desire to have a farm

Chapter 13

Cabin on the Shore. A Place of Change

After work I hung out with my friends, a group of younger folks like myself. Lack of money plagued us all, but it was a time of idealism. We felt the anthem of alternative thinking important and in a perfect world money wasn't the most important thing. Not unless you wanted to buy land, have a child, drive a car that was dependable enough to travel off-island, and a myriad of other choices that required dipping into the capitalist system. It was a conflict.

Most of us worked at the salmon cannery in the summer or construction or seasonal farm work or fished while others grew dope. When marijuana went from a benign hippies' choice of a few plants for personal use to the Mafia controlled underground business of high stakes and mega profits, some chose to play the hippie capitalist and retreat to the paranoid life of a grower. As seductive as it was, my intestinal track couldn't tolerate the tension of such a life. I had too many fears and visions of a darkened Papillon-esque cell, a dim shaft of dusty light, and scratches in neat rows that showed the days and months and years that had passed.

Island jobs were lousy. Everyone who worked at the cannery spent every spare free hour bitching and discussing the horrible conditions of the cannery. Everyone in those days who worked construction bitched and complained about the handful of cowboy contractors. And everyone felt sorry for the waitresses with their minimum wage hopes, their ashtrays full of nickels and pennies, and their hard, armored, calloused smiles that politely fielded derogatory sexual slurs and the occasional sloppy hand.

The 60's were over, according to the calendar, and the early 70's were when our noble and lofty concepts sought a reality. It was time to test the metal of all the talk of the previous decade. The music, politics and discussions pushed handfuls of young people to live the ideals beyond a momentary discussion.

We were a group known as "back to the landers" or the "rubber boot crowd". How do we change the world with practical survival yet retain the revolutionary ideals? Capitalism for us college dropouts was a bitter pill, but it somehow needed to fit. It was much easier to stay up late listening to music as it oiled our existential discussions, with a joint and a bottle of wine, ironing out the precepts of a more perfect society.

On one level or another we all shared a beginning toward realism gleaned from our campus lives ignited by the Vietnam War, archaic racists and a latent acknowledgement of women as equals. Where was one to go after the peace march that took over the freeway chanting for the end of the war? What was one to do when on TV we watched policemen and their dogs attack blacks marching in the South? And what were we supposed to think when fellow white students were shot and killed on a campus not too far from our own? There were hundreds of issues that seemed of concern such as equal pay for equal work and recognition of those with different sexual orientations.

To many it felt like raw indignity to snuggle into the honeycomb dormitory room, after a meal of industrial carbohydrates, only pursuing these questions between nine and five as intellectual abstracts. Too much of college life felt as if we were being groomed for a repeat performance of the ills of a country that needed changing. So in large unprecedented numbers, without any real plans, many young Americans including myself and my friends dropped out.

We were all diving into the pond of the new experience and behind us on dry land were our parents, our colleges, our government and a mind-set that no longer made sense. It was a terrifically exciting time, a dangerous adventure appealing to many of us in our early 20's. The question was could we float, how long could we last, and who among us wouldn't be able to stand the liquid freeform experience and would turn back to shore?

To some the water was great, to some it was not, and for a few the plunge was a lifesaver. We grew gills and flourished. The creative process of this new life and the thought of returning to the existence we'd come from left us gasping for air, flopping on the dock with a hook of dread in our mouth. I embraced the principles of escape.

Living in my little car was damp and cold. It was a continual nest of dirty clothes, a wet dog, steamy windows and a scratchy AM radio. So when I heard of a free cabin far out on the west side of the island, I went to explore it immediately.

Far past the end of the summer road, past the last lights of farm houses, through barren rabbit warren fields, down along the craggy west side where the only thing that grows well is rock, down along the water's edge in a little draw was a cabin. Like the few fir trees that occasionally found footing in the crevasses, it stood proud but weather worn and beaten by the winter winds.

One hundred feet in front, spread out like a ten million dollar movie, were the Straits of Juan de Fuca, ever changing and glorious. This vast sea was home to whales, seabirds, seal, sea lions and thousands of migrating salmon. Rising up from the horizon line some twenty miles south were the Olympic Mountains that in the winter coyly gave glimpses of their snow capped jagged spires—a powerful glory reminiscent of the Alps all bundled and stuck on the Olympic peninsula. And far off to the west was the smarmy glow of lights from Victoria B.C., a dignified little city described once as more English than England. I was in love with this little place immediately.

It was a wintry day when, for the first time, I slid the door open into a small single room perhaps 14 x 18 feet. Overflowing coffee cans littered the floor, left to catch the rain from the leaking roof which spluttered and dripped in an awkward rhythm. It was moist and cold and felt very forgotten, but with a little driftwood gathered from a small cove nearby I lit a fire in the old wood cook stove. The small amount of heat, along with a few stubby candles, brought a flicker of life to the cozy uninsulated wooden walls. The wet wood hissed, and steam drifted aimlessly off the cold cast iron surface as I swept the floor with a handleless broom.

This little dwelling with its ten million dollar view, creaky little walls and leaky roof was a giant step up in the forward motion of the uncharted waters I was traversing. A remote cabin, far from anywhere, a refuge for thought and a place of permission to live the way I wanted.

It was to become the place for emotional transformation. A self-chosen retreat to let myself wander into whatever was to come next by merely just letting what was already in me come out.

I gathered my sleeping bag and few belongings from my little car and officially moved in. It didn't take long. I didn't have much. After a few days of sleeping there, guilt led me to the Assessor's Office for the rightful owner's address so I could make contact and hopefully legitimize an arrangement.

After a myriad of letters to a Minnesota address, Barbara still didn't believe anyone could live there in winter and suggested I must be confused. I drew pictures and wrote elaborately and eventually she was convinced I was spending a winter in her little summer cabin. We worked a deal where, with a few repairs, I was allowed to stay. We wrote extensively after that which was the beginning of a life friendship knitted together over our love for this tiny refuge she'd built some time in the 1950's.

Her generosity and acts of kindness were much appreciated

but, looking back from the vantage of many years, I now see that my friendship with Barbara was a pinnacle point in my transformation of spirit, a life-saving time in my growth as I pushed beyond the first 20 years. I wriggled and squirmed past the rigid molds of my family and school. I felt very alone but reasonably confident as I progressed toward the reinvention of my life.

The following weeks I settled into my hermit existence with a song in my heart. I continued work at the cannery where Russ and I pounded nails with purple blue hands, talked little and ground out the hours for small sums of money. This led to a very simple trip to the grocery store: a 10-pound bag of potatoes and one of onions, instant coffee and a gallon of milk, a loaf of bread, a large can of peanut butter and one of jelly and for the mornings, instant Krusteaz pancake mix. Just add water and pour the mixture right onto the surface of the little cook stove.

Often a gallon of Cribari wine, one cup doled out at night to myself like a prison camp allotment. A cup slowly savored as the kerosene lamps flickered, CBC AM radio driveled from a two inch speaker, and I sat on a chair in front of the woodstove both stockinged feet stretched straight out in front of me into the open cavern of the oven. There with one hand I held my cup of cheap wine and with the other I stuffed chunks of wood into the firebox.

Outside the winter winds howled and the rain smattered against the roof. This point in the day I found great relaxation and contentment. My mind drifted between radio shows and plans for the future. I was finally in a place where I felt happy and moving ever so slowly forward, but forward it was.

Bunnies could be shot from the front door step with my pawnshop 22, this of course if one had not been procured during my drive home. There were wonderful large mussels clinging to the rocks directly in front of the cabin, filter feeding themselves into what came to be known as tennis shoes, nick-named for their large size and shape. These would periodically have small imperfect pearls in them which rendered me, after 13 months, a tiny Dixie cup about one-third full of oddly shaped bluish pearls.

Regretfully, in a Steinbeck moment, I remember walking to the edge of the rocks when I moved out and throwing the pearls back into the sea, no doubt worth less than the Dixie cup which contained them. I wish I'd known I was to be married and have daughters one day. I would have loved to string the little purple imperfections for one of them. But at 21 years old, I was hardly inclined to believe any of that might ever happen and the swells that crashed against the rocks that morning ate them up with a yawning insignificance.

Time spent roaming the rocks and walking the shoreline or evenings in the cabin was the incubation of the dare to let myself change - to feel my way into ideas rather than to employ my over active brain to think myself into a thousand corners. Thinking had become too controlled by childhood perceptions that left me feeling depressed.

Merely hauling water from the little spring a hundred feet away and watching a pod of whales go by was soothing and on some level started to feel important. It was not a conscious effort derived from monastic discipline or meditation but more of whimsical luck, a result of playing with my fantasy and a giving in to what felt good. I had been desperately out of luck, in school and at home, to the point that I felt the gruesome wet cold blanket of depression might always be covering me.

Now I felt aware when the wind was blowing or the sun was on my face or cold was making my fingers clumsy. A spirit was wakening and the first glimpses of it finding time with my heart began to show.

I made house. I collected wood from the beach and made stools. I made a cabinet from wooden egg boxes lifted from the cannery and fashioned them into a box with a door that had a little screened vent, called a cool-cabinet. This was nailed to a shady wall outside to keep milk and eggs. I bought a few kerosene lamps and pots and pans from garage sales. The little space inside felt like I'd moved into a gymnasium after life in my car. I felt the luckiest person on earth.

After driving the summer road of soft silty soil for a number of months, it was necessary in the fall and winter rains to park my car a good quarter mile away to keep from getting stuck and risk spending hours excavating myself out of the mud. This area of the island was wind scarred, had very few trees and little one could winch to or pull from.

One early morning, as the wind and rain pelted, I gunned my way through a risky looking muddy patch in the middle of a large open field, a sort of mud scatting, when the bottom fell out and I slammed to an abrupt halt, heaving Tally dog and me forward into the windshield. I had been avoiding the main path, as it had had too much traffic and was looking too muddy to traverse. I'd unknowingly driven over a rain soaked bunny warren that collapsed under the weight of the car which sunk to its wet muddy bumpers. Armed with only the little jack that comes with the car, a ridiculously impish tool barely made for changing a tire in the best of conditions, I set to work. The car was up to the bumpers at both ends and the rain was coming down in sheets.

Far from any farmhouse, I walked around looking for dunnage to place under the jack. My rubber boots collapsed into deep waterlogged mud holes, spilling cold muck over the tops and down into my warm socks. I scooped out the chocolate ice cream mud with my bare hands to put the jack under the axle as daylight brought a moldy gray light to my dismal situation. As I pumped the jack handle, it was obvious the jack was moving down through the mud instead of the car moving up.

I needed more dunnage, a larger platform in which to build from, so for the next eight hours I hauled and carried old fence posts and rocks as I jacked up one end, and then the other, pushing whatever I could beneath the tires. With grit and determination, and mostly desperation, I persevered. The day passed.

Originally I was fearing being late for work, but the mud was a fearsome miserable opponent and I dug with bare hands and soaked clothing all day and when I was finally able to grind and sputter my way back to harder ground, it was too late to go to work. So I parked and slogged, bone weary wet and exhausted, down the hill to my little cabin and called it a day. After that I never drove closer than a quarter mile from the cabin with the memory of that ugly day well etched into my psyche.

One afternoon as I walked down the hill to the cabin, a small clump of bushes began to shake and from behind came a low grumbling bear like grunt that quickly increased in ferocity. Moments later the familiar face of brother Hughie jumped out laughing, "Did I get yah?" I didn't realize how much I missed him. Hugh had been a long time gone on the East coast attending the university and we hadn't spent a lot of time together in years.

It was a great reunion and we stayed up late drinking cups of cheap wine and talking about where I had come to on this remote island. He loved it. He wanted it as well. He said life at Harvard had grown irrelevant to the questions of the day. We talked late into the night about farming and how important it was.

Just like so many years before in the apple tree playing "little men", we hashed out ideas and concepts that, naive or real, felt important and full of purpose. This was a place where we, as brothers, were very close. We openly shared our dreams and fantasies. Our affection was not flawless, as we had learned affection in a harsh environment. Competing one minute, sharing and caring deeply the next, but I always knew I loved him deeply. With this admission we realized that living on the same piece of land might end us up in a brutal tangle. Hughie decided to look on Lopez, a neighboring island.

Chapter 14

Land

Hughie found a job caretaking the old McCauley farm on Lopez Island, all the while working every odd job imaginable. He built miles of fences, hand dug water wells some as deep as 40 feet, built houses and eventually managed to scrape together enough money with a few loans for a down payment.

I'd called him from a phone booth in town and he told me he'd found a piece of land he wanted and thought he could afford. He had $3,500 he was going to put down and his payments were going to be in the neighborhood of $125 a month. His voice lacked confidence and he asked if I'd come over and help him seal the deal. Neither of us had ever experienced high finance and he wanted a little moral support.

Before signing the papers, Hugh and I drove over to where his dream farm was to take place. We rattled along through the woods in his old truck dodging the crater sized potholes. He was talking at a hundred miles an hour, excitement and fear racing neck and neck through his words, our exuberant dogs licking the spring air with flared nostrils from their toe clawed perch on the back bed.

We came upon a little clearing in the dense fir trees beside the road. It was small, perhaps 30 by 50 feet. Hugh got out and his eyes lit up and he looked at me as if he'd just brought home the most beautiful girl in the world and wanted me to marvel and show a little jealousy. I gave the little brother reticent smile, ever posturing our feelings of closeness, a game we pushed and pulled at. Truck doors slammed and dogs dove off the flat bed like missiles into the underbrush. Hugh sputtered on with ideas, plans and philosophical platitudes as if reminiscent of the days of playing "little men".

"This is where I'm going to build my house, all handmade from scrounged lumber, and over here a barn or shed for some goats and up here . . ." We are now plowing through dense underbrush and thick grabby branches in a dense fir thicket. He plows on and on, rambling on about cows and draft horses. It's impossible to see three feet for all the branches. In fact, it's so dense our faces are being swatted and slapped as we push on through until we arrive at what seems to be a maple tree.

Hugh proudly announces, "There's eight of these. Some kid planted them way back and I'm going to clear all this land with an axe and turn it into pasture." I was stil staring at nothing but branches just trying to see five feet, but he had a vision and he was possessed.

We made our way to Mike Lemar's house, the agent in charge of selling the land. We sat in his kitchen on plastic covered metal chairs at a Formica covered chrome metal table - two long haired, bearded, awkward looking pokes hurting for adventure and terrified of making mistakes. Between us, we had absolutely no experience whatsoever in real estate, or for that matter, in anything financial.

Hugh chewed the corners of his mustache, his forehead a city map of wrinkles, as Mr. Lemar strutted the linoleum floor in his pajama bottoms and a triple XXXL stained white t-shirt. His military haircut looked fresh exposing a large extra white patch of skin on the back of his head, while the little sharp points of the flat top glistened with Vitalis. He marched between the table and the refrigerator pouring slugs of bourbon into glasses of milk, prematurely celebrating his big sale, as we sat somewhat speechless stabbing glances at each other like little boys at the dinner table.

With a glance, I knew what Hugh was asking. He needed my reassurance but it was hard to do much more than shrug as Mr. Lemar explained, with a demeaning undertone, lots of things we didn't understand. Hugh signed the contract obediently, one last glance at me, one last shrug and a sheepish smile back at him, and Hugh handed him a bank check for $3,500. He was handing over hundreds of hours of hard work and signing up for thousands more. They shook hands and we left.

When the truck doors slammed, Hugh, while fumbling for the keys, had a look of terror and excitement on his face. Not quite sure if he'd done the right thing or not he let out a long drawling "ffffuuucccckkk!" We drove away.

When I returned to San Juan I went straight into a real estate office and sat down with an agent. Hugh's land purchase had made me feel confident in the possibilities that he could, as an older brother, break the trail of experience for me, three years younger. A little envy and competitive spirit nudged me along as well.

I explained to Bob, the agent, that I was looking for a piece of land I could farm. I wanted open fields, water and a small forest for building and firewood, fertile soil . . . I sounded like some immigrant homesteader fresh off the boat having just cleared Ellis Island. He looked across the desk and said, "I've got just the place."

As we hopped in his car, I was thinking that he probably says that to every client. We drove a short distance out of town as I rambled about wanting to be a farmer and he politely nodded and acted interested holding his real questions to himself. We stopped in the woods alongside the ruts and potholes on Boyce Road and walked down into a deep green stand of waving fir trees. We followed an ancient road that had grown over and, within the first 100 feet, I turned to Bob and said, "I'll take it."

He smiled, dismissing my silly humor, and we continued walking. The words had just sort of blurted out of me. After all I'd only known Bob for 30 minutes and been on the land for two. I just knew it. It came perhaps from some inner intuitive compass I was not altogether familiar with. "You haven't seen the meadow yet." We walked from the woods out into a 20 acre hidden meadow surrounded by trees, tall grass shimmered silver across green. Several deer took notice and then disappeared into the woods. "There's a stream down here and one over there and they meet right over there." Bob was gesturing in all directions but I was not really listening as much as I was feeling a warmth and a happiness.

I was lost in a dream of where the cabin would go and the barn and the cows and the pond and it was everything I wanted. It was an enormous magnetism of spirit. Something pulled and pushed and held and coaxed me. I was home.

"I'll take it," I repeated. Bob smiled again. "This is only the first piece you've seen. Wouldn't you like to see a little more?" My mouth said yes but my mind said I was just being polite. We drove around and I never got out of the car. Nothing compared and I couldn't concentrate. I was in love. My intuition was running strong and deep and it had made me a believer.

On the way back to town, I explained I had $3,500 and a second job and could give him $1,500 more in 6 months. He told me to come by the next morning with a bank check and I could sign. The owner wanted $1,300 an acre for the 17 acres. I didn't realize at the time I could barter and perhaps offer a little less, but it was only the first of a million lessons I became wiser to in time.

May 1, 1974, the 17 acres became my own. My payments were $150 a month at 8% interest. I was flat broke. I rifled through the glove box for change. I was working but I remember having literally no money for a week or so after I gave over my savings. A tank of gas, a few groceries and a job at the cannery and a promise to pick up extra work when I could. But now I had land.

I'd signed a contract that had a flowery cover sheet and one page of legal statements full of promises and signatures. My fate was sealed and I walked away happier than imaginable.

I moved out of the little cabin on the west side almost immediately and moved on to the land a month before it legally even closed. I wanted to be with this piece of the earth and, like a crazed lover, all my thoughts were in finding out as much as I possibly could about it. I stared at it and walked it for hours. I woke at night and walked it in the dark. I listened to the night animals, the frogs, and the wind, the owls, the stream gurgling and I listened to the deer that passed bashful eyed, curious and alarmed at my invasion. I spent long hours lying on the ground trying to fathom my good fortune, watching the clouds tumble east and west.

I took a long afternoon and lay in the cool shade of the underbrush by the stream and built a fluttermill: two Y shaped sticks pushed into the sandy silt in the bottom of the stream, and a long carefully engineered process with my jackknife whittling a 4 inch shaft with 2 thin reed blades that, with the tender coaxing of the stream, would turn or flutter endlessly. A stolen moment from Marjorie Kinnan Rawlings' *The Yearling* from a memory of lying in bed and my mother's soft voice reading aloud. Each year on the anniversary of my purchase, I repeat this ritual. It's a way of being with my birth mother and my land as mother and to give thanks that I have known them both.

I had purchased a tipi from a friend months before for this occasion and spent the first few days after work picking out small trees. I felled them with a Swede saw and peeled them into long, skinny, smooth poles with a drawknife. I erected these in the prescribed cluster near the stream, wrapped the canvas shell around it and moved in to the 17 foot tapering cone. A small mattress on the left for sleeping, a fire in the center, and piles of clothes and tools and a wet dog who'd drag in delirious from the excitement of chasing bunnies. I was as full of energy as I was of romantic ideas.

The stream, where I'd erected my dwelling, was in the lowest portion of the land and was actually more of a marsh. I'd race home after work and put myself to one of the hundreds of over-whelming tasks ahead, no plans, no experience, no blueprints, only romantic visions and a lot of determination.

I had no tools except a hammer, a drawknife, a handsaw and a tape measure. I stole pouches full of nails from work. Actually I would empty my pouch every evening after work and arrive the next morning with an empty nail apron but made it a rule not to be too gluttonous. I realized I had a terrific stroke of luck and didn't want to jinx my good fortune. On some level of rationality, stealing a little seemed okay.

But down deep I knew it was time to give up my school train-ing as a cheater and klepto. I was ass-deep in good fortune and I didn't want to blow it for some stupid indiscretion. There would be a new feeling of renewal about who I was by changing my re-actions to the world around me. So I quit, cold turkey, but I quit.

I peeled dozens and dozens of poles and framed a chicken coop and made a pigpen and garden fences. All things equal, I was discovering I was pretty good at these homestead crafts. It came somewhat as a surprise, but notching and fitting logs and building with little or no money was an art form that required a creative mind. The same mind that had figured out how to survive in school had finally found a positive place to release its talents.

Animals arrived. Gifts from people who felt they could be nice by getting rid of the problem or neglected animals at their house. A pig named T-boe who was criminally able to escape any pen he'd ever been in. The one I'd labored over held him in for about twenty minutes and he arrived at the tipi, snorting toward the oval hole with the smell of dog food on his mind. I spent many hours chasing and coercing and rebuilding pens for that pig.

One day I arrived home from a long 24 hour shift at the can-nery and T-boe was missing. Bleary eyed, I headed toward the tipi for a sleep and found my pig sleeping contently on my sleeping bag. He'd pushed his way through the door, probably moments after I'd left for work the previous day, gorged himself on a good 40 pounds of dog food and shit his way across the tipi to my bed where he smeared his filth and pig slobber onto my sleeping bag after chewing and disassembling my feather pillow. He was startled at the audacity of my entrance and squealed and grunted and torpedoed out under the back wall of my little shelter. T-boe's life ended shortly after. Sudden death from a well placed 22 slug. I was eating pork for quite a while.

There were goats, a flock of weathered Nubians, cute as kittens, that escaped their little enclosure and pillaged my outdoor camp and had no shame when it came to pooping in camp or eating from the vegetable garden. Poop where you want and eat whatever you want, they seemed clueless to my rules. They left to another unsuspecting goat herder who had naïve notions about their cute little antics.

I had the vision that a farm was to have animals, many kinds, despite any function they might offer or preparedness of feed or pen. Perhaps it was in defiance of Hughie's edict, when we were five and eight years old, that I was to be the truck farmer and he the animal farmer.

As the word spread amongst the islanders that I was starting a farm, people offered me gifts. Would you like a horse, or some goats that could escape Alcatraz? Pigeons, roosters? I was even offered an ocelot by a woman who was moving and didn't want to take it with her. It never materialized but images of this stealthy cat in my chicken coop never occurred to me. "Oh yah, I'll take that. That would be cool."

There was a flock of geese dropped off by a professor who was moving away to study algae in South Africa and entrusted me with 20 some white honking geese. They strutted around camp like a pompous group of elderly women from the PTA, self-absorbed in discussion and self-righteousness, ready to announce to the world any injustices of potential harm or danger with shrill nasal blasts, each repeating the others' cautionary warnings. Other than that, they seemed content eating the grasses and enjoying the waning current of the spring stream. Always single file and a little paranoid, they made an effort to appear in control while clinging to the fundamental principles of the higher goose.

Then, as would happen every spring around mid-June, the stream dried up. I would arrive home from the cannery late in the evening, tired from hours of pounding machines and fish guts, to find a distressed scene from *Animal Farm*. Geese, chickens, Mooch the horse, and various other strays ambushed my arrival protesting the world without water.

I carried a couple of steel barrels in the back of my pickup truck full of water from the cannery and would siphon the water from a garden hose into various dishes and troughs much to the excitement of my livestock. They'd slurp and snuffle, glug and sputter, and the geese would jump in and begin to preen and wash off the day's hot dust. Within thirty minutes there remained only a few puddles of murky mud; animals rehydrated wandered back into the grasses of the meadow, all of us oblivious to any common sense regarding the basics like needing water, clean and abundant.

Rick was with me one afternoon, one who always found the humor in such things, and while watching this Serengeti ceremony said, "What you gunna name your farm? You otta call it Thirsty Goose Farm." We had a good laugh, but the name stuck with variations such as Thirsty Goose Slug and Thistle Farm, or Thirsty Gooses' Boogie Bottom Frog and Cricket Farm and on and on, sort of depending on the events of the day. Thirsty Goose Broken Truck and Smashed Finger Farm. Eventually it was eternalized simply as Thirsty Goose Farm.

Other basic needs found creative solutions. The stream, when it ran, had been a place to do dishes and wash the murk from my body. When it dried up, there were the pay showers down at the Port and many of us "back to the landers" piled precious quarter after quarter into the little slot robbing machines for three minutes of hot water, forever racing to lather up and rinse before the water cruelly and abruptly stopped despite a scalp full of suds.

It became an art form of hyper-active flailing arms in a disgusting cinderblock stall whose grimy walls always looked like undiscovered science, scary and contagious. I walked out into the parking lot looking like I'd just lost a fight with a fire hose. Racing to beat the clock and the fear of having to insert three more quarters to rinse off, I'd stagger out steaming wet, wet hair, slightly cleaner, and exhausted.

Both working at the cannery waist deep in fish, or working on the farm waist deep in dirt of many different flavors, meant clothes didn't stay clean for very long. Between the battery acid holes, the grease that no detergent could budge, the soil that caked on the knees of jeans and the permanent stench of foul fish, most clothes reached a point where they were removed and thrown on the evening fire and burned to ashes after their months of service.

Some of us devised a method, during the summer months, that saved a few bucks at the laundromat and took advantage of the miles of pothole gravel roads on the island. Water was abundant at the cannery so I would fill a barrel in the back of my pickup about half full with clean water, throw in the filthy jeans and sweaters along with a handful of laundry detergent, secure the lid and drive the bumpy road home. Change the water once in a while, slosh about the island a few more miles, and then drape the wet but cleaner clothes over my truck in the sun while on shift in the cannery. This barrel became known as the Broke Hippie Bachelors' Laundromat.

The summer passed into fall and work at the cannery was all consuming when the wild sockeye salmon were running. Large vessels known as tenders swaggered, with their sterns dragging low, into the cannery at any hour of day or night bulging with fish. These boats were hired by the cannery to buy fish in the sheltered waters of the fish grounds and deliver them to the cannery, when full, where they were unloaded into brailer bags or conveyor belts and sluiced into the caverns of the canning facility.

There were concrete bulk headed rooms that were filled to capacity measuring 4 feet high and 30 feet by 30 feet where workers waist deep in fish pushed them with rakes toward gated troughs. Thousands of pounds of fish lay in these rooms waiting to be processed, their vacant eyes staring at the ceiling, life and spirit left in the ocean.

Sledded through a sluiceway onto a table known as an indexer, the fish were one by one conveyored side by side toward a revolving propeller-like blade that would decapitate each just behind the gill plate. This ghoulish invention would and could cut any finger or body part with relentless precision.

From there the fish would flop on their backs and slide into the Iron Chink (named for the dozen or so Chinamen the invention had replaced) and were grabbed by a pointed set of spears at the tail and dragged through a series of knives and brushes that did about 85% of the cleaning of the fish.

This was the machine I ran for a few consecutive summers. It was a loud circular crashing and clanging machine that spluttered and tossed fish guts in a hollow for 10 feet around it. This meant that the entire time the machine was on, I in my rain gear was being splattered by the evisceration of thousands of fish. I used to laugh to myself when I thought of what my parents would say if they saw me. All those years of worry and money put toward educating me and here I was spending 18 hour days covered in fish guts for some $3.50 an hour.

The fish were then dropped on to a table where they were grabbed by any of a dozen workers, known as slimers, and with knives they would clean the fish for the final trip toward the cutters that segmented the fish to specific sizes so they would fit into either quarter pound or half pound tin cans.

Lids slid down log tracks and flipped face down onto the fully packed and salted cans of raw fish. The lids were sealed and the cans dropped into large wagon baskets that were wheeled on train tracks into enormous retorts or pressure cookers where they were subjected to extreme heat and cooked through. This process was loud, wet, messy and exhausting and we had shifts that lasted until the fish were all in cans.

There were no breaks except lunch and dinner, no overtime and I think my top wage was in the $4 an hour range. I remember a shift of 32 hours on the clock and many 18 and 20 hour days.

Fatigue led to accidents. Wet numb fingers, half-mast eyelids and sheer boredom sent many a worker to the emergency room for stitches or worse. One morning early, after working the midnight shift until daylight, I was cleaning king salmon. After hours of hurking bins full of heavily iced fish, some as big as 50 pounds, one at a time on to a table and cutting out the gillrakers and eviscerating their mammoth hulls, the sharp blade of a filet knife and a frozen finger met going in opposite directions.

I yanked my hand free after the electric needles of sliced flesh sent a dreaded sensation up my arm. Blood sprayed and I clutched my hand and squeezed as blood and gurry ran from my fingers. I stripped myself from my rain gear and drove directly to the clinic for repair. I had my "cannery clothes" on, clothes not too far from their own crematorium.

The receptionist at the clinic, who was the nurse, stared at me with a quizzical smile as she filled in my name and address. Around the corner I heard her talking to the doctor and mentioned that I was the dirtiest man she had ever seen. There I stood, dripping blood and fish slime in my rank cannery clothes, long scraggly hair hanging in my face, a beard full of fish scales and gurry. I smelled foul and looked worse. Little did I know at that point that I was meeting for the first time a person I would grow a terrific fondness for and she toward me—my future mother-in-law. I was stitched up and sent back to work none the wiser at the time.

The infernal crashing rhythms of the cannery's machinery was exhausting. In a desire to be frugal, most of the workers, including myself, slipped a salmon into their boot on the way out at the end of the day. These gorgeous fish supplied protein at every potluck and many a barbecue to those of us willing to still look at them after long hours waist deep in their slimy blue backed and silver bellied carcasses.

Chapter 15

Healing Lost Parts of Myself

It was mid-summer and the days were long and the mornings warm. I was niggling my cooking fire into enough heat to make a cup of coffee. Suddenly the dogs jumped to their feet, running into the woods announcing the arrival of someone approaching. I had been given a small St. Bernard known as Tugboat. I looked but nobody appeared. The dogs were out of my sight and had stopped barking.

Curious, I wandered into the woods and there, kneeling on the ground, was a young boy with an enormous backpack easily half his size. "Hello," I said. He was caressing the dogs with hands of confidence. Thinking this tiny person hadn't heard me I said hello again. This time without turning his head, he gave me a slight peripheral glance.

"What's going on?" I was a little taken aback by this tiny person in my woods with the oversize pack who seemed overly interested in the dogs, did not speak, and appeared from who knows where. His curly black hair hung in his eyes as if to protect him from bright lights and nosey questions. From behind the veil of his bangs he could see what he wanted and nobody could see him.

There were long silences as I asked obvious but dumb questions. He finally stood up and, looking at his boots, in a tiny soft voice which I barely heard half of, whispered, "Tim. I'm Rob's brother. I came to find him but we had a fight." He stood silently, his hands reaching toward the dogs, staring at the ground.

I felt like I'd just come across a fawn in the woods. Tender, tiny and vulnerable. I told him I was just about to make some breakfast and slowly walked toward my camp. The dogs followed and slowly, quietly, hesitantly so did Tim. "I was going to have a bowl of granola. Want one?" I looked at him with a peripheral glance trying not to be too intimidating. He stood there with his enormous pack looking away. Silence.

"Tell you what," I said, "I'm going to make two bowls and I'm going to put one right here on the box and if you want it, go ahead and eat it. Just be careful the dogs don't get it before you, if you want it." Silence. I poured the milk over the grains and set the bowl on the box. "You can take your pack off if you want. It looks heavy." The little quiet deer quickly picked up the bowl and wolfed down the granola. "You want some more, you're welcome."

We are now talking in glances only. We were both mousing around a silent situation not exactly sure how to proceed. I was digressing quickly to sideways glances and small quiet words. Tim said nothing, but stood heavily planted next to his pack.

Eventually I told him I was going to see a friend and then to the dump. He peripherally seemed to be fine with that and I told him to stay as long as he wanted and make himself at home.

I jumped in my truck and bee-lined it to Rob's house. Rob was a cannery worker friend, younger than I, a dropout from Los Angeles, who lived on cigarettes and black coffee. He was smart at everything I wasn't and had great enthusiasm for wild ideas and philosophical discussion, his adrenals generally whining at maximum caffeinated RPM's.

He explained over coffee and a cigarette that Tim had run away from home, from their dad who'd married a devil lady, and wanted to live with him. He too was trying to escape and was navigating a relationship with Lisa, his new girlfriend, and between the caffeine, nicotine and her Italian blood he wasn't interested in taking care of his baby brother. He had his hands full already. "Dunnit too much. No fucking way. I left LA to get away from all that BS. And now it's following me up here. No fucking way." I drove to the dump a little perplexed and bewildered.

When I returned to the land, Tim was sitting quietly petting the dogs. "I brought you a present," I said as the truck rolled to a halt. I didn't even listen or look for a response. At the dump I'd found a couch, a nice little well used green grandmother-looking couch. We carried it into the tipi and set it on the side of the fire pit opposite to my bedroll. "There you go. Stay as long as you like." Another mouth to feed, but this one could help take care of the animals.

Work at the cannery was at long last beginning to slow down. I'd saved four months ahead in land payments and had $800 for building materials. The $67 worth of taxes were paid for the year, and it seemed like a good time to build myself a cabin for the winter. Tim was content on his couch and stayed around camp during the day playing with the dogs and slowly feeling a little confidence in the world around him.

I borrowed an old stock truck from Pete and drove to a nearby farm and asked if I could have some of the rocks piled in the corners of their field, no doubt rock and stone their grandfather had collected with an old stone boat pulled by draft horses clearing the fields for planting. The farmer was humored that I wanted the rock and told me to take all I wanted. My initial plan was to build a stone house like the one Solonge had in southern France.

The next morning silent Tim and I fired up the old stock truck and drove to the rock pile to collect material for the stone cabin. I had excavated a ditch in a square about a foot or two deep and about 14 feet by 20 feet. I'd selected, without a lot of thought, a place across the meadow on higher ground next to the trees overlooking the field below.

I'd also spent a day at Jackson's Beach and shoveled a load

of sand, mixed with pea gravel, from the beach into the truck and then off the truck at my building site back at the farm. I'd cut chunks of old barbed wire to use as pliable rebar to bend around the rock and stabilize the concrete mortared into the cracks. Tim helped me throw rocks into the back of the truck all morning. I was singing and making one-way jokes to my now grinning but silent sidekick as the morning passed. The truck tires began to bulge and I decided we had a load.

The old truck coughed, farted and blew a cloud of bluish gray smoke into the cow pasture as we ambled toward the county road. I was making jokes and praying out loud, patting the dashboard, prodding just one more ride out of the old derelict, singing in a holy roller sort of prayer. Both hands pulled down hard on the left hand side of the steering wheel, just to keep it in a straight line, as the mangled steering rods fought hard in the opposite direction.

We cruised out on to the county road—no license, no registration, bald tires, an engine that kept trying to retire and so covered in filth it's a wonder it ran at all. The whole truck was leaning heavily to one side, the bearings were howling and a light plume of steam began to trickle up through the hood ornament and steam the front spider webbed windshield.

As visibility became more opaque, something jumped out in front of us on the road (probably just a bunny) and I slammed on the brakes. With that, Tim's passenger door flew open simultaneously with the glove box. A vintage pair of eyeglasses rolled out, covered in cobwebs and dust. I was playing the preacher louder and louder now asking for the Lord's forgiveness, praying just to get us home. I picked up the filthy broken glasses as a joke and put them on my face, pretending that all was then clear as a bell.

I'd known Tim a couple of weeks and to that point he'd whispered only the basics of one or two sentences. But at that point he let out a squeal, threw his head back and began to laugh uncontrollably. He giggled and squealed all the way home and then he began to talk. And talk he did, endlessly and quietly, but he had found his tongue and had lots to tell. Tim loved the farm, especially the animals, and began to open up and relax and laugh from then on. It was easy for me to make him laugh and we laughed a lot.

I emptied the truck and went back for three or four more loads before returning it. Then I began hurking the larger boulders into my ditch and bedding them with concrete made from the sand and $18 worth of lime and cement purchased in town. I laid in my barbed wire and made a movable form that faced the outer walls. Stones were faced against the walls and shovel loads of concrete poured in between. When the form came off, I filled the cracks with mortar on the outside surface.

It was grueling work. Fingers were perpetually getting in the wrong place which was cruel punishment, but finding that same sore finger with another rock was much the worse. But slowly the walls began to rise. The footings were about 3 1/2 feet wide and the walls about 2 1/2 feet wide at the bottom, tapering as they got taller. I was proud of my work but as my concrete and stone supplies dwindled, I calculated it would take several years at the rate I was going. Memories of Solonge's house would have to be tabled. I decided to switch to wood and use the rock walls as a foundation. Such is the beauty of building with no plans and blue prints that changed daily.

Tim stayed through the summer. By early fall I encouraged him to catch the bus back to LA and go back to school. But in the spring, and every spring until he graduated from high school, he'd show up like clockwork looking a little mournful. Life in the big city sucked the spirit out of him.

After returning to Thirsty Goose Farm for a week or so and being around the animals, I could see the spark return to his eye. A country boy forced to live in the city. Perhaps Tim's greatest gift to me was his spirit. Against all odds, this quiet little fourteen-year old person would slip away in the night and hitchhike hundreds of miles to get to where he wanted to be. Tiny and fierce.

The next summer another young boy showed up and asked if he might stay a while. His family too had fallen apart. And through the subsequent years there were dozens of kids who found the farm, arriving with nothing and staying as long as they needed. I certainly never had a lot to offer more than a meal, a place to sleep and a lot of quiet space to roam and feel safe. My only rule was that there were to be no drugs and no ripping off.

It was just word of mouth that they found the farm and somehow the word got out. In truth they were giving me the spirit of survival my hemorrhaged self-esteem so desired. They were tough in their injured ways and though most have since passed or are lost to jails, drugs or disease, I gained an essential perspective in my own life from these young men and women.

Chapter 16

Building a Cabin

My hands are how I would do this world.

I caught the ferry to Lopez to see how brother Hugh was coming with his little cabin. Hugh had no budget. His entire cabin was built from what he could salvage or scrounge from forgotten buildings on the island. Making money for land payments proved to be all he could do as jobs were near impossible or paid so poorly he just couldn't get ahead. In those days everyone knew the winters were long cold wet and dark. Most lived on savings or hung tightly to the jobs they had.

He peeled dozens of poles and framed up a few little rooms with salvaged windows and salvaged flooring. The nails, the hinges, the insulation, and the shingles all came from old houses he'd torn down for the labor. When it was done, he said he'd shelled out a full $12 to complete it. It never suffered from that new house look where the materials needed time to blend in. When the smoke curled from the rusty stovepipe above the sod roof you'd think a Hobbit was going to appear.

It was a labor of love complete with a rock wall fence that circled the entire yard and when the grass grew long on the roof, Hugh would grab a milk goat and hoist her above the eaves and let her graze from gutter to gutter. It seemed in the years that I visited that little cabin, it was never warm. He had a beautiful old turquoise wood cook stove that, regardless of what kind or how much wood was stuffed into it, let off very little heat. I was always shivering when I was visiting him.

Fisherman's Bay Lumber Company had tall stacks of freshly cut rough lumber piled neatly in golden yellow piles all around the parking lot of the mill yard. I had never built anything but moved toward this project with what was best described as blind intuitive naiveté. I pointed at piles that looked good to me on some level.

I had no blueprint and wasn't tending to move in that direction. I just sort of was going to start and go along as it made sense or until the wood ran out. There is no book for this process. I knew of no mentors or apprenticeships, no bank loans, and did not have much help, but the freedom of such creativity felt good and enjoyably dangerous.

I pointed at one pile and another. I'll take some 2x4's and some 1x8's and some of those over there. In 20 minutes I spent $600 of money that had come from a long summer of sweat and toil, fish guts and noise; and poof, my handful of twenties was gone and the man in the yard with the hardhat and red suspenders said they'd deliver the following week.

The pile was dumped 60 feet from my rock foundation and it was time to begin. I looked at it with bewilderment and nary a clue as where to begin. I know the floor goes on the bottom, so I guess the first thing I need is a floor. I couldn't use rough-cut lumber for a floor; I needed some smooth boards. I had six 14 foot 4x4's and laid them down across the rock foundation and leveled them the best I could.

Then I made one of the rare trips during this project to the local lumber store and bought some smooth tongue and groove lumber for the floor. It seemed the smoothest side was the side with the beveled groove so I put this side up. A momentary decision that I cursed for years afterward as the dust and dirt filled and hid in those beveled grooves and could only be swept in one direction making it impossible to clean the floor. I had no electricity for a vacuum cleaner and wasn't planning on such luxuries, as it was too representative of the capitalist Americana my 22-year old ideals were trying to reinvent. That and the defining factor of not enough money to consider such improvements.

Then I had a rough set back. I was working some long hours at the cannery to keep my cash flow up, as long as the salmon were around and we could fit them into cans. I was a little late getting to work and hurried into my raingear when I realized the call of nature was coming like a freight train down the main track blowing its whistles and not applying any brakes. I quickly ducked into the men's room and sent that train on down the track. I finished, washed my hands, and ran to my station at the Iron Chink and the crew that waited for me to turn on the machines that give that canning line the stuff of our hard earned pay checks.

Instinctively, I checked for my wallet in my back pocket as it was bulging with a land payment and a few extra dollars for food, but it wasn't there. I slammed the machinery to a halt and ran back to the men's room. There was my wallet set up on a shelf in front of the porcelain train station—empty. All my money had been stolen.

I pondered all day how I was going to make my payment and feared the bank would take my land away or I'd incur some horridly inflated penalty. At lunch I told everyone what had happened and agreed to sell to a woman, whom I worked with, my tipi for $150. It was a sad ceremony pulling the canvas off the poles and it never occurred to me it was probably worth two or three times that amount. I was just fixated on getting my payment to the bank.

Until the cabin was finished, I needed to move back in my car or just sleep on the ground. I took three sheets of 1/2 inch plywood and assembled two on the sides, one for a roof, slid my mattress underneath and figured it was good for the time being. The whole incident added energy to the building of the cabin.

From the floor I framed up walls. A friend came by and showed me the rudimentary concepts of framing. I wanted large beams so I walked the beaches looking for large dimensional lumber, gifts deposited from the ocean to the high tide lines and free for the taking. I lugged, with every grain of strength I could muster, some large 6x6 beams that had lost their accurate dimensions but had a unique beauty the artist in me found to be perfect. I spent hours with saw and chisel fashioning them into frames for a loft.

I had one handsaw, a hammer, the occasional tape measure, a shy level that went missing a lot during much of the building, a pencil and a broad hatchet. This broad hatchet proved to save many a day. I was able to notch and hone timber quite effectively with it. When I came to a piece of siding that needed to be ripped or cut in the long direction or with the grain, it required a special rip saw with a different set in the teeth. Cutting an 8 foot plank lengthwise with my handsaw was like pulling teeth out of a snarling dog, as the tool bound and fought and exhausted me. I found I could hone the long direction with the broad hatchet, and finish it with a degree of accuracy with a hand plane.

I needed windows. There was an old abandoned cannery in town due for demolition with a wrecking ball. I asked the owner if I could go in and remove the windows before they indiscriminately reduced it all to rubble. He gave me a mouthful of excuses that didn't make much sense about how he just couldn't let me in; so veiled in the dark of night with a flashlight, a backpack and a penlight, I snuck inside the old building through a loose plank on the back side and collected window panes.

There were dozens of windows made with 8"x10" pieces of glass. The sashes were soft and rotted away, so I carefully pried the panes loose and stacked them in my pack and slipped away early the next morning, just before the wrecking crew arrived with their giant ball of destruction.

I spent rainy days building sashes. The windows would be as big as the glass dimensions and the sash wood dictated. This was how I arrived at the prescribed openings when framing the walls. The south side had three windows, four panes wide and four panes high. This didn't require hours of calculations and mathematical blueprinting. I built around my materials, unlike the more common approach of designing an opening and custom building a window to fit the vacancy. This process of building was full of limitations but worked well enough that it was incredibly enjoyable and made me feel competent, at least to a degree. It also proved to be far less expensive.

I was driven by some small glimmer of light, that often blinked on and off, that was guiding me from someplace deep within. It was me I was feeling. It was intuitive, it was my mother inside me, and it was a feeling of arrival. I drank it in.

My hands were how I would do this world. They were just learning their way, but they were giving me confidence and something raw but something real. My fingers continually got in the way of hammers and chisel, stones and beams, but due to many rolls of adhesive tape, a few stitches and the healing that time can bring, I persevered. I was proud of my rough bandaged hands.

As money waned, creativity found solutions. There was enough leftover hemlock tongue and groove flooring to build a door, which I promptly cut in half to make a Dutch door. A three point buck had left his antler in the trail and it became the outside handle. I cut out a place for a single pane of glass in the upper half and bolted it into place with four large hinges complete with axe handle latches and sliding latch bolt. The tipi poles became the legs of my kitchen table and the railings for my deck.

I'd seen a barn with a gambrel roof that looked like it would give me space for a sleeping loft, so I began to frame it complete with a dormer when I realized I was quickly running out of lumber. There was only enough to complete the gambrel roof halfway across the 20 foot structure so I would have to take the remaining 2x4's and make a shed roof before the winter rains could ruin my fun. I rolled out tarpaper, as the first big drops of fall splattered and drooled rivulets, keeping my little nest dry.

I had two 2x12 boards that were as wide as the building so I strapped them together side by side and made a counter at one end. I painstakingly cut a beveled hole in the middle and inset half a small oak barrel as a sink. From the dump I had found a piece of black inch and a half poly pipe and made a drain down through the floor under the rock foundation and out to a little seasonal stream that ran just outside the cabin.

Lack of money and the need to move in dictated the use of newspaper and old clothing as insulation tacked up on the inside of the framing. A friend and I borrowed a truck and bought two slings of rough cut short cedar boards for $45 a thousand which was enough to cover the entire inside of the cabin walls.

I bought a tin stove and six lengths of pipe and lit my first fire sometime mid-winter and the heat was almost an overwhelming joy. Up to that point I had been living without much heat and donned long johns continually everyday all winter. Initially the heat was like a handful of Qualudes lulling me off to sleep, my body relaxing and giving in to the warmth. Simple and full of flaws as my little cabin was, it was my Taj Mahal.

Chapter 17

Water—A Rant

I dug a hole in the ground 12 feet deep next to a little seasonal stream outside the cabin. A few small poles were set over the top and I made a floor of fir boards with a trap door for access for a bucket on a rope. I never got sick from the water but by today's doctrines of anal-retentive health codes, it was an abomination.

By world standards, I was far and away luckier than most. It made good coffee, washed me clean and helped me do the dishes. It was basic and functional in sustaining my life on the land.

I dug another hole across the meadow next to a larger stream and covered it in the same way. In the evenings of the summer months, I would drive my sputter and chug Chevy pickup across the field, back it up to the well and, with a bucket on a rope, fill the leaky horse trough in the back of the truck. Then I'd sputter and chug back across the field, water sloshing over the edges, toward my garden where I'd ladle out bucket after bucket and drench my thirsty green vegetables. It was a primitive method but it solved the need to grow my own food and water my livestock.

I often joked with friends that I would go to work in the 20th century but return home to the 14th century on the farm. Cows tethered on ropes, hauling water, cutting all lumber with a handsaw and spending the evening with dim little kerosene lamps was all part of what I felt was necessary to live the ideals I deemed necessary for a purposeful life. An effort to repair or examine a world that seemed to suffer a biological disconnect. A life that asked questions of the world that seemed to be so recklessly careening toward destructive values.

It was raw and usually only partially thought out. Diesel was far cheaper than kerosene so I used it in my lamps; the soot and stench were undoubtedly far more hazardous to my health and eyeballs than any assumed benefit, but like most things of its day it was all an experiment.

The island had an increasing number of young people with their anthem for change and experiment. Houses became art projects of collected materials and creative thought. It was a continuation of the Aquarian Age of the 60's and the disgust and disillusionment of the American ideal. It was to disassemble our traditional approach and reassemble in a more harmonious earth-loving manner.

Many of these ideals became clichéd by skeptics but the intention was harmless. The creative exercise in questioning societal norms was exhilarating and refreshing for a generation that had seen their country fight a cruel and unjust war, coupled with the awareness that the environment was at risk due to human kind's greed and folly, and that the corporate world and society were generally moving in a destructive direction. It needed questioning and it needed these unlikely heroes to return to the basics and start over. To feel themselves building a shelter, hauling water, living with less, using less and hopefully gaining more on a level of inner spirit were some important and perhaps only small changes in our existences.

It was a parting of the clouds where, looking back, the sun shown through brightly and perhaps slowed the runaway capitalist ideals that seemed so vicious and planted a few seeds that thirty some years later seem to be sprouting new life. The banned music of revolution and radical thought of the 60's now plays in grocery stores and elevators for your soothing subliminal background entertainment. Solar and wind power are now a national focus.

America has built itself up on the false calories and the maximum consumption of cheap goods. Food in America has long been a race to the bottom for the cheapest, most available, convenient processed items. Most recently with the advent of small farms and good publications, America is educating itself about the environmental atrocities of large corporate farm practices and the subsequent nutritional hazards. As obesity and eating disorders permeate national media, people are flooding to their farmers' markets to find contact with the persons who feed them three times a day, longing for a relationship of trust similar to their desire to know their doctor or dentist or car mechanic.

I'd like to think that these and other social changes came from those ideas and seeds planted by the men and women who were disgruntled enough to dare to try something else. Yes, there are piles of broken inventions and bad ideas out behind the barn, and there are volumes of painful memories and many more worth laughing at, but this is the creative process at its best as we are asking and moving and changing and hopefully getting better at it. Not to be able to try, not to brave the chance, or not to be able to ask the question is to stifle, stagnate and slowly die.

This creative freedom and permission to question is my favorite part of America. It's the water that sustains life in a culture that functions.

Photo Gallery

My parents in the early 1950's.

Brothers Jim and Hughie.

After several long years in and out of the hospital with Crohn's Disease, I am strong enough to take my friend for a ride.

Cabin on the
shore. My place
of transformation.

Zorba the goat, Tally
and me.

My tipi, the car I lived in, my kayak and my dog.

First dwelling on the farm.
(photo by Scott Whitelawl)

Building my first garden. (photo by Scott Whitelaw)

Thirsty Goose Farm's homestead cabin, built with a modicum of hand tools.
(photo by Abbie Sewall)

Interior of cabin. Life off the grid.

Relaxing on the front porch (24 years old) with ever faithful dog Tally and cat Dylan.
(photo by Abbie Sewall)

Building my first fence. (photo by Scott Whitelaw)

Garden. Water hauled by hand from creek across the meadow (photo by Abbie Sewall)

Tansy the cow who helped pay off the farm.

Building the chicken coop. Cost $12, and still standing 38 years later.

Haying with my cantankerous beast of burden.

Rowing to our wedding, Lisa reads
Robert Service while I row.

First days of marriage. Rowing to save our lives.

Salmon dreams (photo by Lisa Lawrence)

Siblings. Jim, Anna and Hugh.

Our beautiful strong daughters, Mara and Natalia.

Adam, Lisa, Charley, Jim, Mara and Natalia. 2008.

Chapter 18

Guatemala

I met Abbie about the time the cabin was complete enough to move in. We laughed and played easily in a heart rescuing sort of way. We shared the need to unravel upbringings that were laced with the trickle down effects of alcohol and overbearing fathers, of mothers, and their children who hit the world like scrambled eggs without a compass full of angst. We had a willingness to chart a course that would make more sense to ourselves and the world around us.

Full of hope, we sped off into our love affair, blindfolded as to how a relationship worked assuming desire would fill in the blanks. And it always does when you're young, at least for a while. Like every generation before us, we felt we'd invented romance. We set up cabin and immersed ourselves in what seemed like a path of great importance.

Abbie had a loving heart, cockeyed glasses and great intention. She wanted to be a photographer and we raced around the island in her little '62 Volkswagen bug looking for the perfect composition, always talking about lighting, looking for the one photograph that was going to get *National Geographic* to beg her to join their staff. It was always our joke. Working for *National Geographic* was pretty much her life's desire. She was seldom without her cameras and spent every extra penny on her craft.

Meanwhile on Lopez, brother Hugh had been making a few long distance phone calls to Abbie's little sister, Laura. They'd met at our cabin and were a couple of giggling goober heads when they were around each other. There was enough smirking and flirting to know they wouldn't take long to find a way to be together. So the Lawrence brothers not only looked and sounded very similar, they both wanted to be farmers and now lived with sisters.

Our lives as brothers would often be eerily in parallel. Without notice we would shave off beards on the same day ten miles apart, or wear the exact same clothes or have bought the same record album. It was something that we initially were proud of but as life went on we struggled for individual identities.

The winter winds were blowing cold when we hatched the idea of going to Guatemala for a month. We packed the little VW bug with the basics, changed the oil, bought rolls and rolls of film and headed south late in January. The little bug buzzed up over Grants Pass and down into the burnt brown valleys of California. Then over Donner Pass and the thoughts of those who'd tried and failed and boiled their harnesses and dug up dead oxen before starvation led them to eating their own perished relatives. Then out across the military-brown desert, flat and continuous.

We arrived in Tucson, Arizona, and wandered the ornamental orange tree lined streets to a cousin's house, stored the Volkswagen behind her garage, and took a train from Nogalas to Mexico City. We bought the cheapest tickets available and rode with the goats, chickens and smiling brown-faced women and their dazed children who smiled through teeth of red, blue, and green candies. We slept sitting up on wooden benches, draped over each other and our backpacks, as the train clicked and groaned its way south.

It was hot and sweaty as dogs, chickens, people, pigs and goats all jostled and bumped, shit and peed, while brakes squealed and Mexico unveiled its unique beauty outside the windows. We ate from vendors at the stations, leaning through open windows, smiling and trying to make sense of the money and language, drinking in the wonderful chaos of Mexican city streets.

Six or seven exhausting days later on February 4, 1975, we arrived in Guatemala City. Darkness had fallen on the city but it was alive with bright lights and a busy hum of clubs and businesses open into the coolness of the evening. We wandered, bone weary, through the streets looking like little kids who'd stayed too long at a birthday party. Worn out and looking for a place to sleep, we inquired about lodging when we heard a voice speaking English in the middle of the sea of Spanish tongues.

The man seemed nice enough and invited us home to his apartment where we were welcome to sleep on his floor. We trudged up some stairs and he pointed to the concrete slab that was to be our bed, under the full-length picture windows. We were sufficiently exhausted to feel appreciative of any safe place that wasn't rumbling and smelling of urine. He disappeared down the hallway. We closed our eyes and all was dark.

The next thing I remember was jumping up to my feet out of my sleep and looking out the tall glass windows in front of us. The room was quiet and the streets were empty except for dim street-lights that guided the way of a prowling alley cat. I was standing, tense fists clenched ready for I knew not what.

Suddenly there was a deafening noise as if hundreds of freight trains were being dragged against their brakes. Then the room shook violently and the wall shifted ten feet and smashed me in the shoulder, throwing me to the floor. The windows over Abbie began to flex and wobble before they exploded glass into the room. The noise continued and the walls shifted, lifted and crumbled with a bizarre surrealism. The world went dark and we were in a crashing ocean of concrete and splattering glass.

People voices began to yell. A woman let out a shrill scream. The man in the room down the hall began to yell something in Spanish and then through a dim night light, I saw him jump out the window in his bedroom toward the street below. His body folded and snapped when he hit the signpost directly under him. He lay motionless on the street. Sirens wailed. Abbie was calling out in the darkness.

In a moment of frenzied panic, I reached down and scooped her up like a small duffle and ran into the darkness toward where I remembered the staircase to be. I clambered down stairs, as bricks and mortar pelted us in the dusty dark stairwell. We made our way out into the narrow street and huddled as sheer terror flooded our veins and emptied our pockets of common sense and logic in the lost darkened streets of this little foreign country where the tectonic plates of the Motagua scraped, shifted and groaned for a mere 3 and 1/2 minutes. People ran past. Others were yelling and some stood petrified looking up toward the sky. Everyone was holding on to one another, children cried and babies screamed. The violent shaking of all things stationary stopped and we all stood still.

Then there were small tremors. The beast beneath our feet was still moving, still angry, bricks and rocks fell, my bowels rolled over and evacuated. In the darkened street, I squatted and eliminated on the sidewalk as my body experienced the physiological reaction to sheer terror. I was readying for a primal fight to live. Some of the old rock and mortar buildings crumbled beneath the shifting strain and fell on to themselves and slid into the streets, covering all in their path. People were being crushed and buried.

Abbie and I held each other in a grip so hard as if to be stronger than anything that might want to harm us. We understood nothing of the language of the people around us and had no idea of any direction to run. For three hours we stood in the dark, waiting for the first signs of daylight.

And then, like refugees on the shore waiting to be rescued, light came. A hot sun, that knew nothing of the destruction it would illuminate, rose slowly over the ruined city. I dashed back up the stairs and gathered our packs and passports and we escaped the narrow little street where we'd stood helpless, praying the buildings around us would stay standing. We walked through miles of rubble and broken scared people.

Sirens wailed as Federales drove trucks loaded with machine gun clad soldiers through and around what looked like a bombed city, declaring martial law on looters, a desperate effort for control. We met other Americans who told us their tales and what they'd heard. Rumors were like runaway horses, dangerous and scary.

"I heard California slid into the ocean. The whole West coast is gone."

"Don't drink any water or eat any food. It's all contaminated. The dust when the ground gets shook up is full of disease."

"The death toll is going to be in the millions, but there's a good chance that as time goes on we'll be targeted and robbed. There's no place to go. The airport's shut down. Armageddon, dude. Survival of the fittest."

Our bodies were in shock, our minds too full to fathom half of what we were seeing and hearing. We passed a hospital where people were backed out into the parking lot, holding the injured, people crying, people clutching bloody stumps and people too dazed and shaken with no expression at all. We passed collapsed buildings with screaming women attempting to unpile thousands of pounds of rocks to presumably find loved ones.

Abbie grabbed instinctively for her camera. An opportunity of a lifetime. *National Geographic* really would be calling her if she documented this. She raised her camera and adjusted the settings, focusing on a woman desperate in search, her face crying wild stares of disbelief and terror.

My hand shot out and covered the lens and I pulled Abbie over toward me. I put my arms around her and hugged her tightly, clutching her with a desperate anguish, and as tears rolled down my face, said in a croaking voice, "You can't do that to these people. She probably just lost her kids in that building. It's too raw, too invasive. I beg you, it feels like we're stealing ... stealing their spirits. Please let's leave them alone." By now I was crying heavily, as was Abbie. We realized this was a once in a lifetime opportunity if we made it out alive but the lens had changed. It didn't seem kind, helpful or appropriate. Abbie, through sniffles, pushed the camera back into its case, and said, "You're right."

We walked on and by evening were at the airport. Darkness came like a repeat performance of the terror filled night before. It seeped and oiled its way over us, blindfolding our confidence. We hunkered down on a grass median next to many others carrying blankets and overstuffed bags of important belongings.

"Senor, es banditos iye?" A slate faced response of "Si." I ask again, hoping he didn't understand my fractured attempt at Spanish. He repeats, "Si senor, es banditos iye." I wanted him to tell me how safe we would be but he had nothing more unconvincing than the concern in his eyes. We lay on the grass clutching our backpacks and each other. I fought off visions of the earth splitting open in a deep crevasse, Abbie on one side and I on the other. The earth shook us to sleep with an after shock irreverence.

The next day we spent waiting in line at the airport front terminal doors that were locked. Long lines of desperate hot people, with waning patience, trying to gain access to a flight out. Rumors continued. "The airport's buckled. No flights possible."

A Lear jet suddenly swooped down on to the runway, taxied up to the terminal and five young men with cameras and microphones jogged across the tarmac and into the crowds. Camera shouldered microphones live, they began interviewing people.

A tall handsome man was ushered to the front of the crowd and the microphone was poked at his face. He seemed calm and sturdy. He was speaking English with a Norwegian accent. I was drawn to his confidence and moved through the crowds toward him. It was Thor Heyerdahl, the famed explorer/anthropologist. He smiled when he walked past and said he had no answers. It was a horrible event. That many thousands of people were affected.

He disappeared and as one of the lingering reporters stood

next to me, I asked with a sheepish, forlorn smile if he would take my girlfriend and me out of here. He barely glanced at the floor in front of me and rapid fired, "No can do, buddy. I've got a story to get out." He too slithered off through the crowd and an hour later the Lear jet blistered off through the mirage heat waves back toward America. I cussed his cavalier nectar-sucking indifference.

Somebody gave us a small bottle of baby food. We hadn't eaten in almost two days so we shared the infant portion of unsweetened creamed carrots. It was like throwing a thimble of water on a house fire. My stomach had been holding the tension and began to clamp down in refusal.

We were hot, sweaty and worn thin after our long nonstop travels down the edge of the North American continent to this foreign land and the subsequent two nights we'd spent in its grips. Trees swayed with freakish spasms as the after shocks continued. My stomach cramped to the point I was walking with a limp.

We huddled on the median of the tarmac for a second night. We spoke softly to each other but we were crying a lot. It felt hopeless. The rumors were almost more than we could bear. And with every subtle shift of the earth beneath our feet and the looks on the faces of the terrified people around us, the destruction and the remoteness and the inability to find solution, we were sinking deeper into a black hole.

The next afternoon Abbie put on an attractive summer dress and made her way to the front of the crowd at the terminal front entrance where officials were talking to people through a crack in the door. An hour later she returned with two airplane tickets for New Orleans. She said that the sexist pigs could be bribed for a wink and a smile. A Boeing 707 slowly taxied up to the terminal several hours later and we boarded.

We arrived in New Orleans the day before Mardi Gras began. As we debarked the plane there were more reporters sticking microphones into the faces of the sad, shocked and grief stricken.

Nobody felt like talking in front of the cameras. We pushed on toward Customs. I felt empty and injured, a post terror vacancy with a hair-trigger for panic. A large spit polished customs official, who'd been looking at Abbie, said with a Louisiana drawl and a smirky little smile, "All Y'all come back here, please. We all need to conduct a search of you and your possessions." He told us to walk behind separate doors and remove our clothes. His attentiveness to Abbie made my skin crawl.

"Sir," I said in a loud confrontational voice. "Sir, you can't do that. You need to get a woman officer. I won't let you do that." My blood felt hot and my nerves ragged and easily pissed off. I'd called this large brute out and told him he couldn't strip search my girl-friend and just as I was bracing for the full brunt of his reaction, two agents walked around the corner and asked what was going on. I tensely explained and the situation was diffused; a woman officer was found.

All-be-it, my interrogation was extremely thorough and full of impossible questions with multiple double negatives. "Young man, is it not true that you've never attended a pot party or have ever used marijuana in a recreational form?" This is a hard question to get right when you're naked and bent over in a chilly win-dowless room while spreading your butt cheeks for two grown men. As soon as we'd escaped the gorillas with badges, we made it to phone booths to call our parents. We both had a hard time fighting off tears when we told them we were alive and okay. In both cases they had no idea we were that far south and hadn't heard much about the earthquake anyway.

The buzz and the hum of the upcoming Mardi Gras craziness was too much for us to handle in our frazzled emotional state so we flew on to Arizona to reclaim our little VW and head home. Abbie seemed to bounce back, the closer we traveled toward home. I, on the other hand, was having a real hard time. I would wake up at night and spring from the bed waiting for the walls to tumble down. And when I lay back down, I was full of tears and torment, my mind racing until daylight.

Several weeks after we arrived back on the island, Abbie mentioned she'd found a job offer in London that would further her photography career and would be real hard to pass up. I had to be supportive, but I wasn't ready to have her leave. Six weeks later I put her on an airplane for England.

Building the farm became all-consuming and I worked myself to sheer exhaustion so I'd sleep through the night. But the nightmares of Guatemala were powerful, and I was convinced I was continually feeling aftershocks. Months passed and my relationship with Abbie was melting away. Her letters were full of her love of the city and her work and mine of the farm. Eventually we let go.

I have toiled with my request that she not photograph the suffering we saw. It would have given her a leg up on the career she wanted, and on the other hand when do you say "no"? Nearly 30,000 people were killed that night and over 100,000 were injured. The destruction was in the multiple millions of dollars. It was a time for empathy and prayer.

Abbie and I have been in contact throughout the years and she never held it against me that I'd asked her not to take pictures. She claims to have never had any lingering negative effects. She said she always felt safe with a big strong man there to protect her. I, on the other hand, became extremely claustrophobic; I have a hard time being in large buildings past the 3rd floor and cannot be either in an elevator or a small airplane. Hours in the counselor's chair have not been able to erode these fears. I carry those memories of that earthquake like an unhealing wound.

Chapter 19

Working the Farm

Tansy

With Abbie gone to Europe and the relationship over, I threw myself into the work around the farm. I had jobs with different contractors and would come home in the evening and work on the cabin or tend to the handful of different animals I had collected. The fields were overgrown and little was used other than for my emotional and romantic pacification.

One weekend I organized a band of friends to come with their scythes to cut the tall canary grass. It all sounded so purposeful and important to our vision of what this "back to the land" life was about. Six or seven young men donning scythes, with long hair and a look of purpose, showed up reminiscent of some ancient clan of protesters ready for revolution in the streets.

We sat and drank coffee and sharpened these awkward foreign tools that looked like giant stiff elbows with two handles and an attached sword. Then we all spread out in unorganized directions, probably as much from fear of each other's wild swinging, and began thrashing away at the tall green grass. Arms swung and scythes slammed bluntly into the ground making elbows and shoulders ache. Frustration ran high as blades bound up in knots of grass or caught too much grass for the human arms to handle.

The preferred method was to present the blade in a smooth swinging motion at a sharp angle that would only cut a narrow but consistent swath laying it over in an organized repetitive row.

Good intention, in itself, seldom guarantees good results. Then there was that subtle niggling in our thoughts, the way men like to compete, even when they aren't trying to. Each of us glanced at the other's ill progress, then at the 10 sweaty exhausting feet we'd covered and then out at the 20 acres of softly flowing uncut grass taunting in the field in front of us.

Pete had figured it out. With neat, effortless little swipes he would swing and step, the grass lying over like artwork in tufted little Van Gogh-like rows. He was 60 feet out and hardly drawing a sweat. His long hair waved in rhythm to the swinging of his arms, his face unable to hide a quizzical little smile.

The learning curve, like so much of our new lives, was steep and with aching shoulders and throbbing elbows along with our miserable unorganized piles of grass, we quit several hours later. I'm not sure what the end result was supposed to be. I had made three or four hay rakes by hand like ones I had seen in the picture drawings of Eric Sloane's coffee table books about old farm life. So I spent evenings raking our work into piles, again without any real reason or use. It felt right, though, a piece of the puzzle for this larger picture I was working on. It was the doing, not the result that mattered. The hay lay in piles and was never picked up.

Some time later I was on Lopez Island seeing brother Hugh and we were visiting our friends, Peter and Julie, folks with a similar affliction to "back to the land" farming. Peter had been milking two cows, and the weaned calves of the two cows had worn out their welcome.

"Wanna buy a couple shit head little cows?" Peter called as he ran through his yard chasing the two awkward teenagers toward an open gate. I wasn't thinking about the fact I hadn't any fences, or feed, or way to get them back to my island. Again I didn't really know what I was going to do with them, but it was the immersion into all things farming that attracted me. "How much?" "100 bucks if you take them today," Peter wheezed through his Nordic beard, fully out of breath.

After several hours hammering and nailing old salvage pieces of lumber, I had fashioned a rack on the back of my 1951 Chevy pickup. Peter and Hugh seemed to be missing when I needed to load the two resistant calves. With ropes around their necks, I pulled and coerced them, one at a time, to the back of the truck and then with all my might lifted first the front end and next the rear end and secured each calf to the front of the pickup bed. I lifted the tailgate and nailed three or four boards in place behind them. Peter got paid and my two new bovine and I sputtered off to the ferry dock looking like a bedraggled chapter from *The Grapes Of Wrath*.

When I got back to the farm, I attached a long piece of rope around the neck of each calf and disassembled the rear gate. There was an explosion of hooves from the slippery pee soaked floorboards of the truck when the two calves leapt free in full flight in opposite directions.

My hands clamped down with a determined grip, unwilling to let my new calves have their way, and the rope burned red tender welts on my bare hands. The rodeo continued and I did wind sprints for the next several hours, finally catching the long ends of the ropes and securing them to small trees. I hauled each calf a pail of water and collapsed in the cabin just before dark trying to remember my original intention.

For the next number of months, once a day, I changed the position of my little beasts to a fresh new patch of grass and hauled them a full pail of water. They settled into their routine, with few escapes, but had me thinking a pasture or at least a corral would be a lot easier.

With time I was able to save enough for a Stihl chainsaw. It felt like such an advancement in my limited toolbox that, every night after working with it, I polished it and set it on the kitchen table so I could admire it and show it off to friends. It was a mini-industrial revelation that my tired muscles easily justified as I modified some of my original proclamations as a "back to the lander." I cut cords of firewood, notched logs, ripped planks and took it to the beach where I cut miles of drift logs of cedar to seven feet and split them into fence posts. This was one of my favorite jobs, wind blowing and storms boxing and pelting the shoreline leaving grandmother cedar trees in the wake.

One winter I spent every day following the storm debris up and down the half dozen beaches on the exposed west side of the island, lugging my chainsaw, three or four wedges, and a splitting mall, looking for freshly deposited logs I could cut and muscle into posts for the farm. The work was strenuous but the winds were fresh and invigorating. Again it felt like a piece of the puzzle from a bigger picture that was slowly beginning to take a shape. I split close to 600 posts that fall and winter and sold nearly 1/2 of them for $2 a piece. That gave me enough to buy wire for the corral.

I was at the post office mailing off my hard earned bank check to Sears and Roebuck when I ran into a group of friends who invited me to go to Mexico for the winter. They said I'd need about $300, about the same amount I'd just put into the envelope for a shipment of galvanized wire.

It was a hard decision to say "no" and go home to my dim little kerosene lamp lit cabin and watch the winter rains drool a monotony of redundant gloom as I chained up my cows, stoked the fire, and looked forward to a shipment from Sears and Roebuck, while friends frolicked half-naked in bubbling surf, eating cheap tacos and drinking cold beer. This felt like a missing puzzle piece. Hard to see the big picture as complete without this piece.

I drove my heater-less truck home and slogged through the woods, where the driveway was too wet to drive on without getting stuck, and threw a damp log on to the hissing fire. I chained up my two bovine who were indifferent to my disgust, and returned to light my little kerosene lamps with the soot-blackened mantels to wile away the winter darkness while rain dripped its relentless water-boarding on my tarpaper roof. It was hard not to feel sorry for myself despite being chest deep in good fortune.

Spring came with a joy only a bachelor Luddite in a wet cabin could appreciate. As March progressed there was a sheen of green grass that pushed up from the belly of the meadow and Tansy and Ragwort (the names of my two cows) ate enough to give themselves green greasy butts. Now yearlings, they were complete with hard pointed horns. I began to tether them from a rope tied at the base of the horns with a ring in it. This gave me a little better chance at pulling a willful head around when they steamed off in a direction I wasn't intending.

One evening while leading Tansy behind me to new grass, I had a screaming interruption of basic primal proportion. In a playful head swinging excitement, Tansy swung her proud new horns around and caught me in the south end of a place where only toilet paper and darkness ever visit. I rocketed into the air from adrenalized toe tips, escaping with no more than a frantically beating heart and a resolve to dehorn the daggers that protruded so dangerously from her head.

Several days later I tied her tightly to a large fir tree and wrapped rubber bands around the base of each horn. A week after that, I readied myself for a blood bath with a hacksaw and a bag of white bleached flour. I re-tied her to a tree, pulled her head around and tied it again. Then I began to cut the horns off with a hacksaw an inch above the rubber band. The flour was to throw over spurting blood as a clotting agent, if need be, as horns are full of blood vessels and directly connected to the sinus cavity. But the rubber bands had worked, there was no blood, and the event was surprisingly undramatic.

By mid-summer, Ragwort earned a one way ticket to the butcher shop, the unlucky consequence of his gender. Tansy, with the luck of her gender, was turned loose into a pasture with hand split cedar posts and galvanized wire from Sears and Roebuck.

In the early 70's, I was the second person living on Boyce Road, the rural country road that bumped past the top of my driveway. Mrs. Cobin was an elderly lady who lived in a rotting little cabin nearby. She ached for company and visits usually lasted far longer than intended.

To talk to her was always to compete with Scruffy, her clueless little yapping canine that stood three feet away and barked shrill warning sirens of fear and protection in a continuous rain of absurdity, competing with a large TV that was blasting a volume her elderly ears could hear from the next room. None of this was the least bit distracting to Mrs. Cobin. She rambled on unfettered. On one such visit she explained that with two of us now on Boyce Road, the Post Office said we could have mail delivered to boxes right out front and save the half mile walk to where they were.

The following Sunday morning, I took a small crowbar in hand and walked to where her mailbox stood and began to wiggle and pry it from the stand. Immediately I heard the report of a gun and the sound of a shell whizzing over my head.

From across the road, standing on his porch, was old Mr. Phillips. Hobbling with canes and sucking on his asthma respirator, he yelled out across the road, "Get away from that mailbox or the next shot won't miss." My knees began to shake uncontrollably as I croaked back that I was trying to help Mrs. Cobin because the Post Office said we could … He snorted some reply and turned into his house. I scurried off down the road with the mailbox under my arm and a pounding heart.

A week or so later I could hear a tractor making its way through the woods toward the meadow and it was Old Man Phillips. He pulled up in front of the cabin and turned off the engine. I didn't see any gun and cautiously walked outside. He sat sucking on his inhaler, canes stowed beside his enormous lumbering frame. He had a two-week beard and an old greasy feed cap on, the worn out version of an ass kicking brute whose prime was a lingering memory. He wheezed and said, "You want me to mow your meadow? Sorry 'bout the other day. I thought you were just some hippie stealing a mailbox." I wasn't sure what to respond, and reticently mumbled, "Ah, Sure."

He'd come to help me out and, with his apology, the old redneck and the hippie became friends. He was old but wise and spent a lot of time trying to tell me how tough he'd been. He never minded referring to hippies in some disparaging way in his stories, somehow insinuating I was exempt despite my outer looks. He also continually bragged of all the dogs he'd shot for just crossing his farm and for that matter anything else that crossed it. It was the way of his experience as a farmer in the 40's, 50's, and 60's on our little remote island out in a lost part of Puget Sound. Innocent and slow to change, the old island way of life had difficulty with those who were new and different.

Clyde was another old-timer on the island and an entirely different pot of soup. The first time I met Clyde he talked to me like we'd known each other for years. Friendly from the beginning, he adored people and the chance to entertain at his kitchen table. He was a tall skinny farmer with enormous working hands; his clothes flapped and hung over him like laundry hanging on a fence rail. He'd taken a job at the Post Office and farmed during the evenings and weekends with help of his three boys and two daughters.

Ruth, the heart of Clyde's life and the heart of the friendliest, most generous kitchen in the islands, always had two coffee pots on and plates full of chocolate chip cookies. The cookies and generosity of time and spirit kept the chairs around that little kitchen table full and open to all. I worked with Clyde often with the understanding that if he needed help, he'd ask, and likewise if I did, but he said just don't ever keep track.

On one such occasion, he and I were putting a small addition on his house when a truck drove up and a couple fellows walked over and Clyde began a friendly conversation full of jokes and friendliness and eventually invited them in for lunch. He never introduced them to me but we all gathered around the table and ate and talked for a good hour or so. As the afternoon wore on, the two men thanked Ruth for her lunch, said goodbye to Clyde and me and drove away.

As we were pushing through the screen door to go back to work, Ruth said in a whispered voice to Clyde, "Who were those men anyway?" Clyde shrugged and pushing his hat back on his head looking baffled said, "I don't know. I thought you did." They both looked at each other curiously. Ruth said, "Well, they seemed pretty nice. It would be nice to see them again."

When Tansy was of age I took her to visit one of Clyde's bulls. Nature persisted in its drive for life and the following spring she had her first calf. I'd built a small shed with a dirt floor and milking stanchion. A bucket of grain convinced her to stick her head between the bars so I could milk her. Her udder was heavily engorged with milk and my only experience had been milking goats in France and their udders were a tenth the size of Tansy's. My fingers ached from the long hour it took to get her teats and my hands into a cooperative effort at releasing the milk, while dodging a swatting tail and the occasional kicking of a manure covered cleft hoof.

I kept hearing the voice of Clyde telling me how young girls would milk ten cows before school. I felt like my hands were in training for some Navy Seal course. And I needed to repeat this all over again in 10-12 hours every day of the week for the next nine months. Then I had to figure out what to do with all the milk. As the weeks progressed, she built her milk up to about 3 or 4 gallons twice a day. I became overwhelmed and was pouring it out for the chickens. Without running water, making cheese and even butter was a chore that proved to be too much.

Mike, Clyde's son, had been raising Holstein calves on powdered milk, and I put together the idea of raising young calves myself on the extra milk. Flies buzzed and the smell of sour milk wafted through the cabin like a bad idea that was getting worse.

I followed Mike to the auction yard to the pens of baffled, lost looking day old dairy calves. The sick and the compromised in with the healthy, all discarded from dairies for any number of reasons. Their suckling soft mouths snuffling in search of a mother's udder found each other, potentially inoculating themselves with every sickness known to bovine science. It was a nerve racking time, picking out and bidding on prospective calves. $100 a calf was a lot to pay for something that might only live a few days.

There was a stiff and ruthless learning curve raising dairy calves. It was always a punishing project, with a sad and angry heart, digging holes out in the woods to bury their stiff little black and white bodies with eyes rolled inside. Many times calves lay beside the wood stove as I doctored their difficult beginnings. But what did seem to give me an edge was plenty of warm fresh milk with Nature's perfect crooning mother.

Tansy murmured low guttural moans as each new calf entered the shed—a mother's welcoming caress with her selfish desire to nurse every calf she laid eyes on. There was a magic to maternal instincts. She proved to be an invaluable link and eventually my calf loss was insignificant.

My unlikely hero was a thousand pound hull of jutting bones and a gut like some bovinic concrete mixer, with liquid eyes and a love for perpetual routine and a can or two of grain. She'd stand and wait, with her head stuck though the milking stanchion, with the same excitement twice a day, her long raspy tongue licking her nostrils, her eyes deep and dark, asking for the simple pleasure of feed—and to please release those calves from their little stalls so I might nourish them from my bulging dripping udder with my given ability as their mother.

I loved milking and raising calves. Tansy made it easy as she was so primal about her mothering. Through the years I tried adding other cows and never did I find any that would compare. Tansy was bred and freshened and raised some ten calves of her own through the next sixteen years and fostered some sixty more. She lived to be twenty (the average life of most dairy cows is three to five years).

Then on one rainy day, as I looked out the window at my old friend, I realized her time was too painful to continue. And years before in a cozy barn, the pens filled with fat happy calves, rain tapping on the roof while she munched her hay, we agreed she'd live out her days and be buried on the farm. I led her arthritic, weary body to the edge of a pit, placed a gun to her forehead and like a scene from Old Yeller, pulled the trigger. My throat gripped in harsh sadness as I sat in the mud and the rain poured down and my tears flowed and mixed in the puddles left by her last footsteps.

I thanked her for her wonderful self. She was simple and she was basic with a strong spirit for mothering. She provided me with enough success to be able to pay off the loan to the bank within six years. I milked and fed calves before and after going to work, hauled water by hand, hauled hay and built fences and drove off island for more calves. I sold calves to pay for supplies and bought more and more calves. Youth and will power are wonderful grease for ambitious determination.

Her gigantic lumbering hull, with the low maternal guttural mooing, is forever etched in the spirit and the wind that blows through the farm.

Chapter 20

Troubled Youth and Foreign Shores

Four or five years on the land and I was feeling a restlessness I wasn't expecting. The cabin was built to a point of comfortable habitation. I had a shed for milking and various other buildings for chickens and wood. I drank from the stream and ate from the garden. It was all just as it should be but it felt like there was a stone in my shoe and I had a hard time admitting to it.

I was 26 years old and had worked and discovered much in a short time about this life I'd chosen but there was a hollowness that wasn't filling me up. I needed more interaction with others. Perhaps I was lonely.

I had spent the previous nine months working a draft horse I'd bought and was endeavoring to do some selective horse logging. This meant I'd spend a good portion of the day with this rangy unbroken brute arguing who was going to be in charge.

It was rough work. Danny was an 1800 pound Belgian I'd bought for $400 and I was a 165 pound scrawny dude with dangerously little experience. His previous life was full of goblins and terrors. Good intention does little to fill in the required knowledge of gentling a near one ton equine that can panic at seemingly nothing and run like a locomotive towing a thirty foot tree and me and anything else in the path down and across the hill and field, harness snapping and shattering like my spirits. I was naive and he'd had experiences in some previous life that triggered his flight response like that of an Olympic sprinter.

The combination could easily have been deadly for one or both of us. I was as determined as he was strong and full of inexhaustible energy to panic. I skidded on my belly across the meadow more than a couple of times clinging with all my might to the driving lines as he charged for distant horizons pulling a stone sled or log inches from my skinny desperate body. Months later and after daily routines of exhausting workouts, we came to a truce that was only mildly confidence building. It had taken hours a day to keep him muscled up, but the reality was that I wasn't getting enough work to survive. I was eating potatoes and onions three times a day, while his feed was costing me more than my own.

After a newspaper article proved to be of little help in terms of getting work, I got a note from a man on a neighboring island that he'd be interested in perhaps buying my horse if I sold him with the harness and my homemade trailer. I explained to the man about his phobic past and his sensitivities but he seemed to think he knew everything about horses. At the least I had not misrepresented the horse.

Blue smoke smeared the air from my old truck as I took that large massively strong brute for his last drive with me as his owner. I felt like I may have escaped something potentially dreadful and I felt light with relief as I drove away with Danny indifferently grazing in his new pasture.

Several days later I was building a fence and heard on NPR an article on teenage foster care in Seattle and it struck a cord. Perhaps through disenfranchised teenagers I would find a part of myself. Their instincts and anger often appealed to me.

I scratched down a number, called, and they offered me a job as a staff person in the soon to be opened residence for street kids. It seemed a little miraculous at first but I soon realized they were desperate for help. The pay was ridiculously low and the work would be some of the most emotionally draining, sad and difficult I would ever encounter. I'm not sure there were any other applicants. I liked the other workers and felt the change would do me good.

Tim had recently come back to the farm and was game to take over the cabin in exchange for care of the animals. It felt like the right move. Purposeful work and contact with interesting people. I had to borrow a truck to move to Seattle as mine was untrustworthy off island. I found a room in a house in the Central Area of Seattle a few blocks from the "residence".

The residence was an old dilapidated house that the collective, known as Youth Advocates, had rented on a chaotic street where trouble seemed to lurk like a three ring circus. We had six beds and being idealistic and at the bottom of the foster care system hierarchy, we trolled the basement of Juvenile Hall for clients. We found a handful of kids, both boys and girls, with rap sheets and emotional troubles that were so long and involved that, from the day we opened to the day we took turns leaving a year later, were so overwhelming that we could hardly function in our own lives.

In 1976-77 HIV was not a large factor on the Seattle streets nor were gangs, but there were plenty of other diseases, drugs, violent injustices and trouble laced with the world of juvenile prostitution, theft and robbery. In 99% of the case histories each kid was fighting for survival in homes where they had been beaten mentally, physically and/or sexually.

These young men and women had thick skin and reacted like cornered raccoons to authority, yet clung together and defended themselves with a strong ferocity. I admired their kinship to each other, their toughness and mostly I admired their courage, despite the fact it was usually misdirected.

Their ferocity kept them well known to the police and Juvenile Hall. Relief was drugs, alcohol and sex with indiscriminate abandon. And from time to time there were moments when they were warm and loveable, beautiful and handsome, proud and hopeful. But there are those that the systems of help do not connect with and of the some 40 kids that we housed and cared for that year many are missing and gone to who knows where but most are dead. Overdoses and murders, Aids and disease. Life in prison. Short lives that struggled and fought and searched for relief.

There were two things that I felt I was able to offer that year that brought relief and happiness. One was Tally, my ever devoted golden dog, who offered hours of comfort and understanding to the kids. Muzzle on lap with dark brown eyes that said it was okay no matter how hard it was. It was the unconditional love they were so starved for.

The other was the farm. On arrival it was like letting caged canaries free from their confines. They were perplexed and awkward. They had never flown further than the width of their cage. The first time I brought six kids up to the farm for the weekend they were caught shoplifting, flipped and rolled a car and one girl took an overdose of Dramamine she'd shoplifted just to feel the buzz. And then there was the irate redneck farmer who drove up looking to twist someone's head off because some kid had stolen his kid's bicycle. Needless to say I only brought one or two at a time after that and kept them in sight. But the open spaces and the quiet relaxed atmosphere gave a pause to some lives that had never felt the quiet of idle time or seen nature, or knew that carrots grew in dirt, or that they could feel safe while they were here.

There were three or four kids in particular that stole my heart. Marianno, a beautiful African-Puerto Rican-American who was thrown from his home at age 12 for being gay; a harmless sweet man with warm brown eyes and a desire to get along. Cowboy actually was a Native American who was prone to exaggeration and street fights but had a loveable nature.

Missy was a child whose fundamental wiring had been tweaked by an outrageously perverse childhood. Rape, incest and years in Juvenile Hall full of bad drugs. She was a mountain lion too long in a cage. Needless to say she was a mess. Between her self-mutilations, prostituting and over the top fighting and drug abuse, she required an inordinate amount of attention that continually exhausted the whole staff. But she had a way of working into my heart. We spent a lot of time on the farm and in her fractured crazed world she was always talking about.

She was emancipated at 18 and dropped out of sight as so many of the kids did. Three or four years later I got a phone call from the Seattle Police Department as they were completing an investigation of the Green River murderer and they had concluded that "Bones 157" was Delise Louise Plager, commonly known as Missy. And there was Vernon, a sexually confused boy-toy who found nothing to be taboo. He was out there and proud of it and so lost.

All the kids were brave, defiant and in a societal subculture of lost street kids, easy for the general population to ignore and punish. They were good people who started out so below the bar of opportunity that it was a struggle just to stay out of trouble. It was an amazing year, like traveling to a foreign country that spoke a language that no one was interested in learning.

The grant for my position ran out about the time I'd had enough. I was exhausted from my time with the kids but not entirely sure I was ready to return to the island. I loved the thought of going back but was still feeling the need to grow in other dimensions. A kind woman, whom I'd shared a house with while working with the kids, was a Peace Corps recruiter. She said "I've seen you put your heart and soul into those kids for the past year." She dropped a large binder in front of me and said "Look through that. See if you find anything you like; I'll make sure you get in."

I was at the kitchen table fiddling with the radio knobs and stumbled on a calypso song by Toots and the Maytalls called "Cola Wine". It was a hard song to sit still to and soaked in deep.

I couldn't sit still; there was so much happiness in the music. As soon as the DJ said that it was West Indian, I flipped the binder of jobs open to the page that said Windward Islands. There was a country called St. Vincent 100 miles down wind from Barbados in a long string of island pearls that stretched from Trinidad, Tobago, to the southern tip of Florida. Flying off to a country I'd never heard of and the fact they spoke a flavor of English made a lot of sense as well as it being a part of the world where great music originated.

I spent the summer back on the farm and with a group of friends we built Tim a small cabin up in the woods overlooking the farm. It was a great summer of notching logs and relaxing with friends and putting the basics together for him to have his own little place.

In early September I flew off to Barbados for training. It was warm and relaxing and the people and music were a delicious time of rejuvenation. After my year of emergency rooms, police stations and late night hysterias the warm breezes, the turquoise ocean and the rural West Indian people were a dream come true.

A month later I said goodbye to the other volunteers and flew off to Saint Vincent. The country was a small island that was merely a volcano rising up and out of the ocean and the population of some 120,000 people lived on the shorelines. It competed with Haiti as the poorest country in the Caribbean. The population was largely of African descent or Carib Indian (the remains of an indigenous tribe) and many of the people in the far northern parts of the country had never seen a clear man.

I rode a bus of jolly laughing people, who were terrifically curious about who I was, to the end of the road to the little broken down town of Bridgetown. It had been a sugar cane town but the West Indians refused to work in the cane fields as it was too reminiscent of the days of slavery and it had been all but forgotten. Its only legacy was a famous folksong, "Joshua Gone Barbados," written about the labor uprising.

I met elderly Mrs. Cumberbach who lived in the upstairs of a shop and with her dog may have been the two oldest inhabitants in the country. I was to remain with them for several days when a certain person was to come by and show me my new job. Days drifted into weeks. Mrs. Cumberbach shuffled about the apartment in her slippers muttering to herself, her old exhausted dog sleeping hour after hour looking as if he might be dead. One day she came to my door and asked me if I'd take her dog out and shoot it. This, my first assignment as a Peace Corps Volunteer. After carrying the poor old confused canine down to surf edge and putting a bullet in his head, I went back to the apartment and packed up and left.

I walked north. I crossed the Rebecca Dry River and walked north on the little sandy road that skirted the shoreline. I walked through villages where poverty blew through along with the Caribbean wind that was ever tugging at the laundry and palm trees. The village children would run out giggling from their yards staring, barefoot and curious. Asking a million questions.

"Give me a sweetie," they'd demand, laughing and covering their mouths with embarrassment.

"Give me some ting man. I want some ting."

There was no electricity this far north but there were lots of transistor radios and there was only one radio station. It seemed the airwaves were full of some new musician named Bob Marley and nobody could get enough of him. Including me. Walking though a village everyone's radio was on the same one channel, everyone listening to *Exodus* and "Rastaman Vibration, Got to Have Kaya Now". It was so wonderful to listen and carry the song from one house to the next uninterrupted. Everyone from grandmas to little kids sang and danced along. Bob Marley was unifying the country with a joyous musical connection.

I followed the road up a steep hill and on top was a small

group of houses and a view out over the vast Caribbean Sea. White cumulus clouds puffed by in the wind and far off through the haze I could see the twin spires of St. Lucia. I asked if there were any houses to rent and a gaggle of willing children led me by the hand to a small green one room house overlooking town and mile upon mile of open blue ocean.

I lived there for the next four months. I climbed up the mountain with different people and basically saw myself as a friend who wanted to help, with no real job description. The village took me in. There were always dozens of giggling kids smiling with excited eyes as they waved and called out, "Mr. Jim. Mr. Jim."

Because I was single, different villagers took it upon themselves to send a kid over every night with a plate of food suspecting an inability in cooking anything for myself. Most West Indians had a partner and three to five kids by my age of 27.

Several men in the village brought home some empty oil drums and began to cut them into different size pans and pound out the tops into segmented dishes. Within several weeks our little village had a steel drum band. In the evening, as the stars began to twinkle overhead and white rum began to limber up inhibitions, the villagers would turn out to dance as the steel drum band practiced.

I was very close to one family in particular and worked with them often. At four in the morning there would be a soft knock on the door, "Mr. Jim, Mr. Jim. Are you ready?" Sherman Bynoe, with several of her young children in tow, was heading to a remote hillside to a planting of sweet potatoes and was taking me along. We walked in the dark down the dirt road that followed the shoreline, padding on the soft dirt listening to the ever blowing Caribbean wind rustle the coconut fronds. Crickets were finishing their nocturnal chorus.

Until the sunlight glimpsed over the ocean horizon of the wide Atlantic to the east, we spoke very little. But like the birds in the trees the children began to chatter and warm with the new day. We walked for hours laughing and bantering, hoes over our shoulders. A 12 year-old daughter balanced a large plastic bucket full of cooking pans on her head as we walked which gave her the posture of a model walking elegantly down a runway.

The road ended and we followed trails through steep ravines and along dangerous cliffs, past waterfalls, dripping mango trees, wild avocados, tufts of sugar cane and up and down impossible hills. We laughed about everything, charmed and warmed by one another's presence. The children running to hold my hand, the men and women shyly covering beautiful smiles with a hand as they laughed.

The trail dipped down by the sea and someone bought a small fish and then we climbed unbelievably steep terrain for another hour to a small patch of potatoes hanging on the edge of the slope. Looming in front of us straight up was Mt. Soufriere, the disgruntled volcano, and down over the rich green slopes, down across the white-capped sea, I could see the spires of the southern shore of St. Lucia.

We worked hard hoeing weeds for hours. The wall of potato planting so steep in front of us there was hardly need to bend over. The sun high above relentlessly crashed down and seared us. Sweat and good humor flowed as the strong humble bodies toiled away.

We stopped and sat in the delicious shade drinking broth made simply from the small fish boiled on a fire in several gallons of water with salt and butter. I stared out over the steep green hills, transfixed by the water and the sun, watching a sailing cargo ship traverse the wide open ocean. With both hands I held the broth to my lips and I drank. The fish water, the children laughing, the jungle, the love of my friends, the view, my sore and exhilarated muscles, the frigate bird in the breeze, I drank it in. I drank and drank and drank. It all seemed so simple, yet so perfect. The love and happiness of wonderful people, bodies maximizing their utility, laughter in ample quantity and food simple and perfect. It was a moment when a tear mingled with the sweat on my face.

We had walked four hours, to hoe for two and then we walked four hours home. I collapsed on my bed and napped until I heard the steel band begin its evening workout. I passed by Sherman and she was crouched on a stoop of her forlorn little house breast-feeding her infant child while an impatient older brother waited his turn.

Several months along without any real job and, as much as I loved these people, I was having trouble finding what seemed like an adult conversation. These were people whose ancestors had been ripped from the jungles of West Africa, loaded on ships, beaten into submission and bred like cattle for a strong docile labor force. The indigenous tribes of the Arawak and the Carib either died off or would not cooperate. No spirit, no language, no freedom allowed.

Then in 1833 slavery was abolished in the Caribbean. The colonial system in the Caribbean was useless without labor and the Afro/West Indian was not interested in working for the people who had enslaved him. Industry faltered, population and poverty grew, and St. Vincent became a forgotten island far from anywhere, far from hope and far from any possibilities.

Education was minimal and the language was remedial at best when slavery was abolished. The people of my village had a very small working vocabulary.

"Good morning, Mr. Daniels. You going to work today?"

"Yes, Morning, morning Mr. Jim. Yes, I be going to work."

"What are you doing today?"

"Oh, I'll be going to work, Mr. Jim"

"What kind of work, Mr. Daniels?"

"Oh, I be going up de mountain, Mr. Jim."

"What are you going to be doing up de mountain?"

"I be working wit me cow, mon."

"Oh yah. Is your cow okay?"

186

"Yah mon. I have me pon and I going to milk me cow in me pon."

Mr. Daniels smiles. He looks content having had such an in depth conversation.

"Good luck Mr. Daniels."

"Right, right Mr. Jim."

As much as I loved these people and their rural subsistence world, I needed more. I wandered off in search of something that was more fulfilling.

I spent time on a little island to the south and ran into a unique little school where an expatriate was teaching teachers a new and progressive approach. Classes were held in an old house that spilled out on to white sand beaches and where children spent their recesses frolicking in the blue Caribbean or playing makeup cricket on slanted sand.

I was offered a job and excitedly rushed into the Peace Corps office to tell them that I had found work and was feeling really optimistic about my future. The two gentlemen at the Peace Corps office listened to my enthusiasm, then excused themselves to conference behind closed doors. A few moments later one of them returned and informed me in a very official voice that I had 72 hours to be out of the country. I was incredulous and begged to know what I had done wrong. I reminded them that they had never secured me a job in the far north and I'd taken initiative on my own and found purposeful work. He reminded me of how much time I had and disappeared back behind closed doors.

I had no choice according to my agreement with Peace Corps and I flew back to Barbados for my exit physical and related paperwork. At the end of several days of processing I demanded to know what had led to such drastic actions on their part.

The officer in charge explained that by wandering in to the southern district of the country it looked very much like I was supporting the government's current opposition. A man named

San Mitchell was posing a threat and was thinking of running against the president and it looked like I was in his support by living in his district. I was entirely naïve to the situation but got a lesson in Third World politics.

I was released from Peace Corps. I took a bus to the airport, tucked my Peace Corp official passport in my pocket, presented the officials my regular average-Joe passport and re-boarded the plane back to St. Vincent.

I returned to the district in the south, rented a dumpy little cabin high up on a hill overlooking the harbor and went to work for Lower Bay School. My savings were meager, but my heart was light and I so enjoyed the kids. One in particular.

Aku was a beaming young boy with a heart-warming smile and a golden tipped Afro. Aku had no family less a brother a few years his senior, a catatonic mother and an elderly grandfather whom everyone called Papa. Papa, a strongly religious wizened little man, walked with a cane and didn't mind using it on young boys he reasoned were out of place. His religion was rigid, angry and condemning. He saw himself as a conduit from God and hobbled around the almond tree in the center of town explaining his divine knowledge to anyone who would listen.

There was very little to eat at their house. Aku spent afternoons looking for discarded food in the dump or husking coconuts for a drink of the clean coconut milk and a meal of the hard white copra inside. At school lunch time he usually wandered off by himself in fear of taunting by the other kids as he often only had a piece of what was known as prison bread and a jar of sugar water.

Despite all, Aku was a joyous young boy full of laughter and pranks, singing and dancing. Like so many parts of the Third World it is the kids who show you the way. He and his friends showed me where the best diving was and we'd spend hours diving for our dinner. And on nights when bands played and music engulfed the islanders, we'd go and laugh and ogle at attractive women and wish we could dance as well as some of the young village men.

"Take me to America with you, Jim," Aku murmured quietly one day. "Take me home with you."

AKU

Aku's request was farfetched, but the real issue was money. I hung out with a handful of ever changing little boys. Neezi, Nobi, Richie, Colon and Aku were the most consistent attendees to my morning rice and pigeon pea breakfast. They'd show up in the morning about 8 o'clock and rummage through my stuff, ask me about America, guns, women, TV, anything that popped into their excited minds. Curious and charming they were always excited for a large plate of food. Inadvertently they taught me more than I would ever share with them.

"Jim, Is der a Jumbyman in America?"

"Jim. Don't sweep towards the front door, mon.

It be bad luck."

Paramount was their infectious spirit. It was their joyous youthful happiness and the excitement that someone was paying attention to them. They were brave and honest and pushy about it. It's how they got what they wanted. They took chances. Characteristics I had lost as a child. Illness and fear were my memories of the same age so their brown little barefoot bodies running, laughing, carrying on with a million ideas and questions were a way I was living it all again, this time with excitement and gusto.

Phil was a little taller and lighter skinned than the other boys. He had scrambled yellowish hair and a face of adolescent acne that played to his shyness. He'd show up and lean against the opened front door, silently waiting for me to notice him. In his mysterious understated way, Phil was different as he always seemed to have money and was generous with it. Where did this guy come up with cash when he didn't seem to work or be from a family with much money but always had a fresh $20 American bill? West Indian kids generally had nothing and when they did come into a little change it was always spent fast. One day over slices of greasy pizza I put the question to him.

Despite his shyness he almost seemed relieved to be able to tell his story. "Long time ago, every day I passed up de mountain I seen a red bag in de gutta and one day I hop down and look inside and der is so much money. I hid de money under me house and I just take one $20 out every time I needs money and cash it here at de pizza house. But dat was two years ago and I tink dey are getting wise to me. Maybe you could help me cash it. I have thought a long time about whose money it is. I tink it might be drugs because I never hear nobody talking 'bout it in town. Dey might be marked or something." My eyes were lit up like porch lights as his story unfolded. He agreed to bring the money to my little cabin and we'd count it and talk over what he might do.

The next morning Phil was standing silently in the doorway holding a little red nylon bag. The blue Caribbean shimmered far off behind him and a morning breeze drifted up the mountain carrying the raspy yodel of crowing roosters. "Come in, come in," I say, trying not to let my enthusiasm seem too overly eager. He pulled the contents out of the bag and handed me a large roll of wet American bills about the size of half a roll of toilet paper. They weren't just wet but soggy.

"First thing," I said "we need to dry these out so we can count them." We painstakingly separated the mushy wad and set the bills out on the uneven wooden floor of the cabin in the shafts of light that came through the front door. By the time we were done we had the entire floor covered with wet green leaves that puckered as they dried in the strong sunlight. We rotated and turned some 300 soaked bills until they were all dry enough to stack.

The bag of bills had come from God knows where and had sat in the gutter for who knows how long and then two years under Phil's house slowly rotting in the warm Caribbean moisture. Many of the rectangular bills began to disintegrate into hundreds of fractious pieces when we tried to pick them up and flatten them out. We stabbed unbelieving looks at each other as hundreds of dollars crumbled into so much valueless confetti. It was an excruciating process.

By the end we had a stack of taped and crinkly $20 bills worth just over $4000 American. Piles of cash have a way of making you want to stuff them in your pockets and run away. There was an excitement to our task despite the enormous loss of what may have been around $3000 in hopeless green-composted paper.

"Can you take dis money to de states and cash it in?" Phil was anxious to get away from the burdens of the paranoid. He was convinced the bills had been marked and the officials were close to catching him and he'd be in trouble for not turning the money in. Prison to young West Indian boys was a fear of unthinkable dark wet cells filled with big men that had nothing to lose and would violate and abuse them beyond their deepest fears. It seemed unlikely to me but I had an American sensibility and this was the West Indies.

I offered to buy the money and take my chances. I realized that if I walked into a bank and exchanged the money as a tall white American I wouldn't draw the suspicions a young dark skinned West Indian would.

Phil blurted out an idea that had been rolling around in his thoughts. "Jim, you give me $400 American of clean money and you can have the rest. I'm not kidding, mon, I tinks dey is on du me." My mind raced around. I was thinking of 50%, that would be $2000 for each of us. Then I wondered if perhaps it was really marked in some way and perhaps my risk was bigger than I thought. After all I was just going to use the money to bring Aku home to the states so it would be for a good cause but the karma of ripping Phil off was not good either. But ... but ... "Okay, man. I said I'd do it." Later that day I gave Phil his money and he was thrilled. He marched off with the weight of the world off his shoulders.

So what I thought was going to be the deal breaker for Aku's trip to the States was solved. What was needed next was a passport, which required a birth certificate, which would then allow us to buy a ticket to Barbados where we could hopefully secure a visa and be on our way. If I only knew how naïve I was in my thinking process, I may never have proceeded.

We caught the sailing ferry, *Friendship Rose*, the next morning and headed for the official offices of registry in the smary filth of Kingstown, the capital and largest city of this little country St. Vincent. Aku's eyes were full of joy as we dodged traffic and crowds and headed to the dirty brown building where all the births were registered. We skipped stairs as we hurdled up the three flights and entered the large stuffy room where all Vincentian birth certificates and records were kept.

Secretaries shuffled us about until we arrived at a very slow moving elderly gentleman who sat and asked us questions. Name: Gilbert Dennis Delves. Aku's enthusiasm was contagious. Date of birth? May 3, 1970 or thereabout. West Indians don't always know their birth information which worried me but not Aku or the elderly clerk who disappeared and returned with an enormous hand written ledger that he slowly thumbed through. He stared down over his glasses and studied the pages of hand writing for an excruciating amount of time. Aku looked so little, his golden tinged Afro racked to perfection in anticipation of this event, his eyes dancing about taking it all in. This was the beginning of his dream to go to the States, and a life that would move him from abject poverty to opportunity. He'd have a clean bed and regular meals and be able to go to school.

The elderly man set the ledger down and peered at us over his glasses and said, "I'm sorry we have no one by that name registered here." His eyes were old and bloodshot and he was so preposterously slow at everything, I impatiently asked if I could see the register.

My fingers scrolled down the rows of hand written entries and I could see he was right. My brain shot off in all directions. This part was supposed to be easy. How could he not be? He definitely was sitting right here and obviously no one ever registered him. Wasn't that sort of the point of why he needed another chance. He never had been a very high priority for anyone.

Then my eye caught the name of a boy registered right next to where Aku's name should have been. Rupert Harold Delves it said. Died at one year of age. I kicked under the table toward Aku whose expression was of tragedy and sadness. "Rupert!" I exclaimed. "Here you are. Rupert Harold Delves." I kicked under the table again and caught one sad and confused little boy on the shinbone, getting his full attention. He looked at me with a quizzical questioning. "You know that's why everyone calls you Rupe. Hell, you're not dead. You were born in 1968 not 1970. This is the certificate we want sir. I'm not sure why it says he's dead but you and I can both see he's not."

The elderly clerk sat looking at us without expression. He picked up the ledger and left the room. Aku began to ask whispered questions and I shushed him trying to decide if I had made a major mistake. We were borrowing this dead kid's identity. I suppose he wasn't going to use it, and besides it was a means to an end and no one was getting hurt. The clerk shuffled back in the room and handed Aku a certificate. "Here you go, son."

We leapt down the steps like fleeing dogs, laughing uncontrollably at our caper. We entered the hot confused streets of trucks, buses and sweaty hurried pedestrians. A world Aku would be leaving. We dropped by the office and applied for a passport before we took the boat back to Bequia. The seas were big and the wind strong on our way back. The rigging creaked as the four men hoisted the main sail in a rhythmic dance of down pulling arms that reached up high on the manila line and heaved downward. T-shirts whipped in the breeze as the large cargo sailor healed over as we pulled from Kingstown Harbor on the broad reach for home.

Aku huddled silently on a pile of rope, his forehead in a quizzical frown. Gilbert Dennis Delves had vanished in the ether of paper work in the same instant Rupert Harold Delves had risen from the grave and Aku was suddenly two years older. We both knew we had pulled off quite a little scam but it seemed somewhat harmless despite its dishonesty.

Ten days later Aku's passport arrived. We'd done it and no one was the wiser. Now we needed to get a written letter from his elderly grandfather who had verbally agreed to let Aku go. It all felt so simple. Then we'd catch a flight to Barbados and we'd head home. How hard could it be?

Papa was a tiny little man, close to 90, walked with a thin cane that he waved wildly at the world around him as he hobbled into town. He was Aku's guardian. His eyes yellowed with cataracts, he'd mutter Biblical truths as he fussed about his little board house, threatening the world with the wrath of his interpretation of the Anglican Bible.

Aku's mother lived there too. Her name was Queenie. Queenie never spoke. She walked slowly in her garden tending to her pigeon peas, or just stood quietly with a gentle smile letting time wash past her like a warm breeze. When Aku was just a little boy they lived in a remote village where Papa and Queenie had held strong oppositional convictions in some heated political discussions. The villagers were outraged and Aku says he remembers the angry people throwing stones and hitting the metal roof of their little one room house. Then Queenie was at the standpipe in town retrieving a bucket of water and the villagers began to throw rocks at her. They nearly stoned her to death rendering Queenie an emotional mess. The family fled in the middle of the night and eventually found their way to the small island of Bequia south of the large island.

Queenie's emotional state didn't improve and eventually a doctor prescribed a pill that relieved her anxiety but in the process cancelled all emotional contact with the world. For the remaining years, she was silent and simple. This is the best one gets with mental health issues in the Third World. Neither Papa or Queenie offered much to the growing precocious youthful ways of Aku. His father was a drive-by sperm donor who was around long enough to father Aku and his brother. He disappeared shortly thereafter and was never again seen or heard from.

I spent hours crafting a letter to Papa trying to reassure him of all that I would and would not do for Aku. I promised his health and safety and that I would never hurt or harm him. I told him he would be able to go to school and would generally have more opportunities in America. I copied the letter over in easy to read printing and delivered it to Papa who sat in the dark interior of his little board house. I took a seat across from him on a metal mattress spring that had a few pieces of cardboard on it, no doubt Queenie's bed. The room was without a window or any light less a few beams that lay across the center of the room from the front door. I handed him my document and told him to read it and ask any questions he liked.

His thin hand grasped the pages crinkling them without regard. He stared through dim light at me and said, "You know I am a spiritual man and I want to look you in the eye and then I will know all I need to know." It was obvious the work I'd put into writing down my thoughts was going to be useless.

Papa leaned forward and quoted some scripture as he stared through the darkened room at me. I was barely able to see myself but this was his process and spiritual seeing is not a physical thing. We talked awhile and he said what I was doing was a good thing and that he would pray for both of us. He let the paper work drop to the ground and reached out for my hands. His little wiry thin fingers wrapped around large white hands. He paused and then said, "Praise God. I wish you luck in your travel."

Aku packed a bag for his new life. He had two dirty t-shirts and an extra pair of shorts. He had nothing else. I took the cash that was left over from my deal with Phil and taped it to my mid section, about $3500. We flew to Barbados and took a bus to the office where we were to get a visa.

The room had bare walls and a ceiling fan that clicked a rhythm of monotony as a flock of dimwitted flies buzzed semi-circles back and forth. We sat in metal chairs for hours trying to be patient, fighting off the dread of failure, and waited. Eventually a lady from behind a large plate glass window with a six-inch hole in it spouted the name Rupert Delves. Aku didn't immediately register it was his turn. I gave him a shove and he jumped up with a look of dread and shoved his paper work through the little hole. It was a startlingly short time before she shoved the pile of papers back and without looking said, "Visa denied."

Aku looked mortified. I jumped up and protested. The woman was well armed with responses. "If I let every West Indian who wanted to go to the States go, there wouldn't be any West Indians left." I kept protesting to her non-eye contact while trying to make my points through the six-inch hole. Finally I said, "Do you have a superior?"

I was ushered into a large office with air conditioning and shook the hand of Mr. MacNamara. He was jovial and polite and I emphasized Aku's situation and my intent. After a discussion he said, "So you have intent to adopt?" I paused. I hadn't really thought of that. My mind was clicking hard. I looked at the man behind the desk and he was staring right at me. "Yah, sure of course." The words just sort of slipped out. The tape on my skin around my chest was pinching and I realized I'd not discussed this with anyone, particularly Aku and Papa. I started feeling like the water was inching up around my nose and I was about to blow the whole thing when Mr. MacNamara said, "Okay. A six month visa with intent to adopt."

We boarded the big jet. Aku was dazzled by everything from the magazines to the seat recliner button. No one ever enjoyed a meal on an airplane as much as Aku did. He smiled all the way back to the farm and every day after that. It was a great time. One of the first things I did was buy him some clothes. It was a simple remedy for happiness. Aku had experienced so little that everything seemed like a huge deal.

A friend gave him a bike and immediately he rode that old single speed Schwinn into the school and watched all the kids coming and going. After being at the farm five days and riding the five miles back and forth, he told me I could take him in and enroll him or he'd do it himself. He was the only black child in his class and for that matter the entire school. He walked into class the first day grinning so hard all the students were bedazzled by his charm and elected him president of Miss Hannigan's 3rd grade class.

Spring came early that year. The mornings came early and were warm. Aku loved to dance and show off his moves, so every morning before school we'd get all the chores done, crank up a little Bob Marley, and dance like laughing idiots until the school bus blew its horn. That was a wonderful time.

Aku and I were like brothers from different worlds. Our friendship was of mutual benefit. There was one nagging question. What would happen when the visa ran out? Being the only dark skinned boy on the island he was noticeable and people asked questions. I invested the remainder of the cash I'd smuggled home in a lawyer who knew nothing about adoption and managed to use up all my funds and I learned nothing helpful.

September arrived and Aku was overdue to return. I knew if he was asked by any official anything about his status it would be a fast and ugly departure, and perhaps ruin any chance of returning someday. The adoption idea was stuck hard between unrelenting forces. He could not leave the country without the adoption being completed which would take Papa's signature. Papa wasn't against the idea but being old, basically blind and very spiritual, he said he needed to look into Aku's face and see for himself. He couldn't sign him away before he saw him and if he left the country without proper adoptive papers he'd not be able to return. We agonized over what to do.

I couldn't have a ten year old become a fugitive even though it made no sense to have him go home, but I really had no choice. I'd given Papa my word I'd honor his wishes and so we regretfully booked his flight. At the time we were hopeful we could get Papa's signature and he'd be back before we knew it. When he left, I truly missed my joyous friend with the West Indian accent.

I devoted my time to his return. This time I had no slippery shenanigans to finagle what we wanted. Aku's letters on his return were depressed and angry. Eventually it looked hopeless and our lives were moving forward. The joyful boy had become a serious brooding young adult and his experience in the States had made him resentful and angry. Over the following six years, and after several tries, we never got past the visa office in Barbados.

The laws were impenetrable for my moderate income and by then Aku was a young adult. It was all a very unhappy situation. Having seen a better world Aku found little happiness in the limitations of his own country. This became a huge feeling of guilt for me. Again, like so much in my life, it had been a seat of the pants effort. Slipping past the rulebook on every turn had I created a sorrowful tragedy? I felt I had.

Aku was 18 when I cooked up my final effort. I sent him money for a ticket to Toronto, Canada. St. Vincent was a member of the Commonwealth with Canada so securing a visa was not a problem. Aku showed up at the bus terminal as arranged and we headed south to the Canada/US border in Blaine, Washington. He had not eaten in three days, a skill he'd learned in childhood when money was scarce.

I'd secured a few bumper stickers with suggestions of my devotion to Christ and put them in obvious suggestive locations on my car. It was Easter Friday when we pulled up to the booth and the officer asked the requisite questions of entry. Aku said nothing. I yammered on about Easter and the blessings of my work in the church in the West Indies and the providence of Aku's visit on this wondrous occasion of Easter, and except for my regret that he'd only be able to stay for two days, we felt blessed. We both gave the officer a long sincere smile and he handed Aku back his passport with a 3-day stamp. As we motored away, we whooped and hollered and celebrated a long and difficult return.

Aku couldn't stay with us for fear we might be visited by someone official, so he stayed with a friend in Seattle, found work and attempted to fit in. The years had changed Aku. There was a hardness that had developed. He was angry at me for the years he was trapped back in the islands, not understanding how the bureaucracies and his papa had kept him from returning.

Sadly we drifted apart. I think our time on the farm so many years before had been so ideal, and life was harder now. Aku became interested in the teachings of Louis Farrakhan and loved to needle me with jokes. But he wasn't serious about being a Muslim as much as he was disturbed by the role of the black man in America. He'd never experienced racism and America was teaching him the sad truths that run deep just beneath our outer surface of multicultural ideals.

He eventually fell in love and married Lorette in a big wedding and was given his green card. That was a milestone in his life in America. He was legally able to live and work in America. The triumph was lost in the demise of our relationship as Aku continued to see the white man as the "oppressor man" in a "Babylon system". It was hard to win. He broke up with Lorette and spiraled into a world where he trusted few. When we spoke he was angry or wanted money. We drifted further apart and eventually lost contact.

The last time I saw him was when I drove to Seattle and begged him to meet me in an anonymous location so as not to disturb him and his family. He sat nervously across from me at a Starbucks. His dreadlocks pushed up under a large beret, I felt like he was forcing himself to be friendly. He said he was a father of five children and they were the center of his and his girlfriend's world.

We talked about the old days and it was clear he still wasn't clear on how and why he'd been stuck back in the West Indies. He wouldn't let me meet his family, but I was encouraged; perhaps we'd started something new. The next time I called the phone was out of order. It's amazing how something so good can get so far out of kilter. I am sad when I think of the dozens of things I might have done differently so I might have an equitable relationship today with my little brother from another world.

Chapter 21

Cowboy and King Edward

I needed a break from the farm. A farm has a way of being all consuming. Tim said he'd watch the animals. Money was short. It was summer but I needed to do something different so I headed for the Seattle freight yard to hop a train and go find something different.

"The 87 Hotshot leaves on track 9 for Cicero, through Dayton's Bluff, St. Paul over there at 2:30 this morning. They'll be makin' her up till then. There's lots of empties. Be careful." The tall dark man slipped back in between the looming freight cars and continued his work with a flashlight, oiling the steel fist couplings. From the dark he warns, "Be careful of the dicks in Spokane. They're the ones without the oilcans. They'll bust your pink little ass."

I turn and walk across the field of filthy creosote ties and bright stripes of steel tracks reflecting light and sooty large cobbled gravel to the underneath side of an overpass. It's about midnight. It looks like the place all the bad stuff happens in movies. Past the chain link, past the no trespassing signs. Industrial noise, diesel smoke, roaring engines, train brakes groaning and squealing, and the percussion sounds of steel boxcars, tanker cars, flatcars banging into each other coupling and uncoupling, booming, squealing, air blast whistles. This the Seattle freight train yard moving megatons of cargo from the protected port city in Puget Sound on ventricle lines throughout North America.

Under the overpass a small fire built from pallets flickers, and I find two men warming cans of food. They invite me over. Two men as filthy and forgotten as the broken pallets they're burning. They ask if I have any wine. We talk awhile and it's clear things would go better with a little hooch so I scurry up the gravel embankment and find a 7-11 that seems to specialize in wines specific to the world of hopping freight trains: Ripple, Annie Green Springs, MD 20-20 (affectionately known as Mad Dog) and a wonderful cozy little cough syrup-like number called Night Train. I bought all four and slipped back down under the overpass to hobnob with my two new friends. They called themselves King Edward and Cowboy, two professionals at hopping freights.

King Edward was a tossed salad of disheveled filth. It was hard to tell his age but references to "Nam" and "growd" children made me think he was somewhere near forty. He looked as if there had been a lot of potholes on the road less traveled as well as a few flat tires driven on hard. His eyes lit up when he heard the sweet clinking sound of bottles in the brown paper bag.

Cowboy, the quieter of the two, looked like a bar-beaten version of Trotsky. His long square beard hung down to his chest and a filthy bandage covered a swollen crusted left eye. He stirred his can of warmed beans with a switchblade. His quiet side, as well as the knife, had me keep a peripheral eye on him at all times.

I passed King Edward the bottle of Mad Dog and he promptly snapped open the metal lid and took a long hard vengeful pull. His eyes closed as the wild dogs ran barking down his throat. He passed it off to Cowboy while his eyeballs came up for air.

Cowboy tilted back his head and let the sweet purple tangeree gurgle like the fountain of forgiveness. When he stopped, Cowboy looked straight at me and said, with a voice smooth and clear,

"Look at my eyes—been snow blind twice;
  Look where my foot's half gone.
  And that gruesome scar on my left cheek

where the frost fiend bit to the bone.
Each one a brand of the devil's hand,
where I've played and I've lost the game,
A broken wreck with a craze for 'hooch'
and never a cent to my name."

"Jesus Christ! What is going on here?" I say out loud to my-self. This man of soot with the Trotsky beard and switchblade, at 1:00 in the morning, is reciting poetry, and quite well at that.

King Edward picked up on my incredulous look and ex-plained, "That's all he does is talks poetical like. He was in the Hanoi Hilton for five years and someone gave him some book and he memorized it cover to cover and now that's all he does is talks poetical. I don't always get what he's saying, but he's pretty good at it." Cowboy is staring at the ground as King Edward talks about him and I'm trying to fit such an amazing idea into my preconcep-tion of these men under the overpass. I swig the Mad Dog, ponder what I've just heard, and pass it on.

King Edward drained the bottle and began to talk profusely, words and ideas barreling out of his mouth in rapid-fire uncon-nected abstractions.

"Where you going again?"

"Stay out of Portland. I did 30 days there for 'conduct', that's misconduct and no relation to Miss January. That was the last hot bath I've had."

"Seen a guy cut in two once by a train. Fell in the track as the train was moving out. Too drunk. Couldn't get in and slipped down and under."

"Where'd you say you were going again? We're heading for Cicero. We'll drop you off in St. Paul on the way."

I got the impression King Edward hadn't talked to anyone for awhile who didn't answer poetical like. We all drank and Cowboy and I listened until we figured it was time to find an empty and settle in for our trip across the country. We weren't very sneaky as we staggered drunk out of the campsite, across railroad ties and train tracks looking for a suitable freight car on track 9. Freight cars are as dirty as their last load and filled with swirling questionable dust. We all three rolled in and King Edward's drunken voice echoed in the large chamber. His monologue was 80 proof and was losing all punctuation.

We were sitting with our butts on large piles of corrugated cardboard (a hobo's thermorest) when the precocious beam of a flashlight wandered into the boxcar. Immediately, a large man jumped into the car with his blinding light and a booming voice that shut King Edward up mid-sentence. With his gun drawn, he backed up swinging it and the light between the three of us.

"You men are trespassing on the private property of Burlington Northern Freightliners and you are all under arrest. I need ID from all three of you. What the hell did you think you were doing here? Now move slowly and we'll have no trouble."

Dead silence. There was a long anxious pause. My heart was pounding in my head somewhere between my eyeballs and my mouth. I was fighting off panic and thoughts of bolting through the open door. Long seconds passed. We all just sat there pulsing, waiting for something to happen when Cowboy began to speak in a voice low and steady as a locomotive,

> "There's a race of men that don't fit in,
>   A race that can't stay still;
> So they break the hearts of kith and kin,
>   And roam the world at will.
> They range the field and they rove the flood,
>   And they climb the mountain's crest;
> Theirs is the curse of gypsy blood,
>   And they don't know how to rest."

The train car at that moment made a huge lunge forward and

we began to slowly move. We were moving out. The man with the gun stood there, baffled, wondering what he'd just heard as he added up his possibilities. We were picking up speed when he decided to cut his losses. In a voice of practiced authority he said, "I'm glad to see you boys aren't drinking. Can't have any drinking on these cars. Let's not see you boys around here again." And with that he jumped out the large steel door and disappeared as fast as he had appeared.

King Edward began his monologue again cursing the yard cops and laughing at our bizarre luck. "Not drunk," he howled. The adrenalin rush and the cheap wine began a prison riot in my gut and I sat looking out the door holding down serious bile. The train kept speeding up, click a tick, click a tick, click a tick and the scenery of heavy industrial gave way to urban and quickly sped toward rural. Two long snorts of the air whistle and we were on our way. To the east the very first prisms of light were pushing up the dawn. I slid back to the far wall, lay on my pack and fell asleep.

I awoke suddenly to the loud clicking and thunderous roar of the freight barreling through the Cascades. My head felt like a thirty-pound steel ball, cracked and weeping important fluid. I sat up and stared out the door, wiping the spittle from my face and taking in the careening view of green firs and lush ravines, when all went dark.

The train thundered on, but we'd entered a tunnel and there were no lights—nothing. I couldn't see my own hands. This, along with having a terrific hangover, was real uncomfortable. The train was climbing a long low grade and we slowed as the engines put their diesel puking shoulder to the harness and pulled the half mile of steel freight cars up the incline. Five long minutes passed and our boxcar was filling up with noxious foul diesel fumes. No place for them to go in a tunnel.

I lay back with a handkerchief over my mouth and fought off my gag reflex and sheer terror. In the dark I heard King Edward stir, "Longest tunnel in North America. Takes 15 minutes but it feels like the rest of your life. We're too close to the engines. Should of looked further back. Less smoke." It felt like it might be my life.

When we finally cleared the black gloom and shot out into the clean fresh mountain air, I could see the heavy blue fumes swirling in the boxcar. I crawled to the door, hung my head over the edge and vomited onto the speeding tracks below. I've never been hit in the head with a splitting maul but I have a pretty good idea of how it might feel. A freight train of a hangover coupled with a migraine from toxic inhalation. I slid my hammered physique back to the opposite wall and sat staring out the big picture window of open door.

My two companions slept while we clicked and banged along, steel wheels, steel tracks, steel car, while I made promises to myself about drinking and tried to take in the dazzling view. Hours passed and I continued my bobble-head pose, watching America slip past the 10 x10 foot open door. Through the countryside with no commercial distractions, sliding through the back side of towns, through the industrial centers and right across main street in the small towns in Montana and the Dakotas.

Across the prairie I could see grain silos that within the hour would pass directly in front of our car. Traffic backed up several blocks as cowboys sat impatiently in their hot pickups waiting for the train to pass. On one lonely intersection we were plummeted with rocks as four little boys stood straddling their bicycles causing mischief and passing time in their town with too little to do.

Cowboy and King Edward were having a rough day as well with hangovers and we all just sat and let time and miles and the Midwest prairie click and tick away beneath us. Once, while sitting cross-legged in the doorway, Cowboy came and sat beside me not saying a word. We stared out for a long time at the hot afternoon. Then, as if scripted, he began to narrate:

"Sky so blue it makes you wonder

If it's heaven shining through.
Earth so smiling way out yonder,
 Sun so bright it dazzles you.
Birds a-singing, flowers a-flinging
 All their fragrance on the breeze.
Dancing shadows, green, still meadows
 Don't you mope you still got these.

These and none can take them from you.
 These and none can weigh their worth.
What! You tired and broke and beaten?
 Why, you're rich—you've got the earth!
Yes, if you're a tramp in tatters
 While the blue sky bends above,
You've got nearly all that matters,
 You've got God, and God is love."

Cowboy looked at me sheepishly and smiled when he saw me grinning at the wonderment of him and his dusty, brilliant contradictions.

The Midwest loomed wide and flat as evening and darkness swallowed the train chugging east. I woke and watched the stars and the night pass and somewhere near Bismarck we slowed to a dead stop. In the distance there was the sound of the freight cars coupling and uncoupling and then there was quiet.

The silence was comforting and we all slept well, healing hangovers and killing time. In the morning, there in the doorway, were the bashful heads of four or five horses exploring the cargo of the freight train left in their prairie pasture. We looked to be hundreds of miles from anywhere. Far to the south, perhaps six or seven flat miles away, I could see the interstate or at least the occasional semi, tiny as a toy, passing to the east or to the west. After sitting and waiting with no luck for most of the day for our train to move, I told my friends I was gonna switch to hitchhiking and it was time to go.

King Edward had enjoyed my company, or at least my wine, and tried to talk me out of it. I wished them both luck and took off on foot across the sage brush prairie toward US 87. I'd walked about a hundred yards and I could hear Cowboy saying something he'd memorized in a bamboo cage in another time and world. He was too far for me to hear what he was saying but my heart smiled just the same.

Chapter 22

Slip Sliding into Love

"All I want to do to you is what spring does to a cherry tree"
Pablo Neruda

The attraction to the opposite sex has always been very present in me. When I was in first grade the first feelings of amour swept over me like a warm wind. It made me happy, yet confused. Shy, but primarily determined. Girls were curiously desirable in some ether-soaked basic way. I was in love with a helium dream. It swept through the room unpredictably, occupying hours of silent distraction.

By the 5th and 6th grades I had learned to acknowledge and articulate privately to my brother inklings of desire. But attraction to girls remained something like the lights of a disco mirror ball reflecting off the walls of my imagination, strong feelings that evaporated as I moved toward them. This made me simultaneously find girls lovely and desirable with an undercurrent of angst all at the same time.

By junior high, love and desires had me like a hay hook in the gut, attached somewhere between my heart and my dick. It pulled me painfully over a field of hormones, curiosity and doubt. But primal desire is a strong thing and despite the rigors of incessant self-pleasure and awkward attempts at communicating with girls I so wanted, I lived in a silent self-perpetuating misery. I wanted girls, in some abstract way I wanted them a lot, but the truth is I had no idea what it was I would do if I were ever successful.

Other boys were good at making contact. These were testosterone bullets, blasting through the odds of rejection, with their muscle covered confidence. They oozed the language of connection. Highly excited talks, with equally excited dazzled girls whose eyes fluttered and bodies squirmed like bags of warm puppies that my repressed spirit would have loved to see set free. By 6th grade, Bill was making out with Carol at every party. Tim was with Becky, and Bruce with a different girl every week.

I sat in those dark living rooms as a designated disc jockey playing the slow side of "Paul Revere and the Raiders" over and over again with my socially crippled friends, pretending these people were being gross and "moving too fast." Besides, our desires had settled for the more fantastic girls in *Playboy,* keeping us safe from ever realizing any real contact with the opposite sex.

The truth of the matter was we all were aching to trade places with any one of them. Down deep I wanted to move too fast and be gross more than anything else in my life. Take me, take me, and let's be gross.

It was a Friday night before spring break in 8th grade. The room was dark less a few muted candles. We were in the basement of Chrissie's house; her parents were out of town. "Paul Revere and the Raiders" side 2 repeating its dizzying anthem music of the big make out heavy pet. Couches and overstuffed chairs were full of couples crumpled over one another, slurping long audible kisses as hands wandered and discovered some of the answers of our youthful incessant curiosities. The less confident sat in the deep shadows secretly eyeballing the pursuits of their classmates. Any one of us would have paid large money for night vision goggles.

Ellen stood up in the din of hormones and bad lighting and walked over and asked me for a slow dance. Petrified, excited and nervous, I accepted. We stood in the middle of the living room floor, our bodies hugging, our stocking feet barely moving, her arms around my neck like I had just single handedly rescued her from the depths of Grandpa's well, our heads tightly pressed ear to ear. I could feel the eyes of my two disc jockey friends drilling holes in my back. I didn't have to hear what they were saying to know that I was being kicked from the club of the inept.

I was crossing a line into a new dimension. Ellen's body pressed against mine. She felt warm. I liked it. I could feel her breasts against my skinny chest and I felt I could have danced all night and for that matter the entire spring break. A lot of things started making sense. An hour passed and our footsteps had barely completed a circle on the floor. We began to stick together in a hot sweat. Ellen pulled her head back to change sides from left to right and as her mouth passed my face our lips so gently touched in a brief pause. I think my knees buckled a little. That's what I had wanted. Oh, soft lips, how good and warm they were.

Mark, watching from his dark perch, played the comedian and flashed the room lights, swallowing muffled guffaws as the remaining nerds took count of their diminishing ranks. I had made out with Ellen Wolf. I was dishonorably discharged with extreme jealousy from my role as a geek disc jockey.

In my late teens and early 20's, my love of nature and time alone pulled me away from a lot of possibilities. But confidence was growing despite a few collisions of the heart where injury left me limping and shellshocked. The primal need to couple was and always had been a strong organic pull. Brain, stomach and genitalia yearned for the warmth and pleasure of sharing.

Somewhere in there the road divided. Sex was the original call of the wild, but the large pervasive and demonstrative beast that sought guttural pleasure wasn't love. And love, the dreamy juicy splatter of happiness that was full of tears, of joy, a safeness and connection, wasn't sex.

It was more complicated and the deeper I wandered into this wood the more lost I became. Both had far more dimension and discovery than a lifetime might allow. I wanted it all.

Memorial Day 1981

"You looked to me like misty roses, too soft to touch, but too beautiful not to try." Tom Rush

It was the spring of 1981, Memorial Day weekend. The pastures and fields across the island and around my little one room cabin were an electric green, dripping in spring rain and abundance. I was milking my cow, Tansy, and raising calves that made a real regular routine seven days a week.

Friends had invited me to a party on the beach that Saturday night and I accepted, regardless of the nagging reminder that all in attendance were happy little committed couples who drooled and giggled over themselves and I was the only single person they'd invited. My mood capitalized on self-pity as I realized there was precious little time spent on my primal needs as a healthy young man. I'd set and caught myself in a trap and I was pissed. Here it was spring, the island was full of life and lushness, of new buds and wet warm rain.

I left the party and headed to another one where I knew the opportunity for a little action was higher. A lonely violin rolled into loud crashing rock and roll as Bruce Springsteen lyrics thundered around my head as I drove my motorcycle down wet roads.

> "Baby this town rips the bones from your back
> It's a death trap, it's a suicide rap,
> We gotta get out while we're young
> 'cause tramps like us, baby, we were born to run.
> Wendy let me in I wanna be your friend.
> I want to guard your dreams and visions
> Just wrap your legs round these velvet rims
> And strap your hands across my engines.
> Together we could break this trap.
> We'll run till we drop, baby, we'll never go back.
> Will you walk with me out on the wire

'cause, baby, I'm just a scared and lonely rider.
But I gotta find out how it feels
I want to know if love is wild, girl,
I want to know if love is real."

The party was an old island standard, basically a three day drunk and pig roast. Lots of just hanging out in a mix of hippies and redneck logger types listening to loud music from speakers propped up in windows and cranked to decibels that warranted the occasional police visit. Lots of smoking and bloodshot pie-eyed smiling. Cars loaded and unloaded with people looking for connection, going on beer runs and stumbling around having fun. Women dressed in their "come hither" tight clothing, preposterous for the rainy weather, and the men in their predictable machismo tough-guy sawed-off work shirts and dirty jeans. I looked the part easily.

I'd made myself lots of rules in the world of romance and number one had always been not to date anyone from the island. This was founded on the ridiculous principle that if things were to go bad, I wouldn't be embarrassed if we saw each other afterwards which was basically, in hindsight, kind of a chicken shit approach derived from a basic lack of confidence and fear of failure.

None-the-less, I'd had several relationships with women from Ohio to Switzerland and repeatedly learned that the functioning of long distance relationships was a good way to make myself extremely miserable and waste lots of time. I pulled my long wet hair back into a ponytail and felt ready to break some rules if the opportunity availed itself. I was sick of my uptight ways and lack of satisfaction.

I parked my motorcycle and began to mosey the crowds and the wet afternoon. The rain was coming down hard and the fir trees dripped, soaking those of us outside around the fire pit. I stood like a hunched dog trying to suck some happiness out of a can of beer, but the wetness began to have a damping effect.

My spirit was waning as the evening grew dark, and as the cigarette ash and beer cans splattered with rain I began to feel the predictable outcome of yet another evening alone. My peripheral glances at the women I'd seen around me were not getting me excited. Should I just suck on beers till someone looked better or until I can't remember all my stupid principles? I had a cow to milk early, and drinking heavily in the rain seemed too painful an idea. I muttered my farewells and slunk toward my wet motorcycle.

As I turned to leave, there was a young woman standing beneath an enormous fir tree. The rain was coming down and light was beginning to fade. I remember she was wearing a white Icelandic fisherman's sweater and an old brown cowboy hat. She smiled as I walked near, not a passing smirk pretending to be cordial, but a smile as big and warm and wonderful as the bonfire I had just turned away from. This was not a smile an intelligent person could just walk by. It was a smile you want to jump into and swim around in.

Two raspberry blond braids hung like strong ropes beside her dimpled cheeks at which point I lost my bearings. There was the overwhelming sound of screeching metal train brakes in my ears. Was she saying hi to me? She stood above me on a small hill and that smile just kept gleaming and she may have said something else or not.

I had been so far away in my mind seconds before, I was completely off-guard. The more I took in those quick seconds the more I felt befuddled. Moments before I had been standing wet as an old rooster there by the fire trying my best to see the light in the eyes of the few women who smiled and looked my way.

I didn't want her to hear the sirens going off in my ears and the screaming masses in my head yelling in chants that this is a beautiful woman and "Don't blow it. Don't blow it." She was talking to me and I was nodding and murmuring still taking in this package of warmth and light. At 30 years old, I knew what I knew. And I knew.

I was terrified and little voices began to pester me. She's a local so you can't . . . She'd never stay interested in me. She's way too full of life and beauty. Blah blah blah. My ears cleared for a second when I heard her say, "You're a farmer, aren't you?" I couldn't believe it. She looked so delighted. Not like you're a farmer with that insinuated image of Ma and Pa's little goon-shaped kid with the too big overalls who's dimmer than a bucket of dust, but "You're a farmer, aren't you?" like I've heard about you and am real interested in your farm, tell me all about it. Like do you have cows and stuff? I always wanted to live on a farm.

"Wanna go out to that big barn over there and tell me about it? It's dry in there." I nodded and tried to unlock my knees and jaw. Could I handle this? Yes, I could talk about farming and yes, I have a cow and yes, this was such great luck. I lost track of the rain, there was no cold, time turned into a rubber hammock filled with wine and poetry. Within a small moment of time, my life was to change forever. She slipped her warm soft hand into my rough callused mitt and led me willingly through the house and out the back door through the rain to that barn.

Once we were inside the looming black pavilion, we climbed atop a large stack of hay and, staring through the horizontal cracks of fading light from a soft cradle of loose hay, we talked until the morning sun pried gleaming bands of light through the opposite wall. And sometime in the lonely cool before dawn our hearts reached out arms that began to pull us together.

Chapter 23

Marriage

There is nothing so life affirming and spirit enriching as falling in love. There wasn't a cell in my body, a thought in my mind, or a footstep on my path that wasn't renewed, inspired and full of hope. I disregarded all my internal noise and jumped into the river. Lisa too let go of the ropes and slid out of control smiling all the way.

The next day she showed up with a friend on two horses, and with her long hair flowing and the smile that opened my heart, they cantered around the meadow. Then just to put the final nail of attraction deep into my yearning neural data, she swam her black horse across the pond. When they lunged up the opposite bank only the horse's nose was dry and between that smile and the wet clothing that clung to 22 years of Nature's marvels, I realized I was either going to be with this woman or spend a life in misery. She trotted over and asked if I wanted to try. The horse made a second plunge and there we stood in the sun, smiling, shivering and making plans.

One evening several weeks later I drove through the rain to pick her up from the ferry. I parked where I could see her, in my rear view mirror, walk off the boat and up the ramp to my van. She walked behind a building and momentarily my door opened and a fist and a yelling man, flailing and punching, came through the door. I was in shock. I didn't know who he was. I was expecting a loving hug.

Why was this person hitting me? He was hurting my face with

each blow. "Stay away from my girlfriend!" came the drunken angry voice. I jumped from the van and there we were in the middle of the street, in the middle of all the walk-off passengers with a ferry load of vehicles waiting to unload. Confusion gave way to embarrassment and it occurred to me nothing was going to get figured out unless this man stopped yelling and swinging at me; so I kicked him.

One kick, a hard blunt thud that would have scored the winning field goal, landed right between his legs. He fell back onto the wet concrete and lay there, in front of the dozens of onlookers and the fifty or so stalled cars that were trying to get home, clutching his crotch. Embarrassment and pity led me to walk over, pick the man up, carry him to the van and throw him and the now astonished and yelling Lisa into the back seat and drive off post haste.

The cosmic vibration caused by Lisa's and my affections was becoming evident throughout the universe and old girlfriends and boyfriends were nervous as the door closed on their possibilities. This man was sent home eating his humble pie and for the next weeks several former girlfriends of mine from far off places showed up unannounced, eyes a flutter. It was all rather strange but our union made a lot of sense to us both and the world could be damned.

About six weeks after our first meeting in the rain, Lisa told me it was time to register for her last year of school at Western Washington University and she needed to move back to Bellingham soon as school began in several weeks. I took the words at the time with a certain indifference. But I was clearly driving with one flat tire for the next couple of days.

We were living toward a "count down" and a long distance relationship and different worlds and when you have fallen for someone, you're supposed to be supportive and happy for them. But I knew how the dice would throw. I'd live in anguish and wait, and she'd be going to school and those "parties" on campus, and someone else would be there when loneliness set in and the mortar that was so good would begin to crumble as we'd live in those weekends of long talks and efforts to understand. And slowly the tides would erode our sand castle to be just a couple more grains of sand on a beach in a beach of millions.

We sat on a small stack of hay when the words slipped from my mouth like a bird free from a cage for the first time. It was simply said, enduring a long pause, a scary silence, words I'd never said before or since. "Lisa, will you marry me?" There was a pause, a peripheral glance and the long hug and kiss. We were in love. After only a few weeks we were going to dive off the high dive into deep water. Perhaps reckless, but perhaps divinely intuitive.

Chapter 24

Wedding

As we dissected wedding options, we concluded that the best thing to do was disappear over the horizon and have a private ceremony. We couldn't seem to visualize our families together. They were from two different worlds and it felt like more conflict or unease than a joyous celebration. So we left.

Lisa's family was from a small town. They were fishermen with strong Catholic roots who limited themselves largely to the extended family and seemed a little threatened by our differences. They were brave, competent, hard working fishermen who didn't venture socially too far beyond their own tribe.

My father was a very bright, highly educated man who thought his blue blazer or doctor's frock demanded a certain degree of respect. He'd struggled with alcohol for years after he'd finished a life of personal debauchery, and the world with sober eyes was a scary and intimidating place. My mother lived in struggle between these worlds. I was not close with my family and the whole situation felt awkward and we wanted to cherish and nurture this feeling of safe love. There would be time enough to squirm on our chairs when these different families met, but that would have to wait.

We packed the van and caught the ferry to Vancouver Island. We struggled my brother's 17-foot Glouster Gull rowing dory onto the roof and headed to Barkley Sound on the remote west coast of Vancouver Island, British Columbia. Our resolve was strong as we drove up the inside coast of the island and over the mountains to the wild rainy shores of Toquart Bay.

I had one strong request: that we make sure we married when the weather was clear and sunny. A number of years before, I had attended a cousin's wedding of great fanfare in the hills of Vermont, gushing with champagne, catered lobster and black limousines, all perfectly timed but with torrential rain dripping from the fall colors. As the bride and groom left under a flurry of rice and good cheer, the elderly snockered priest, who stood beside me, shook his head and muttered, "Damn, they never work out when it rains." He was right. A year and a half later all that was left of the marriage were some expensive receipts and sad memories.

My request of sunshine was going to be difficult, but marriage had rough odds at best and we needed every boost we could get. We launched our little boat into Barkley Sound in the middle of this giant rain forest in late September and headed west.

The seas were calm as we rowed away, no doubt flattened by the giant raindrops that pelted its surface. Lisa sat in the stern seat reading Robert Service poems as I pulled on the oars. We were star struck in love and the rain and gray sky didn't have a chance at dampening our spirits as we rowed hour after hour out into the outer islands.

We camped in the rain and spent the first two or three days wandering from island to island immersed in the sullen grayness. We fished and read and dried out our gear by the heat of hissing wet, smoky fires. When gray and rain sets in on these coastal fall and wintry days, it feels as if it will never clear for months.

On the fourth morning we awoke and the skies were bright blue, the seagulls flew high and the world around us took on a vibrancy of colors that the muted cloud cover had not allowed. Lisa sat in her little seat, now reading *Malabar Farm*, while I with a fresh oar plied the waters further west to the last outer group of islands. These are a small buffer between the waters of this wild Sound and the Pacific Ocean.

Just to the west, if we turned right, Japan was the next stop some 4700 miles later. I have always been drawn to the edge of life: drawn to the edge between land and sea, the edge of the strong current and the soft, the edge of the wilderness and to the edge of cultural norms. We were now on the edge of the Pacific Rim.

We landed on the lee side of a tiny island called Dicebox on a beach where the ocean swells landed us high on the gravel as they eddied around the shores with their vast and daunting power. We pulled the boat up and started exploring.

Up over a small rise we could see the vast expanse of the Pacific, momentarily behaving itself shimmering with the sun on its shoulders. We walked the small beach and found a little cave with a delicate dribble of water from high overhead that splattered down into a lush mound of green grasses complete with Monet-like purple flowers. The sun was warm and strong, the ocean still.

There was a pause and we took a long look at each other. There was a wildness in our eyes. This was our moment. This was our place. We gathered bouquets and climbed up to the top edge of a rock buttress and stood facing each other, the sun glimmering off the wild Pacific, our only attendees three or four clueless seagulls.

We looked into each other's eyes with clarity and great intensity and took our words to heart as we talked of our love and our families, problem solving, and a life of hope and joy and the family we hoped to have. We prayed to the world, to the ocean, to the warm sun and to any and all gods listening that we were sincere in wanting happiness together. And of course we had to add if anyone in attendance disagrees with this notion, speak now. We giggled in the long silence but not even a seagull cried out. With that we said, "So be it." and threw our bouquets into the froth of salty ocean below us.

I looked at Lisa and my face blurred with tears until I was fully sobbing. I had to sit down and just let myself cry. Lisa was a little disarmed by this, but I was so happy and felt such an enormous sense of relief that it just felt good to cry. I think Lisa was wondering about her big, strong, macho husband who in the first minutes of marriage was in a puddle of tears.

We decided to celebrate and deep within the duffle emerged a bottle of St. Thomas rum. We decided to go fishing and toast our little secret to all those in our lives that we cared about despite their absence. We rowed offshore a short distance and each dropped a line as we handed the bottle back and forth. Here's to my Mom...bang, Lisa reeled in a rockfish. Here's to my Dad... bam, Lisa reeled in another rockfish. And my brothers...bam, Lisa reeled in another rockfish. The little boat probably measured 24 inches across, my line off one side and Lisa's off the other, and we both had the same lures on at the same depth. And here's to your uncle who will be pissed we eloped...bam, Lisa caught another rockfish. After too many toasts and a few primal yells into the wild wind and open sky, the total was Lisa 18 fish, me 1. Humility started early in our marriage.

We rowed ashore and stumbled to our tent as a new crisp wind blew in with the shifty eyes of a coyote, but we were too happy and drunk to notice. "I love you, Mrs. Lawrence, goodnight." "I love you, Mr. Lawrence, goodnight." By three in the morning the wind whipped the nylon tent and the rain sounded like pinecones splattering on the rain fly.

By daylight, winter winds and rain engulfed our world. My head felt like cotton hay and rags and, with my eyes at half-mast, I could see that not only was there too much wind to row anywhere, our tent was not sufficient to keep us dry another night.

We decided to move our hangovers into the cave at the end of the beach. We set up a piece of the tent to catch rainwater from the dribbling little stream, lit a fire with damp wood and moved into our new honeymoon home overlooking the wild and windy Pacific Ocean. "Think they have room service here, Mrs. Lawrence? Order Eggs Benedict and some strong coffee, ASAP." Lisa groaned, "Well, at least we have fish."

We wiled away the hours trying to stay warm while overlooking the mighty ocean and the increasing whitecaps and thundering swells. The fire's blue-gray smoke whisked about the cave opening and disappeared into the strong wind. The storm persisted for the next several days and we collected water, ate fish and rice, and yearned for room service.

On the fourth day, probably as much from boredom as anything else, we decided to try leaving. We loaded the boat, lashed down our duffle, took our seats and pushed off from our little marriage and honeymoon island. I rowed with a determined stroke and things went well for several hours.

We crossed behind islands when we could and stuck to the calmest waters possible but eventually we found ourselves a long way from shore with a shifting tide and ruthless wind. The rain took its turn as well and we became an insignificant speck as we crossed Loudoun Channel, 4 miles wide and 12 miles long. The wind humped in from the west off the ocean with a careless disregard for our little vessel. The boat swallowed the pestering swells with ease but as they rose above Lisa's head and disappeared beneath the transom, I pulled even harder and with more determination. "God help us if I break an oar!" I said, sweating beneath my raingear.

Lisa looked at me with a slate gray face and tried to smile encouragement but fear was as strong as the wind. In the chaos of the ocean, we managed to find a rhythm and we pushed through our two-mile passage and ducked behind an island. Finally in calm water, my oars went limp and we knelt on the floor of the little boat and hugged. "Jesus Christ, Mrs. Lawrence, I was thinking of being married longer than four days," I said, relief in my voice. "Me too, Mr. Lawrence, me too."

We kept our runaway marriage a secret when we got home. On our trip home we'd stopped off at a municipal building in the sleepy town of Ucluelet, British Columbia, and paid for a generic wedding. A ceremony performed in front of strangers in a small cinderblock building felt like a day in court for a traffic ticket. It was an effort to formally legalize the ceremony of the hearts that had taken place on Dicebox Island.

We left Ucluelet with the crumbs of our $6 reduced for sale wedding cake on the floor of our van. With the boat loaded on the roof, we sputtered back up over the mountains toward our little farm on our island. Our married lives were ahead of us but, to be honest, there was an awkward silence as we reviewed in our own heads the events of the past several days. Our own little ceremony was warm, personal and real, but there was reality as well to those generic words uttered by the constable at the Traffic Violations Bureau, "I pronounce you a married couple."

The long drive gave us the opportunity to think. I could tell Lisa was lost in thought and when I'd smile at her she was a million miles and many more thoughts away, but smiled back with only a second's delay. Would this all be hard for her to explain? I think she was working out the details.

Suddenly there was an awful whine and a growling thud and the engine disengaged. It was running, but the gas pedal gave us no forward motion. I coasted to the side of the road. These types of incidents were not uncommon in my life of vehicular ownership, but they never ceased to fill me with dread. As we coasted to a halt across the crackling gravel, my imagination feared the worst. We were already a little overdue with the delay from the storm and real close to nowhere familiar.

I walked back to the rear of the van, didn't notice any telltale spurting arteries of black crude oil, which eliminated some major terrors, but didn't solve my problem. I opened the engine cover and there was the engine, right there, much closer to the door than it was supposed to be. I slid under the van, over the wet ground alongside the remote highway, and stared up at a crowded turnpike of dusty rusty metal and cables.

Eventually I was able to discern that two of the four engine bolts had lost their nuts, and the engine had fallen backwards thus disengaging the drive spline from the transmission and rendering it powerless. The bolts were stripped and nuts lost forever, hidden along the mile of gravel roads behind us.

The only solution I could figure was to pry the engine back up and into place with one of the oars from our rowboat. This was good for getting the engine upright as long as my 165 pound body was bearing down on the long end of the oar. The creative process, driven by our remote setting, led me to take the second oar and lash it to the center of the roof rack at the back of the van; then while pushing down on the first oar, thus leveling the engine, I lashed the top oar to the one below. The awkward protrusion held and an hour after we were sidelined, we were back in the game growling down the freeway somewhat relieved but with just another niggling detail to worry about.

We held our secret silently to ourselves as it was a moment in our short time together to hold close the spirit of us as a couple—letting the paint dry before we told anyone.

Chapter 25

Cabin on Fire

When we came home from Canada, we went back to our routines. Lisa worked for her parents at night on their fish boat and I worked on the farm. It was October and our firewood was yet to be cut. We had a dozen new day old baby chicks in a box next to the stove and winter was coming. I rumbled across the meadow in our 1948 flatbed dump truck and over the stream to the far field where I'd seen some downed alders.

I looked back and saw the cabin through a small gap of trees that lined the shores of the creek. A small sniff of smoke from the chimney disappeared in the breeze. It looked so peaceful, nestled in the corner of the hidden meadow. I remember thinking that this is our little home, our little nest where my new wife and I would live. I felt glad to have it, simple and rustic as it was.

I cut firewood for several hours, piling freshly split chunks on the steel bed of the truck. The midday sun was hot as I put my splitting mall down and leaned against the loaded truck. My gaze fanned out across the meadow and through the gap back at the cabin. I was shocked.

Smoke was billowing from a window in a thick gray plume that raced around the outside of the cabin disintegrating into the wind. I felt panic as I sprang into the driver's seat, rolled the old flathead 6 engine over several times before the engine started, and drove like a lunatic across the field over the stream and across the meadow with the accelerator jammed firmly to the floor boards.

Water sprayed from the creek and firewood bounced and clattered to the ground. I crested the hill and shot over to the house. I left the truck on a dead run, jumped up the stairs onto the porch, swung the door open and charged in. It was black with smoke and being startled, I inhaled a gulp of thick gray fumes. The smoke knocked me flat to the ground, choking for air. I quickly crawled back outside retching in pain. I could hear the crackle of burning wood inside the cabin.

As fear shot through me, a fury took hold of my senses. I needed to fight to save my little home. I ran back inside this time holding my breath and, although dark, I groped around, found the phone and pulled it outside.

With fidgety fingers I dialed 911. It rang twice and an operator said, "Hello?" I yelled into the phone, "My fucking house is on fucking fire. I'm not fucking kidding. This is no fucking joke." I was yelling and sounding serious as I had heard about pranks and wanted them to know it was the real thing. "Send a fucking truck to Boyce Road, please!"

"Yes sir, we understand. A truck will be on its way momentarily." I slammed the receiver down and raced from the deck down to the pond where there was a gas water pump that I used to fill water troughs. I poured water in the primer hole and pulled on the starter cord. It fired off on the first pull, which was unusual. I hurdled a fence and yanked the pipe out of the water trough and jammed it into the black poly pipe that ran across the field to the house. I leapt back over the fence and sprinted the 100 yards to the cabin.

I grabbed several five-gallon buckets by the door and stuck one under the now flowing pipe from the pond. As soon as it was filled, I stuck the second one under the pipe and took the first, sprinted up the stairs into the house, swung the door open, gulped a lung of air and flung the water in the dark room toward the fireplace. A large crackling hissing noise erupted from the gloom as water doused the flames. The fire was far from out and I sprinted back to the poly pipe and changed the buckets. I repeated my run inside and flung water wherever there seemed to be flames.

As I was leaving, the phone rang and my reflex was to answer it. "Hi Jim. It's me, Lisa. We're in from fishing. Anything going on?" "The fucking house is on fire. Get out here quick." I slammed the phone down and ran back to the buckets. I could hear sirens wailing in the distance.

With the next bucket I clambered up onto the roof and poured the water down the chimney. A police car with sirens wailing blazed down the driveway and parked, leaving the lights flaring. A large officer got out adjusting his belt loaded with Billy club, guns, ammo, mace, cuffs and other irrelevant items. I was racing back and forth with buckets and yelled to him to pick up a bucket.

More sirens and the phone rang. For some idiotic reason, I picked it up again. It was Chris and Marsha, the neighbors. "Hey Jim, What's going on? We keep hearing sirens." "My fucking house is on fire." I slam the phone down and continue my steeplechase with full buckets.

Next the fire department steamed down the driveway, more lights, and more officials in uniforms. I had the fire pretty much out but was still in overdrive racing back and forth. I glanced out the window as the policeman stopped momentarily and pulled a comb from his celebrated black belt and took a few swipes at his hair in the reflection of the kitchen window. A moment of levity in an otherwise frantic time.

Lisa showed up and suddenly the little cabin was full of people. The air was wet and heavy with the stink of burning fiber and plastics. I felt dizzy and suddenly exhausted. The fire was out but a good portion of our belongings were ruined. All the books in the bookshelves had their backs burned off. My camera had melted, our little 12-volt car stereo and the tape cassettes were melted and our couch was a toxic, wet half-burned relic. The steam and heat had permeated our bedding and clothing.

The only plausible cause seemed to be the chimney. Strangely

I had just upgraded it a day or two earlier from the seemingly more dangerous single wall pipe to the very expensive new double Metalbestos triple wall. Who knows? Little cedar cabins of that era often burned. A rite of passage for the "back to the landers". Thankfully nobody was hurt, including the dozen day-old chicks who had found plenty of oxygen one and a half inches off the ground.

We'd been married three days. That night we slept in our little half a cabin snuggled to the one corner that offered shelter. One whole side had burned and the rain poured in with a depressing persistence, reminding us how tentative our world can be. The next day we tore away the wet charcoaled wood and stacked and burned it while friends dropped by to assess the damages and lend a hand. Their help was our only insurance but it reinforced our feelings about our island community.

Over the following months, we rebuilt on the same foundation, saving what we could of the original cabin. Beams from an old barn and more from the beach all added to our low budget Zen nest. A continued act of non-traditional creativity.

Chapter 26

Fishing

When we did let the secret of our marriage slip out, we got the full gamut of reactions. Friends were delighted with a skeptical eye. My mother blurted out something about grandchildren, my brother angry we hadn't been more traditional. My father didn't say a whole lot.

Lisa, the youngest of four, and the only girl in her family, got a different reaction. None of her family could believe she'd do something so reckless. She was supposed to marry her high school boyfriend, the drunk who'd tried to punch my lights out that rainy night at the ferry dock. Her brothers dubbed me "the root eater" as a cynical response to their dismay. Her father cried and her mother had twenty reactions that covered all spectrums.

We had disrupted the family process, broken all the unwritten rules and declared our independence. It was a tough time and I'm glad we lived our little secret for as long as we did. Lisa's heritage was from two of the original families that came to the islands and there were a lot of relatives and old timers who had a lot to say about our disrespectful audacity.

Prior to this time I had enjoyed a degree of anonymity, but when the word got out, the way it does in small towns everywhere, I was the butt end of a lot of secretive whispers. "If that was my daughter, I'd of horse whipped her," one woman said. "Whatever kind of hippie marriage they had I'm sure it wasn't legal and should be annulled," an uncle announced at a party. Her father was the postmaster, one uncle owned the hardware store and the other the drugstore. The streets were full of her aunts and cousins and word got around that the beloved daughter had run off with that tall hippie guy with the ponytail who seemed to always look dirty and was a farmer. I guess it was all true.

It took some time to win them over. But time is a great healer and there was an amount of acceptance that came with repetition. We would show up at their large family gatherings and eventually the eyes of disgust ran out of ammunition. In fact a year or so later, everyone seemed to enjoy knowing a harmless tall guy with a ponytail, despite my liberal opinions and odd lifestyle.

After all it was the early 80's and they were high-liner fishermen with boats and permits in both Puget Sound and Alaska. Money came relatively easily. They drove nice new pickups and played hard on plush vacations to Hawaii. It seemed silly to them, eking out a living as a farmer. They literally could make in one night of fishing what I made in an entire year on the farm.

We were living without running water and electricity and it was always a crap shoot as to when and if we might arrive somewhere because of the older temperamental cars we drove. I carried a full toolbox, jacks and spare tires at all times and developed the habit of backing up any incline just in case the battery decided to play dead. We lived on an exceptionally small budget, with no emergency funds and nothing extra.

Then in the rapid-fire pace of our life together, we got pregnant. It was an exciting, planned, yet a daunting reality. I had no idea how we were going to afford such an undertaking, another mouth to feed, diapers and clothes. As principled as I was about a simple life, I felt a deep need to give everything I could to raise our child.

It occurred to me that perhaps we should go fishing. I would need to overcome my fears of the ocean, largely brought on by my insufferable seasickness, not to mention I would need to learn how to fish, operate a boat and work on nets. Fishing of one type or another had been a part of me since I was a little boy. Digging worms and fishing for perch off the dock with Hughie, Pots and DJ was standard boyhood entertainment. Worms graduated to fly-tying, faraway rivers and fly rods with brother Hugh to remote, wild uncharted rivers in the interior of British Columbia where the fish were hungry and ample. River fishing taught me how fish moved, where they held and their relationship to sun and dark and light and all that's in-between.

Fly-fishing became some of the first real spiritual time I'd spent as a young man. Partly immersed in water and lost in my primal desire to hunt and catch, it gave me inspiration and relationship to the world of the river. The water running past me, through me, became a mantra, a baptismal that flowed and washed clean all of my trivial thoughts. It allowed me to slow down my thoughts and to ponder my life. It felt safe and a comfort, a belonging. If life were music, a clean river pushing downhill to meet its mother ocean full of fish pushing uphill to meet their final home is my grand concerto. Put me in the middle of that anytime.

Lisa's family owned gillnetters. They all owned and operated their own boats. Highly skilled, highly competitive and highly successful. A gillnetter is a small work boat about 32 feet long, has a large deck and fish hold, with a strong engine and a small cabin to shelter the workers and the electronics from the weather. It's generally equipped with a large reel that hydraulically winds up and stores a long piece of gillnet. This net (up to 3/8 of a mile long) is set out into the sea and drifts between tide and current, between logs and kelp, and is brought aboard every hour or so. Each fish is hand picked from the meshes and thrown into the fish hold. This is largely done at night, when the net is least obvious visually to the migrating salmon that swim into the meshes and become stuck by their gills. An easy concept with a dramatically different reality.

Weather, mechanical difficulties, and locating the fish are the big three difficulties while hundreds of other different obstacles lie in wait like tigers ready to pounce on the unprepared and weary. Necessary qualities for this job are the ability to work without sleep for long drudging hours, sometimes for little or no pay, mend nets, perform on the spot mechanical repairs, cook, navigate, find fish, pick fish out of the gigantic nets, all despite the weather, and also maintain a home life.

Lisa's oldest brother, Nick, took me fishing my first time. It was an act of generosity to me and his little sister. We plowed out of the port and up San Juan Channel, the large diesel engine brattling a monotone dirge that was lost in the wind behind us.

I had always grown up afraid of the water and my idea of becoming a fisherman had lots of personal obstacles to overcome. Fears of open water, of deep water, of monstrous sea animals that lurked below that would love to suck the juices from my flailing desperate body. Inside the cabin the stink of warm diesel swirled around like the stench of strong bad cooking, so I stood on deck to keep myself from throwing up. The inland waters were calm and the sun was bright. I partially convinced myself I would be able to handle it.

I stared down at the blue green water wondering how deep it was, how cold it would be if I fell in. I envisioned leagues and fathoms of black suffocating liquid that would steal me from life within moments, not to mention the Jules Verne animal life that would gnaw and slash at my body before devouring it in a haze of red-stained water.

We ran close to the kelp beds that rumba danced in the currents and alongside Goose Island where gulls screamed and hovered over fuzzy gray chicks. The diesel growled out past the lighthouse, sitting quietly yet proud, high atop the cliffs over Cattle Point. The white building waited for nightfall when it would perform its lifesaving simple task as a land star that blinks nocturnal marine voyagers to safety.

The boat began to rise and fall as we rounded the point and

headed westerly toward the Salmon Banks. The wind was cool and my stomach tightened as we headed straight into it, splitting whitecaps with our solid little bow. I moved into the doorway where I was warmer and tried to pretend I wasn't smelling the bilious fumes of warm diesel wafting up from down below. Nick was studying charts and talking on the radios seemingly unaffected by the motion, the noise or the diesel smell.

I began a white-knuckle grip on the door jamb, as we beat into the weather, wondering what I was bargaining for. We stopped in what seemed like a totally nondescript place about two hours after we'd left the port. The boat flung about in the waves as Nick donned his rain gear and moved to the back deck. He yelled over the wind for me to steer back to the lighthouse after he threw the boat into gear.

I took a deep breath and stepped back into the cabin to the helm and watched the enormous net unravel off the stern in an even straight line into a sea of chaotic waves. Some minutes later the boat hung off a long tether attached to the net that worked as a sea anchor and the waves took turns smashing into the stern as we shuddered and rolled in every disorienting direction.

My entire mental and physical understanding of being on planet earth began to unravel. Nick reacted as if he were sitting at the kitchen table having a cup of coffee. I on the other hand was tense and banging from side to side, feeling greener and greener, clutching the doorjambs trying to stare at the horizon. Late afternoon and evening evaporated the light, and the horizon disappeared into a black windy and rolling world where seasickness grabbed me like a gorilla and beat the guts out of me.

Nick was just getting to know me and he was assessing this stranger who had stolen off and married his little sister. I think he was looking for a manly tough guy who would understand the world of fishing the way most understand how to drink a beer.

I began to puke. At first it felt like I was being discreet as if it was something that would disappear and we wouldn't need to say a word about it. But "manly man" went over the side into the raging green froth of the sea as I puked or sat staring at the waves for the next several hours. Bile and meals of days gone past reversed order and blasted upstream blowing past tongue, nostril and tear duct and any form of dignity one may have ever possessed. And after the stomach was empty, the reflexes continued hammering away with nothing but the sounds of a large dying cat that hollered at the swirl of the ocean that swallowed one's grief with total disregard. Seasickness is a time one contemplates the rewards of death. This is entirely inconceivable to those who do not experience it.

I was exhausted and it was only 9:00 at night and we would fish until 9:00 the next morning. I stood on the back deck to help Nick pick fish as we hydraulically reeled the massive net aboard. My knees were rubber and unsure, my arms weak and unable. I felt it was all I could do to stay awake and survive.

Nick looked at me with a skeptical eye and no doubt a fair amount of disappointment; that which felt like a noble cause in fact became a pain in the ass to have on board. My position in the doorway, out of the wind yet breathing a little fresh air, couldn't be a worse place to park myself. Nick was working hard between the radios and the aft deck and this tall green skinny guy was in the way both coming and going every time.

A mile or so to the north, I could see the lights of the islanders. House lights of people in warm, motion-free houses who were probably eating dinner while watching TV, beginning their first notions of a large warm Posture Pedic where they would slip safely into a world of dreams. At that moment I wanted a boring life: flat, bland and predictable. My body ached for shore, for terra firma. So close, yet we thrashed about in our diesel bean can only a mile or so away.

Nick was cursing the fact that we'd found some seaweed and kelp islands and there weren't many fish. I was thrilled yet acted disappointed for Nick's sake. This meant we might be quitting. And if I were asked I would try not to act too enthusiastic, but act as if it didn't seem worth the wear and tear. By the time we'd picked out all the kelp and sticks, it was close to midnight and Nick said we'd set her out again and wait for daylight.

By morning light the entire night had been a nightmare of sickness and exhaustion. I was so tired I felt barely conscious. The sea didn't settle until we motored back around Cattle Point into sheltered waters. We pitched our fish off onto a tender anchored at Fish Creek and Nick took his disappointing check for some $380.

It seemed like a lot to me. $80 a day was good wages to me, when I could find steady work, and he was disappointed at $380. Wow, I had to figure this thing out. After all I was going to be a father, it really didn't matter how I felt. I just needed to provide for my family.

Seasickness afflicts 5% of a population all the time and 5% never get sick at all. Everyone else falls somewhere in-between on a sliding scale. I was at the bottom end and Lisa not far behind. I convinced myself that I needed to overcome or learn to deal with this self-inflicted bar beating that happened whenever the wind blew.

We convinced Nick to lease us an extra older boat and he agreed if his friend, Mel, would come along and show us the ropes. Mel was more experienced at fishing, as well as drinking and smoking. The boat was an old slab that gushed and sputtered noxious fumes but it managed to get the net in and out and us to and from the fishing grounds.

I was constantly asking and then pleading with Mel to not smoke in the cabin as it made us both nauseous and it seemed risky, considering Lisa was pregnant. The issue persisted and Mel began to chain smoke four packs a day without regard for anyone else. There was a grimness and under current of anger, no doubt a hangover from his tough times in Vietnam. Just short of coming to blows I insisted, due to the health of our unborn child and our continuing battle with seasickness, that he get off the boat and Lisa and I would go it alone. It was a hard decision as I liked Mel but his habits weren't just his own on a small boat with three people, one of whom was pregnant. I felt protective of the child we hadn't even met yet.

I remember the first opening we motored the boat out. The water was calm cobalt blue. There was a frisky wind that chipped at the surface but died away as evening dimmed the lights. We drove the boat as far away from the fleet as we could get and set the net out and waited the requisite hour or so before hauling our net back

My stomach was in knots while I tried to remember everything in this new world and new profession that I was so determined to figure out. The net crackled as it tightened through the stern rollers as the large hydraulically driven drum rolled forward and then, like a miracle, a large sockeye salmon flashed and flopped over the stern. This was our first fish together. Lisa watched from the deck and we grinned as I flung the large five-pound silvery bullet into the fish hold. It was the first of many hundreds that we would be so fortunate to catch in the years to come.

We fished on through the night and made some $400. I was so happy the next morning when we sold I could hardly contain myself. One-half went to Nick, some to fuel and groceries but I was beginning to see that it was possible. As long as the weather cooperated, Lisa and I would be fine. The only fallacy to that logic was that seldom did the weather follow my rules.

We gained courage and confidence, however, despite our old boat and inexperience. When the wind blew, we invariably got sick and struggled. Lisa would hit the bunk and I'd just tough it out. Pick fish and puke all night long. Reminiscent of my child-hood, it was perhaps the most difficult work I have ever endured. The vomiting was an exhausting distraction to deck work, churning my guts into a tense rope and draining me of energy and spirit. Many a night I had to really reach deep to find reasons to stay out on the fish grounds and fish. I'd walk out on deck, puking, cursing the wind and waves with every breath. It was the plight I'd chosen and I was going to be a father. I had to tough it out.

One night we went particularly far off shore. We were hoping to cut off a run of silver salmon running down the north side of the Olympic Peninsula. The weather was choppy and a black line lay across the darkening horizon to the west. Lisa's belly was showing enough we were making jokes about her not fitting into her oilskins. The lumpy seas sent her to the bunk.

By the time I got the net off the boat, the sea was four or five foot with a menacing wind that was gaining energy. The VHS radio began to come alive with fishermen as if the wind might somehow be different a mile away as it howled down the Straits, asking for weather reports and wondering how it was wherever their buddy was fishing. You could hear the tension in their voices. Lots of nervous chortle. People needing each other's comfort as they readied themselves for a real tough night.

"There better be some Goddamn fish around is all I can say," a voice in the dark blurts over the speaker. It sounds like one of Lisa's brothers. "I hope my hydraulics can pull against this wind." "We're so far out here and with this tide, hell, if we need to pick up and run it'll be closer to run south to Port Angeles," another brother chimes in. I sit in the chair at the helm.

I've never been in anything like this in my life. The boat is rolling and crashing and banging like one long accident; and my pregnant wife and I, who don't know much of anything, are stuck here inside in the dark with our net out not knowing what to do and praying that there are no breakdowns or that one of us doesn't go overboard trying to get out on deck to pick up the net.

We were in the middle of the straits, which is the middle of the freeway of wind and waves blowing in from the west. This storm felt like it probably got started in Japan, pummeled west unobstructed and gained speed right down the Straits of Juan de Fuca where it crashed about our little boat. Radio chatter became more revealing and it looked like it was time to run for cover. "My net's heaving around so much, no fish is going to stick in there." A voice from the speaker that sounds like a cousin of Lisa's mom. Then someone pulls the cork by saying, "I'm getting out of here. I'm gonna run for PA." Everyone collapses and begins to pick their nets.

Within minutes, deck lights were on all across the fleet and the little voice on the speaker somehow gave permission to the rest of us to pull her back and run for cover. I told Lisa to stay inside as it seemed too dangerous for her on deck. I put on my rain gear and flipped on the picking lights. My stomach was in an awful knot and I was vomiting as I lurched and fumbled my way to the back deck. The lights revealed the furious sea.

The bridle line heaved and sprung tight as the waves lifted and dropped the boat at their will. I stepped on the hydraulic pedal to reel in the net and the bridle line caught the top of the stern roller, snapped it off, and it sailed through the air right past the door of the cabin like it had been thrown from a catapult.

Lisa had just appeared in the doorway to check on me and the large metal bowling pin missed her head by inches scaring me in a deeply profound way. I began yelling for her to get back in the cabin and shut the door. My voice had grizzly bear in it laced with fear and anger.

The net would be difficult or impossible to get in without this roller. I stepped on the pedal and the boat slowly backed into this large webbed net that was as tight as a thousand banjo strings. The green water smashed and pounded from every direction and I vomited now, without even turning my head, letting the fury of the salt water thrashing about clean my face and oilskins. I was in an angry terrified misery.

The net slogged on board as the hydraulics cursed and moaned. The wind blew the web over the broken stern roller and as the hydraulics wormed their way in, meshes snapped and tore as they ripped over the jagged metal edges. I didn't care. At that point I was concerned for my life and my wife's and our unborn child's.

I was in survival mode and didn't give a shit for the net. I just wanted it on board and I wanted to get the hell out of this nightmare. Finally the end of the net appeared and with the jacklight on board, I struggled my exhausted body into the cabin. As I switched off the deck lights, I could hear the muffled deep growling sounds of Lisa vomiting below in the bunk.

I switched on the radar and the sea scatter cluttered the screen to the point it was useless in such a rough ocean. The radios were alive with chatter again as people were looking for anywhere to get out of the gale. "Winds at 40 knots gusting to 55," a nervous voice I didn't recognize. "Head for PA, just head south and you'll see the lights. Hell, you'll run into something eventually," a chuckle that sounded relieved. I looked at the compass, pushed the throttle into gear, swung the boat around and headed through a chaotic mess of waves in a southerly direction. The windshield was awash in water but the bright lights of Port Angeles glimmered above the fray.

Then an hour later, like the magic of prayers heard, we rounded the breakwater and with one last swell surged forward into calm water. We idled up to the dock, dropped bumpers, and tied bow and stern.

The boat was a mess. The cabin had leaked and was awash in the contents of emptied drawers, vomit, and a sheen of diesel-stained water about four inches over the floorboards. Lisa lay in the bunk and cried softly to herself, quiet muffled whimpers. I was so exhausted, I was no comfort. I climbed into the bunk next to her and murmured softly. "We made it. That's about as much fun as I can handle in one night." We fell asleep in our wet clothing, in our wet bunk, with vomit on our breath and no fish in the hold.

We tried anything and everything to cure us from seasickness. There were the drugs Bonomine and Dramamine which rendered me comatose in about 20 minutes and were unsafe for pregnant women. We tried wristbands that had little knobs sewn into the fabric, worn tightly just below the hand. These worked about as well as the Umeboshi Plum pit we taped into our navels. These only satisfied the persons who sold them to us.

Mildly successful remedies were soda crackers eaten on a continuum that delighted *Nabisco*, but rendered a dry mouth and restricted the use of the feeding hand when endeavoring to pick fish. Then there was chugging a lukewarm *Budweiser* that seemed to settle the stomach and give a degree of energy. For me, working hard and drinking beer put me to sleep but occasionally it really made sense on a long night in a rough ocean. I knew fishermen who drank a case of beer a day and it never seemed to affect their ability to work.

Then we discovered what NASA had developed for their astronauts: a transderm patch that was stuck to your skin behind an ear, infused with a drug called Scapalomine. This became a lifesaver. There seemed to be few side effects, less getting some of the drug in your eye which dilated your pupil to the likes of a snowy owl. Eventually all macho fisherman who were afflicted with the dastardly despair of seasickness wore these little patches.

Chapter 27

Juggling Nets, Tractors and Money

The first year of fishing was exhausting. There was so much to learn and it was all happening out on the fish grounds without much help, except what we could glean over the radio. We had to solve our own problems and learned most lessons the hard way, usually at some ungodly hour when the sane world was fast asleep: like after struggling to get the net off the reel and brushing past the control knobs at the stern station and not realizing the boat had shifted into reverse.

I walk into the boat cabin, relieved I have a small break, take off my rain gear and hang it by the stove as the engine idles obediently. Then there is a low muffled groaning noise throughout the boat and the engine quits for no apparent reason. Intuitively I know it's bad.

I rush to the stern to stare over the transom to find the net sucked up into the slowly reversed rotating propeller into a wad of web the size of a big round bale of hay with the rest of the net stretching out an eighth of a mile behind. There are no pretty or easy solutions to this. The boat is crippled and drifts with the net out in whatever direction wind and tide desire. Neither wind nor tide make an effort to keep you from running into the side of the island and helplessly dashing yourself to splinters on the rocky shore. Tugging on the net by hand is like tugging on the bottom.

The web of the net, when compressed together, is like steel

and impossible to break. I have even seen them render large slow moving freighters dead in the water if enough web catches around the flukes of the large propellers. One method is to gather all the web hanging off the end of the boat and, securing it as tightly as possible to a cleat, restart the engine and rev the RPM's up reasonably high and pop the shifter into forward. With luck, the prop blows a hole in the web and clatters free; then all one need do is spend several hours on board trimming off and re-sewing the net into shorter yet fishable net.

What can happen, however, when the boat is thrust into forward is that the propeller lurches and the web prevents it from turning, whipping the propeller shaft out of alignment or bending the shaft. It can also blow apart the coupler that connects the long expensive stainless steel shaft to the engine and back itself out of the shaft housing leaving you with a big shaft size hole in the boat. This most often happens in the dark and is not kind due to rough weather.

Sometimes all that happens is more web is rolled around the prop and your situation becomes more dire. Often one has to pull the rest of the net aboard into the stern of the boat which requires Herculean strength, if possible at all, and then sit and flail around in the trough of the sea (while everyone else is catching fish) and wait to see if any partner boats will tow you to a shipyard where you can hire a diver to cut the web away.

Ever inventive, I produced another method that worked, but never became very popular. It started one night on calm seas with the net out. The light breeze from the west shifted and the boat swung around and the net went under the stern and tangled in the prop. It was 3 a.m. and only a small sliver of moon shown.

We had been resting and the calm had lulled us to being careless. I wasn't ready to explode the end of my net with the propeller, or hang crippled, drifting until daylight, so I figured it wouldn't be hard to dive down and untangle the web. There would be minimal net damage and I could keep fishing, keep making money.

I taped a large spotlight to the end of a pike pole. Lisa was to hold the lantern over the side, pointing roughly at the propeller so I could see what I was doing. She came out on deck full of doubt, "It'll be too cold. Are you sure? Let's just rip off the end with the propeller. Are you sure? Oh God, Jim, be careful." We were several miles off shore in perhaps 600 feet of icy green water and the world was dark, less our deck lights and the spotlight.

I grabbed a sharp knife, pulled off my clothes and stood up on the gunnels of the boat, a silhouette of a primitive cave drawing complete with bandy legs and hanging genitalia. Below were my worst fears: a cold bottomless ocean that would swallow my insignificant body and lose me in a million miles of flesh eating monsters. I jumped. "I love you," I yelled into the darkness.

The cold felt like I was being crushed between two cars in a head-on collision. The air in my lungs seemed to vanish and I immediately began to hyperventilate. I forced a gulp of air down, ducked my head under and kicked beneath the boat. I was moving at a hectic, frenzied speed. I swung my arms with the knife and slashed, then went for air. When my head bobbed up, I sputtered, "Fuck, I'm cold." I gulped more air and went back to my vague world of cold, deep, green water and invisible web, slashing at windmills, fighting the meshes that were meant to be invisible. More air, the cold was beginning to slow my movements, my legs and arms were a flurry of scrambled chaos.

One last effort and panic sent me to the surface and I scrambled up the net bar and onto the deck. My skin was reddish purple and deeply numb. Lisa and I stood next to the little diesel stove, she rubbing me with towels and me shivering to an almost convulsive state. "Don't ever do that again!" she scolded. "Jesus Christ, do you want this baby to grow up without a father?" My teeth were clattering as I said, "Yah, but I got the net out." I paused as droplets hissed off the stove's hot surface. "Pregnant?" She stared at me like the lunatic I was with a real questioning worried look in her eye.

These nights of learning were compounded by several things. I was still trying to farm as well. We were growing u-pick strawberries and spending the late summer bucking hay bales after long nights of fishing. Sleep came easy whenever and wherever I could find time. Place was never a problem. I learned to nap anywhere for only minutes at a time and was able to drift swiftly into a REM level of sleep. Often my worlds would chaotically mix and my dreams would be filled with gillnets floating in the strawberry patches, or salmon amongst the hay bales. Life was rich and busy and Lisa was gaining a rounder little belly by the week.

We had gained our fishing license through Lisa's heritage. Her mother was a member of the Swinomish Indian tribe. Lisa, by tribal rights, was given permission to fish as was I, her husband; the only criteria was that Lisa was to be on board at all times that we were fishing. There had been a long standing heritage in the island of fishing, but when a controversial ruling in court allowed local Indians the ability to take half the allotted catch, the docks were a broil. The white fleet's time to fish was cut drastically and the Indian fleet, with only a few boats, fished constantly to catch their half of the quotas.

The white fishermen were incensed. Indians were making more money than they were and it provoked a lot of tensions with racial undertones. There were fights and provocations everyday on the docks. We lost a lot of important friends who just couldn't stand the fact that Lisa's family would benefit from such an outrageous ruling.

Oddly, Judge Boldt, the acting judge during the trial, was only upholding a treaty that had been signed like thousands of other treaties but not upheld. It's something about the difficulty the proud white American has seeing women or a minority gain a foothold in our culture and the result is extremely ugly.

Life became difficult during those early years. Walking the

docks was treacherous. Passing the white fleet tied to the dock, crews sitting idle on deck, I generally expected to be harassed. Dogs were sicked on me, my tires were flattened and name calling became a regular ritual. Eventually I learned to stay out of town, certainly out of bars, and never engage in any conversation with anyone who was drinking. We hid our boat at obscure moorages and socialized less and less with anyone who was involved with fishing with the exception of the other members of the tribe.

It was a sad chapter in our life on the island. Yes, the ruling by Judge Boldt infused the local Indian tribes with an important shot of money, and yes, they weren't always wise with how they spent it. But then again white America hasn't been a great role model either. In the end, the fisheries for both the "Cowboys and Indians" were to lose. Fishermen are too independent for any organized effort to lobby or politic and consequently watched the industry vanish like so much water through the scuppers. The fight never really left the dock until it was too late and the political process swept it under the rug and focused on other industries that had a unified lobby.

Fall of 1982 came and we were ready for a break. We piled the firewood high and readied the cabin for our first little family member. By February, Lisa was as round as a buoy ball and several weeks before the due date she woke me about 3 a.m. and told me it was time. I missiled from our bed and ran around the house totally berserk as she lay in bed timing her contractions.

I cleaned and I danced and I sang and I worried. I called my mother in Portland, Oregon, at 3:15 a.m. and told her we were on our way to the clinic. I remember looking around the house and feeling love for everything, an endorphin gleam in my eyes. I was going to be a father.

At daylight we drove to meet the doctor at the clinic. Midway we pulled over to the side of the road in Clyde's driveway and worked Lisa through a tough contraction. As we were practicing our breathing exercises, outside in the cold blustery sky we saw a group of wild trumpeter swans fly by. This was the first time they'd ever been seen on the island in anyone's memory. It was a very powerful thing to observe on the morn of our firstborn child. A number of hours later, just as my mother walked through the door, our first little girl was born. My mother, excited to meet her first grandchild, endured six hours on the freeway and two on the ferry and timed it within minutes of her birth.

I always thought I'd fallen in love with Lisa quite fast, but when that little wet muscled body popped into my hands, I was in love like never before. When the nurse said that she'd take the baby and give her a bath, my elbows went up. I scowled at her and said, "If the baby needs a bath, I'll give it to her." We were protective proud parents and would sit and stare at this child for hours at a time. Her name became Natalia Swan Lawrence.

Spring came and the money was gone. Our roles were defined by our gender. Lisa had the equipment to nurse our thriving baby and I had the ability to swing a hammer. We still had no running water and electricity and our 14x20 foot cabin was feeling small.

We needed a pocket full of money and working for wages made it all seem unattainable. Wages always seemed to spend themselves, regardless of how high or low they were, on basic survival needs with nothing extra. The price of day old dairy calves was escalating and their sale price as springers two years later wasn't. We could have bought the laundromat for all the quarters we were stuffing in those little slots. Our car had a few major medical problems and Natalia was growing almost as fast as the things we seemed to need. Clearly pounding nails and working the farm weren't going to solve my problems.

The truth of the matter was that the farm was using some of the important funds that should have been kept for the house. But a farm is an emotional and physical ball that rolls hard and isn't easy to stop or start, and it was an important personal commitment I needed to keep. The bottom line was my two jobs weren't making it and I wanted to get my own fish boat for the summer season. We suffered from lots of desires and not enough money. At night, listening to the baby gurgling away, my sleep was tormented by the fear I wasn't going to be able to give her enough. Age and reality began rounding off the edges of some of my Luddite notions and I felt it was at least time to hook up to the 20th century.

I was a farmer. I needed money and I could grow things. I would compromise my original convictions and grow dope. I would grow just a little pokalolo, ganja, bud, weed. I would grow some marijuana. I knew others who did it. I wouldn't get greedy, just a few plants, besides I hated smoking it myself so I wouldn't get caught up in smoking all the profits. How hard could it be?? I procured a dozen seeds and germinated them on the windowsill. In the back of the orchard I dug a huge hole and filled it full of rotted cow manure. A week or so later I took three or four little green two leafed plants to my plot and tucked them in for the summer.

Two days later I went to water them and found a sheen of slime where my little plants had been. Mr. Slug had devoured my crop and no doubt was feeling pretty good about it.

I repeated my grow-op and the next time my three or four little plants had copious quantities of diatomaceous earth sprinkled in circles next to little Dixie cups filled with beer. I'd switch those slugs from desires for THC to alcohol. The slime veered away from the fossilized diatoms and straight into the Dixie cups where they drank themselves into a coma and drowned.

The plants grew. The two leaves developed two more and within a month they were attractive small bushes. I invited my marijuana specialist friend (formerly a large grower in California) over to marvel at my success. Greg studied the plants and said I had only one female and needed to pull up the other three. This seemed nuts as they were so pretty and doing so well, but I yanked their strong little root balls from the moist soil and flung them deep into the woods. The remaining little girl thrived and grew disproportionately against the backdrop of grasses and weeds.

Greg showed me how to bend the plant over flat to the ground and tie weights on the branches keeping it from looking like a dope plant as well as stressing the plant which works as a positive. The life force of the plant wants to survive and be as big and productive as possible to be able to receive the pollen from the now missing male plants. I named her Hope, and Hope grew and grew, all-be-it sideways, with dozens of rusty bolts hanging from each little branch that struggled to grow upright. With no male pollen and with her foot up to its thigh in rotted composted manure and watered daily, Hope spread lushly out over a 12x12 foot area.

Fishing had started and we were working away at a miserable season. An El Nino had warmed the currents in the straits and all the fish headed north in a cooler heat gradient around Vancouver Island missing our fish grounds entirely. Nonetheless I would rush home from fishing to water livestock from the little hand dug well and spend time keeping Hope alive. By late fall she'd begun to develop large buds just aching for male pollen. They grew in long twisted tubular cylinders rich in pitchy THC. Before the weather turned, I cut through the 3½ inch barked trunk and hauled the mass of branches into the cabin.

It was late afternoon and the paranoia was running strong. I prayed we wouldn't have any visitors and instructed Lisa to intercept anyone who came, outside in the driveway, and explain I was deathly ill with a contagious disease. The plant needed to be cleaned. Rid it of stems, branches and leaves and pick and clean the massive THC laden buds.

Darkness came and it was taking much longer than anticipated. The baby slept and Lisa's and my fingers picked and cleaned until they were dark and stained from the pitchy resins. We sat at the kitchen table stabbing glances out the window up the driveway searching for headlights. Lisa knocked her cup of tea off the table and it splattered across the floor. We were both tense; we looked at each other and then again out the window to the driveway.

"Did you hear that noise?" I'm concentrating really hard to hear. I look up the driveway and see six cop car lights blazing toward us. I feel panic and blink my eyes and look again. There's nothing there. But I knew there was. "Oh fuck, I'm going to jail," I say, but the words are distorted and Lisa begins to giggle. She collapses backward into her chair and begins laughing with a full body Jello-wiggling posture.

I'm terrified she doesn't understand that we might be in serious trouble and she may become a single parent because I'll be doing life without parole. She'll end up on welfare and eventually divorce me because she's lonely and kinda horny for some guy who's also a checker in her minimum wage loser job. Tears are now rolling down her cheeks and she's complaining that laughing that hard makes her ribs hurt. "You're stoned, you duffous," she blurts out between hilarities. "We're getting high from Hope."

She realizes how funny that sounded and rolls off her chair and is on all fours trying to keep the laughter from sending her into convulsions. "You're just paranoid, relax." I walk outside and try and breathe deeply. I look up the driveway once more. It's dark and quiet. Lisa is repeating herself about Hope getting us high.

I hate the feeling. Something in my life or my body chemistry doesn't work when it comes to dope. My legs feel unattached and keep floating away. My head aches and none of it's any fun.

The next day we cleaned what little remained and stuffed it into bags and weighed it. Hope gave us two pounds of number one bud. Several days later, fearing the paranoia was becoming a permanent characteristic in my personality, I boarded the ferry with the two bags stuffed into the engine compartment headed for a farmhouse in the Skagit Valley to a guy whom I didn't know but had heard would buy.

His driveway was long and I felt ready to abort at any second.

I would speed away and throw the bags off the Skagit River bridge and drive hard and away for hours. I hated all this part too.

I pulled up to a house that looked like a transfer station for junk. The yard was filled with "reduced for sale" broken crap littered by the wind. Inside looked like the yard. The guy I'd come to see sat on a dirty couch piled high in laundry, some dirty some clean, watching his large panoramic TV. Suzanne Sommers was bouncing her floppy ponytails and gigantic boobs and spouting one-liners to an audience of canned laughter.

"Have a seat, brother dude." His hair was long and looked as if it had been affected by some ineffective electroshock treatments. His belly pooched under his filthy t-shirt monogrammed with the slogan, "1 tequila, 2 tequila, 3 tequila floor." The brother dude part and the fact that my dealer buddy hadn't taken his eyes off the TV was starting to bother me. "Hear you got some good shit there, brother dude." We struggled along like this for awhile and eventually "Three's A Company" went to advertisements and he sampled "the shit" and disappeared into the back room.

This is when I knew he would reappear with a sawed-off side by side 12 gauge shotgun and blow me away right there in that torn under-stuffed chair. These feelings led me to accept and promise that I had no future in the drug world. After all, this was a misdemeanor amount of pot.

He reappeared with a tobacco stained smile and handed me an envelope. I smiled back and trotted out the door and sped off feeling relief in every nano second that passed. I didn't look into the envelope until I was on the ferry hours later. Hope had given us 20 crisp $100 bills. It still hardly felt worth it.

Comparatively, I was willing to power a fish boat out into a storm in the dark and deal with half a dozen life threatening possibilities but getting high from the marijuana resins was a far more unpleasant reality. It made me curious about why I had such a different reaction to the same drug that gave pleasure to so many. It felt like it perhaps opened some vault into some proverbial childhood nightmare, something ominous and terrifying, too big for me to look at. I was a child, a victim by innocence and age, and the marijuana took me back there and reminded me of some dark horrid place, some unforgivable sad event and I will never know what it was.

When I arrived back on the island, the mail had a letter of solicitation from the power company looking for new customers. The power company would pay for the first 1000 feet of power cable and after that it would be a dollar a foot. I told them to go ahead and sign us up. 1000 feet was about 12 feet shy of where we needed the power to end, so we paid $12.50 to hook it up.

It had been nine years lighting my night life with kerosene or some jury-rigged car battery and a single 12 volt light bulb. I had milked my cow by lantern. I had gone through countless batteries in countless flashlights and even sat in my car in the evening to read magazines because the cab light was the best light available. I was a full-fledged American now with my own power bill. I had mixed feelings.

We spent the sum total of Hope on a 160 foot deep hole drilled through the earth's crust that produced an amazing five gallons of clean water per minute. My summer with Hope catapulted us forward, but it hadn't felt worthwhile considering how we got it. I liked growing things but that was a one-time crop.

Lisa was pregnant again, so I did most of the fishing that summer and Lisa slept and when we got to shore she was rested enough to take care of our growing energetic little girl who was usually starved for attention by the time we were reunited. The sadness of that summer was Lisa had two miscarriages. These little discussed medical events run deep in the heart and I have carried them as silent personal wounds for many years.

The farm had taken a back seat to fishing purely due to finances. The margin of profit, if there was to be any, was so slim that fishing was our best bet. We still had a herd of a dozen Holstein calves and Tansy, the ever-steady Madonna of the bovine world. One of the myths of farm life is that it's always the bull that aggressively plows through fences and causes problems wanting to breed cows in estrus.

At our farm it was the young heifers that would cycle into a romantic mood and go looking for love. That meant walking the fences head down bawling, calling for a bull, pushing on the fences, and eventually catapulting themselves through the air over the top, or at least half way which would result in a tangled mess of wire and calves. The rest of the calves, aspiring to the greener grass theory, would quickly follow, jumping with shit splattering kicks. They disappeared quickly off down the road with one horny young heifer leading all the way.

They'd usually get about as far as the neighbor's house and stop to trample a few flowerbeds and eat expensive plants. We were lucky if we were home when they called, but fishing led us miles from the island. It did nothing for our relationships with the neighbors except continue to aggravate and piss them off. With the first offense, there was usually an air of tolerance and understanding, but after that no amount of apologizing would suffice.

We'd drag in from a long three day opening, not that any neighbor cared, with no sleep, a needy child and come home to the phone ringing that our goddamn cows were standing outside the kitchen window eating all the zinnias and trampling the begonias. Legs were heavy running these animals back home and good sleep time was spent fixing trampled fences.

One spring when Natalia was three, I signed on to fish the halibut opening in Southeast Alaska. We motored north but after three days of running were blown into Prince Rupert, British Columbia, by a horrific windstorm in Hecate Straits. I climbed the ladder at the dock and made my way to a telephone to call home. Natalia answered and, not realizing the 800 miles between us, cried into the phone.

"Daddy, Daddy, come home right now! The cows are out and Mama's chasing them and she's been gone a long time and I'm here alone and it's getting dark and I want you to come home now. Please Daddy, please Daddy."

It became obvious we couldn't both fish and farm and do them well. The farm seemed empty after we sold our beautiful calves but there was less anxiety. For the next handful of years it lay fallow. Stretched out in its fertile beauty, the farm waited while we harvested out at sea. I had a family to raise and only so many calories in me.

Chapter 28

Another Fish Story, and Another

It's 10:05 p.m. A light cool breeze blows across the water. An early rising moon and a light wind that usually dies with the onset of darkness. Enough of a breeze to stir up the sockeye salmon and confuse them into the net. I am a handful of miles off the west side of San Juan Island. I hear the lip lip sound of water on the hull as I rest between sets, my head leaning against the window listening to the chortle on the VHF radio.

Lonely fishermen just passing time after too many days alone. Talking about pretty near anything that comes to mind. After days on the water, the world and friendship are communicated by a 1-inch speaker and a mic.

"Yah, I'm gunna heat me up some tube steaks and a *Cup o Noodles*," *so*meone drones on or there's some breakdown on their boat they've jury rigged, complaining as if the problem was part of some conspiracy that the boat and its builders had against him. "If I'd just done it right the first time," a remorseful voice laments. "Yah man, a poor man can only afford to do things once," crackles back another voice trying to sound like they give a rip. There's talk of wives at home, or wives who aren't at home when they should be, and there is relentless complaining about money or cars that will get rebuilt next winter.

Tonight, though, there's reference to the good conditions: the timing of the moon and the tides and the time of year. It could be good. I smile and figure I have perhaps an hour if my net holds its shape or I don't run into any junk - junk being the tidal rips of seaweed and driftwood that mysteriously appear in the tides' ebb and flow and clog and sink a net, or at least take up one's complete night picking and hacking at it. Junk makes a net unfishable, fishermen miserable, and is a horrible waste of otherwise good fishing time. Everyone hates junk. I say my junk prayers and close my eyes for a short nap. One learns the real value of prayer at three in the morning when there's junk around.

There is a mystery to late night on the water. There's menacing horrid things that can really ruin a night's fishing from junk to breakdowns to no fish. I have endured most of them. Disappointments that destroy all self-esteem and attitude. "Missing the fish." Going east when I thought I was outsmarting the fleet and going west resulting in the entire fleet catching boat loads. Or there's fish around and you're where you should be, in fact you might have the best set of the night, but that damn hydraulic motor you were too tired to fix, against your better judgment, takes a crap and you spend eight hours playing Hercules pulling your net in by hand.

All mechanical systems, astronomy, laws of nature and timing have to be on your side or piles and piles of serious luck. It's funny how often one holds out for the luck, particularly as fatigue plays with the mind.

But tonight things may be different. I step out on deck and listen and look into the darkness. I have a good set. My radar screen shows a half-mile between the next boat and me. A good distance. I'm a half-mile off Eagle Point and beginning to ebb west. The net is stretched tight with the tide and I'm heading to deeper water. Off maybe two miles to the east, I see a boat up to the banks already and he's got his picking lights on and his engine groans and grumbles like an old dinosaur choking and farting out exhaust and water.

I watch to see how long it's taking him. Some guys work with rundown equipment and their boats pick up slowly, but maybe he's "into 'em" as we say and he's got a hell of a jag to pick before he snags up on the banks. I'll let my net soak. All calculations say we're safe for a couple hours and the conditions are too good.

I return to the cabin and feel the delicious warm heat of the oil stove. Lisa is sound asleep on the bunk. She hates fishing; most wives do. She hates the smell of diesel, rough weather, no fish and the whole awkward possibility of making a living this way. She was born into it and it never held much intrigue. I married into it and love it.

We've had horrible fights out here. I threw a salmon at her once. I missed but I might as well have pulled a gun on her. I'd been up four days and was getting tired to the point of being sort of in a calculated drunkenness. Having just set the net out at about 3:30 in the morning, I gently shook Lisa from her four day sleep and told her I needed her up to help me pick the net by at least 6:00 a.m. After 96 hours with little or no sleep I was walking road kill. I slogged into my rain gear and groped my way on deck.

It was breaking light and the sky and sea were the same color gray. We'd been catching fish all night and we were gonna make some money. I could tell my last set of the opening was good and in order to get the net out of the water on time, I would let it soak as long as possible but then I'd need help. It was 6:15 and the net crackled as fish came over the roller three and four at a time. Experience told me we were "in 'em" and we'd have to work like mules to clear the net by 9:00 a.m. so as not to get a fine by the dreaded fish cops.

Where was my help? Goddamn it, Lisa, get out of bed. I'd latched the door of the cabin open to hear the radios but the low rumble of the idling diesels swallowed my voice. Lisa lay in bed, oblivious to all. I started pouring the coals on in a combination of nervousness and anger. I was thrashing through the net, cutting meshes and flinging fish into the hold with extraordinary speed. My muscles ached, the fish came unrealistically well, the sun was rising and it looked like there was no way of making it without Lisa's help. She lay sleeping only 30 feet away, lulled to sleep by the engine and not heeding my calls for help.

" Fuck!" I say, as I wrestle a little humpy through the meshes. I'm feeling hammered from exhaustion, abused by my life and taken for granted by my wife. Fuck this and without thinking about it, that three-pound fish went whistling into the cabin like a missile. It cleared the doorway going end over end at about 20 miles an hour and hit the back wall of the cabin right above Lisa, and splattered to an undignified rest next to her.

I was yelling by now, sort of in an effort to cover some tracks for such an outrageous act. This had not been a part of our relationship to date. Best defense is a good offense. I was picking fish furiously and feeling fully angry and not very willing to let down my guard in fear all hell might really break loose. After fifteen years of calendar marriage, I knew I was not living with any shrinking violet.

Lisa was up in a moment and I hoped responding to my threats and act of violence by hustling out on deck and apologizing. I knew who the captain was or at least was trying to. On the boat I kept a sacred sweater. This was a garment not for wearing on deck during fishing, but for that time when fishing was over and I was dry and didn't want to smell like fish or feel the sting from jellyfish in my clothing. It was waiting for me in a dry cabinet next to where we slept. Some long moments had passed and I was trying to take in what I'd done, how I'd created a new level to our marriage.

I glanced into the cabin from the deck where I was working away, freeing fish from the net, and saw Lisa, red faced and furious, consumed in her own anger, showing me a thing or two. She'd taken the sacred sweater from the cabinet, put the smashed salmon into it and was jumping up and down on it cussing at my evil existence, mooshing that mealy fish into every fiber of the sweater. Tempers escalated and then in our delirium, total ridiculousness conquered. The whole situation seemed hilariously funny and like a hot wave on my face I broke into hysterical laughter until I thought I'd pee my pants. It took a few moments, but Lisa joined me and we laughed at ourselves and apologized profusely for our utter ridiculousness. Many marriages didn't survive. We were lucky. We gave ourselves two years of marriage for every year we fished together.

Our second child was born just six weeks before the first opening in the summer of 1987. Her name would be Mara, which meant "from the sea". So little six week old Mara Winslow Lawrence, no bigger than a long skinny minnow, was loaded on board on a windy afternoon along with a few days' groceries and we headed out to begin our season with our new baby and our new boat. We passed the Cattle Point lighthouse on an ebb tide and the southwesterly was blowing hard across it, creating a big chunky sea. We motored slowly into it, thrashing and banging our way over toward Eagle Point, and set the net out down wind about a half mile off the point.

I took a break into the cabin, concerned about Lisa and our new baby. They lay asleep, mother and child lulled by the heavy seas. I sat in the captain's chair and listened to radios and watched the wild ocean as the sun set. Several hours later I could see other fish boats with their picking lights on. It was hard to tell if they were taking so long because there were fish to be picked or if was just that the sea was so rough and work was hard or both.

I flipped the FM radio on to NPR as a diversion and figured I'd let the net soak a little longer and wait to see what other fishermen had to say on the VHF radio about the fishing. It was clear in this rough weather, if there weren't some pretty good numbers of fish being talked about, that I was going to run for cover.

The commentators on NPR were talking about the record setting stock market and what it all meant. The Yen was strong and America was in the strongest growth it had seen in decades. The only thing I gleaned from this was that if the Yen was strong we might get a fair price for our fish as the Japanese were buying all our fish. I was crossing my fingers for $1.50 a pound. This made a 5.5-pound average weight fish worth about ten bucks. Catch a couple hundred and make myself a payday.

The radios were silent and all across the fish grounds I could see picking lights still on as the boats heaved and bobbed in the turbulent sea. I donned my rain gear and pushed on the hydraulic pedal. The strong wind moaned and the bridle line whined through the bow rollers as the reel made its first revolutions. Then came the net and within only a few feet there was a fish and then a few more. My heart began to race.

I leaned over the edge and stared down into the frothy green sea below. The picking lights would normally show the white sides of a fish if one was hanging in the net. The bow rose and fell and there beneath the boat hundreds of sockeye salmon were hanging in my net. If this was consistent throughout the net, we'd have an unbelievable payday.

Everything was working well except the weather, but most likely it was the wind that stirred up these big numbers so the wind would have to be thanked as well. I began picking fish at around 9:30 p.m. and for the next five hours, five and six fish at a time came through the rollers. Each one had to be struggled out of the net on my rolling dance floor of a deck. The lurching boat flung me from side to side, banging me off both sides of the boat, as I separated web looking for the fish to pull through the meshes.

On one such jolt, my reaction was to spin and put the cork line under my butt and pin it to the opposite gunnel when the bow crashed into the trough. But then the sea heaved up and the cork line tightened like a banjo string and I shot like an arrow from a crossbow across the boat and was sailing over the side into certain death in a horridly raging sea but was just able to catch my fingertips on the gunnel and hold myself back. It was a wrestling football match with no pads, no breaks and no rules.

When the jacklight at the end of the net was hoisted aboard, I was completely beat. The seas seemed to have been increasing through the time I was picking and I had no idea where I was. I slid the lid on the fish hold and worked my way into the warm cabin.

Lisa rolled over in the bunk and mumbled, "Are there any fish?" I was always incredulous at how out of it she got on the boat. "A couple," I say nonchalantly, excited to surprise her in the morning. "How's little Mar Mar doing?" "She's fine as long as she can breast feed."

"How you holding up?" I say, worried about her seasickness. "Just kinda tired. Is it okay if I sleep?" she says with such a groggy voice I know it wouldn't matter what I needed; she was worthless in this weather anyway. I peeled off my steamy rain gear and looked into the radar trying to figure out where we had ended up. The radar shows no land shapes familiar to me.

The sea scatter is thick, less one dark mass a mile behind us but mostly I couldn't see anything. I look at a chart and there it is, Smith Island. "Shit, we drifted clear out here!" I say incredulously out loud. "We've drifted over 10 miles offshore." Lisa inquires from her sleep, " Is everything okay?" "Go back to sleep." Everything's fine.

The seas are huge and it takes several hours to idle back to the salmon banks. Many boats have quit. It's God's own rough and a lot of the boats figure they'd had enough. Caught a few fish and didn't want to risk anything foolish. I struggle with my exhaustion and the desire to quit. Nick gets on the radio and tells me through a series of code words how many fish he'd caught. He's so calm and, as with all Lisa's family, they are always so calm and collected on the radios it is as if they were back home in arm chairs with a cool drink wiling away an afternoon in front of the ball game.

I feared my greenhorn disposition always shone through. But

my competitive spirit got the best of me and I figured if Nick was staying out on the banks, I too would tough it out. I growled back over to Eagle Point through the acres of wild waves and set the net out about a mile offshore. I stumbled into the cabin and napped in the pilot's chair with my rain gear on and my head against the window. My thoughts were a mix of turmoil and satisfaction. Lousy weather and a big load of fish.

By 5 a.m. I began to pick and it was almost a repeat performance in numbers. Our new boat was pretty close to full and it was time to sell. With our hull low in the water, we idled into Fish Creek and carefully bunked up next to the tender. When the hatches were pulled off, none of us could believe the amount of fish. Several hours later as the fish were pitched off and into totes where they could be accurately weighed, the count came in at just over a thousand sockeyes.

Doreen, the bookkeeper on the tender, beckoned us to come in the cabin. Lisa and I huddled around the little settee and with a grin she couldn't hide, Doreen said, "I don't entirely understand it but the Japanese are paying $4.15 a pound. Something to do with the Yen being so strong." and she handed us a check for just over $30,000. I had never seen so much money with my name on it in my life. It was a day when everyone was grinning. We threw the hook in the calm shallow waters of the protected little bay and slept feeling safe, thankful and blessed.

There were other great nights of fishing as well. Perhaps my favorites were the nights it was calm and the net was out and fishing well and we'd stand on deck and watch the sunset—the sky and water a post impressionist palette of lavender, blues and oranges, the ripples each carrying their own color in a world that blended into a painting few could imagine. Each passing moment a slightly changing paint box of pastels in a motion picture that enriched the spirit as only nature can. And the nights with a glowing moon. Being on a boat, floating at the whim of the ocean in the middle of the night, can be a lonely place. The moon always felt like a friend with its steady beam of warmth as it lobbed itself in a slow motion arc burning a hole through the stars as it passed.

Sometimes standing on deck listening to the lapping water, a pod of killer whales would pass through the fleet. You could always hear the exhaling breath as they steamed along. There might be dozens of boats hanging off nets completely filling the salmon banks and in the dark, with their moonlit dorsal fins, they would hunt and magically navigate without disturbing one mesh in a net. To have dolphins ride your bow wake reminding you of what fun and joy there is in the natural world.

There was much beauty, many thankful moments. The hunter-gatherer in me is basic to what allowed our species to survive. To be your own boss, to do meaningful work pulling a bounty from the sea, to work in nature and to work with your family are truly blessed events.

The mid 1980's were a time of much growth, both mentally and physically. In 1980 I was a single person living in a one room cabin off the grid, milking a cow and getting by on the basics. By the end of a decade, I was a family of four, owned a fish boat, had built a wing or two on the cabin and had my own power bill with running water. We were fat.

Through fishing I explored miles and miles of waterways, from just a few miles outside our front door to the wet cedar covered shores of southeast Alaska to fish halibut. In spring I'd spend a month with some five thousand other highly motivated testosterone driven men chasing salmon in the wind blown tundra of a small bay in the Bering Sea. I towed boats down the I-5 freeway to the mouth of the mighty Columbia River and fished from the oldest town west of the Mississippi, Astoria, Oregon, all the way up to the Bonneville Dam in one of the world's great rivers.

I crossed the infamous Columbia River bar and fished several estuaries up the coast. All these waters filled my spirit and sense of adventure with memories of richness that only the natural world could ever provide. And along with their beauty, a reminder of their precarious fragility.

Toward the end of the 80's the runs began to decline. There is always much speculation as to the cause. In Bristol Bay it was said to be the high seas drift netters whose miles of nets indiscriminately harvested birds, juvenile salmon and anything and everything far out at sea. No regulations, no biology, just a greedy harvest far out in international waters that had no thoughts of tomorrow. Our smolt (young fish heading down river to the sea) migrations on many of the major American rivers, as observed by leagues of marine fisheries biologists, would never return from their sojourns out at sea as they are caught in miles of foreign flagged gillnet.

In Puget Sound there were crucial questions and the war between the "Cowboys and Indians" distracted fishermen from any real concerted effort to save the fisheries. The Columbia River had as many issues as miles in its tremendous 1200-mile drainage. Dams were at the top of the list constipating the wild clean waters, that raged freely downhill toward the ocean in the name of hydraulic power and irrigation.

The bottom line is that all humanity is guilty. Populations that soar to epic proportions desire and consume resources from the planet in unprecedented numbers. In the Northwest, logging and dams were tragic steps backward for the salmon, all so we could build our houses with 2x4's and have lights to stay awake later so we can work harder. We desire pavement to drive our cars on and pavement creates problems with water run-off. We desire much and it's our desires that indirectly cost fish their habitat and then their viability as a species. We are outraged that rusty trawlers from Taiwan should harvest the high seas to feed their population but there are no innocent parties when it comes to the over-consumption of the planet. This is all a simplified discussion that can and has filled volumes.

My life had started in the late 60's with these questions a foremost issue and I was determined to live a way that modeled a gentler approach. But I, like so many, got caught in the strong currents of societal desires and like so much of life, compromise slides the reality curve to the center. Our human condition is at odds with its own future. The answers, my friend, are blowing in the wind, that dreaded wind.

It became increasingly hard to make a living. The price of fish dropped, the numbers of fish declined and the costs of fuel and airplane tickets and nets all went up. Lisa was becoming increasingly sensitive to the whole proposition of our profession. Her seasickness was enough in itself. She lay in the bunk for days at a time in a continuous low level nausea. And if there's one thing about seasickness, it's the miserable attitude that accompanies it.

We were unraveling and not making any money to speak of. It was time to quit. Sell the boats and go back to the farm. It was a sad departure for me. I had grown to love the hunt and capture of salmon and halibut. I will always miss the sound of the crackling web as it brings another fish aboard. I will miss the surprise that every hook brings from the bottom, the ocean and her diverse moods, her temper and the awe inspiring magnificent beauty of it all.

With two growing children, I was nervous about how I would support the family. I was not confident about making enough on the farm now that we were raising two kids. I became a licensed boat captain for 200-ton inland water vessels between Washington and Alaska.

I had notions of running vessels back and forth to Alaska but made a decision to abandon the idea just after an interview with a man in his wheelhouse when we talked of our families. His eyes lit up as he asked if I wanted to see his kid's birthday party and with that he shoved a cassette into the VHS. The little VHS screened away as we watched a bunch of toddlers push red and blue blocks around the floor and then jerky home movies of birthday cakes and a woman saying, "Wave at Daddy now," and she grabbed his frosting covered little fist and waved it at the camera. "Say goodbye to Daddy, say goodbye."

I knew I couldn't watch my kids grow up on air mailed video tapes. The thought made me panic a little. I would have to figure out how to make a living at home. I lay awake nights in a semi dream state worrying how to make ends meet. There were long uneven columns of numbers that I would add and subtract with different answers every time. It felt like school and I was failing the test. I didn't know what I was going to do.

Eventually I saw a counselor and we struggled through all my difficulties bringing up thousands of unrelated and related information. Then I heard an abstraction meant to calm myself and steady my thoughts. It was about not thinking my way through but feeling my way forward. Let my instincts guide my path. After all, they had led me to the land in the first place.

There was something about putting my hand on my mother and grounding myself. It all felt a little new and weird to solve problems this way, but I trusted my therapist and frankly the abstractions felt better than my linear head bashing sessions where the numbers never added up. And that notion of putting my hand on my mother. My first reaction was that she meant a literal laying of hands on my Mommy, but quickly realized she meant something else. I spent a lot of hours preoccupied with these thoughts daring myself a new way to approach my dilemmas, learning to trust my intuition.

I was working in the garden planting a row of carrots or peas and I stopped to look at the soil. I brought a bit up in my hand and then without thinking I reached over and set my hand on the ground. "Grounded," I said softly to myself. "Put your hand on your mother." I sat there for a long moment. A vague notion crossed my thoughts. I could feel I was on to something. The dusty stuck wheels of reinvention turned just an inch and then my well greased reactionary mind shot off in reaction, "Yah but, Yah but, Yah! You can't make a living… you have kids now!" My cognitive mind quickly tried to cancel what I had just felt. The feeling felt so good, I was aggravated by my own yammering self-destruction. It was time to go back to the farm.

Chapter 29

Meteorites Do Fall

One weekend my mother showed up, unannounced, which had a weird awkwardness about it. She sat playing with Natalia, drinking tea, when she turned to me and said, "I'm not going home." Her face welled up and she fought away urges to cry. This had a very ugly reminiscent feel of a life I'd gladly left behind years before when she came to me almost daily to worry and complain about my father. "I promised myself I wouldn't cry," she said in a bumbling jerk of inhales. I recoiled inside. I'd made a concerted effort to get away from such details in my life.

I felt protective of Lisa and our child and it felt both embarrassing and all too familiar. "It's his drinking, again," she said. "But I promised I wouldn't do this in front of you and your little family so I will leave you now." We were all standing in a silence not sure of what to do or say when there was a knock on the front door.

Lisa opened it and my father marched in like a soldier in an invading army. He threw out a few insincere hellos, marched over to my mother and requested they talk outside. Lisa and I sat in silence as we could hear the tops of the sharp words through the walls of the cabin. Things were always big and a little overwhelming when they were around.

A while later my mother stuck her head in the door and apologized for disturbing us and said she would contact us later. They left and I realized there was a big part of my life that Lisa wasn't aware of; sometimes that part seemed pretty messy and it had just shown its messy self.

Several days later my mother and father showed up again and

sat themselves at the table. Awkward silences had us scurrying around making coffee and trying to spontaneously act hospitable. Baby Natalia gurgled and sputtered but it was obvious it wasn't altogether a social visit.

My father began with the tone he no doubt had practiced when talking to people after he'd performed surgery on a family member. His volume was up, his diction was direct and there was never any doubt he was in charge. "Your mother and I have decided to move to the island. I'll be retiring and your mother will be closer to you kids." My knee buckled and smacked my kneecap into the lower cabinet door.

This is my island, I thought, this is where I live, you can't live here too. I found it first. I'm your kid, too, not just my mother's. My mind was slamming a shoe on the table yelling No, No, No! but my mouth just said "Wow, really." The obedient child was behaving and minding his manners. My mother chimed in with an attempt to sound cheery. "We'll only be a coffee pot away," she said with a cheery smile. I could tell my father had won her back and the compromise was to move to the islands.

We all smiled and pushed cheeriness into the room like a defiant child, forcing it to sit with us at the table as we sipped the last of our coffee through forced smiles. Before they left the island on that visit, they'd purchased an old farm a short mile down the road from us. It all happened very fast and I struggled between the good son and the angry as hell son.

Three Legged Table

Truth has a million perspectives and perfect families don't reveal secrets; they carry on, they smile and they make the best of it. Real families have flaws and hopefully eventually learn to laugh at their humanness, while simultaneously trying to evolve. It's certainly more relaxing, if not a little more honest, than a continuous requiem of excellence. The cold rod of perfection is an uncomfortable place to sit while ever climbing the ladder of achievements.

It was where we started and not far from where we ended as a family. We had a hard time evolving. The perfect family always smiles in the photographs and has a hard time telling the truth. The truth within about alcohol, anger, failure, betrayal, inadequacy, falling in or out of love at inappropriate times. The list grows with neglect.

I was always told that I was dwelling on the negative but I was only trying to understand and work out what was happening. The neglect seemed to keep us blind to evolving. Sometimes little messes weren't just little messes, quickly cleaned up, swept away and not talked about. In truth a lot of our blemishes were unintentional gifts from the generations before us, that my elders no doubt received at their births, that they had just cleaned up and deleted from their vocabulary. They were never dealt with and ended up festered messes too scary to deal with. Like physical illness, issues of the mind and heart can seem like enormous ridiculous burdens that are too hard to deal with in a logical day. At least until the doctor tells you your leg is broken or you have cancer and then it becomes everything. It is your life.

The emotional issues of our family needed to reach this level and never did. We all tried advancing our process from time to time in our own ways, but the emotional cancer was larger than any home remedy and we never collectively sought the help that might have unleashed the chains that held us in our predicament.

My father had the blazing issues of alcohol, anger and control. He seemed obvious to pick on and I spent a good 40 years angry as hell about it, reacting and becoming angrier, justifying my life and feeling sorry for myself. But my two cents worth was part of the soup. It helped hold us in our own sad stuck way of relating. We all contributed to our failure. That was the real sadness. Unknowingly we were all part of a wobbly three-legged table. We'd do fine if we only used about half of it. Some did better than others.

Within months my folks had settled in to the island and all the newness brought them much happiness. It was awkward and close for me, but I wanted it to work. For many years a small part of me had missed my parents in a sort of primal way. I wanted their love and recognition. We had each other come for dinner and we all played like nothing had ever been a conflict in our lives. The years I had disappeared were never mentioned. Maybe that was the way to have left it.

They threw parties and were quite the toast of their own arrival. But down deep I felt like Geronimo not trusting the white man's peace treaty. What I couldn't accept is how physically close they were all the time.

Too many hard memories and the messy room I thought I'd slammed the door on years before had not cleaned itself up, nor had I done well to gain a new perspective in my absence. They were now a constant backdrop in my little life on our little island. Our boat floated unevenly and although that was normal for us, we were ever taking on water and I often felt like I was drowning.

I wanted it to work. I wanted parents who could be loving and supportive, happy to see us and show up at the occasional soccer match cheering jubilantly for their special grandchild. Be non-judgmental about my life; in fact I wanted praise. My mother tried to do this and was good at it, less her distraction of keeping the peace at her house. She would drop by and visit spontaneously but she always acted as if on a short leash and, having made the effort, would only stay several minutes and then announce she didn't want to overstay her welcome. Despite our insistence she stay longer, it felt obvious she didn't want to have to explain the missing time on her trips to town to my father.

When she was there the love among all of us was obvious. We wallowed in it, like seal pups on a warm rock in the sun, but she always disappeared pulling the rug out from under a normal setting, leaving us feeling somewhat bewildered. She was always running home to tend my father's desires.

On one such trip my mother asked if we'd like to run a small herd of sheep on their vacant fields. She and my father had talked it over and it would help keep the grass down. It felt like a kind gesture and I took advantage of it. After working on the fences for a week I moved some twenty ewes to their pastures.

A couple weeks later I dropped by horrified to find half the sheep sick and the other half dead. My father explained he had left a full sack of opened Dipel (a poison for slugs that looks just like grain) in the pasture. The sheep gorged themselves on it before succumbing. He delivered the information in his usual commanding tone, facts, no empathy - deal with it. I was shocked. It was a tragic mistake and a big loss. I spent the day wrestling dead animals into my truck and taking them away to let the crows and eagles devour their remains.

As I look back I realize how weird it all was. There were no apologies or suggestions of compensation, only the suggestion that maybe it wasn't going to work out that my animals be there and that I should take the rest home.

The really sad part was that I didn't feel the "cahoness" to ask for it - to talk over what had happened. If I confronted my father on any level about the mistake he made, that wobbly table would tip and fall.

It would start a huge riff between him and me; lots of old garbage would be pulled from the festering mental file cabinets, where previous failings in our lives had been categorized according to unresolved angers, and be flung about like the toxic spoils of a piñata. Then a riff with my mother would ensue because he and I weren't getting along and then she'd come to me and complain that I would have let her down as a son who should just "get over it" and realize my father would never change. "Is it really worth all this anger and fighting, Jim?"

The table would fall over spilling anything and all we might have gained and we'd retreat to our corners. I was real good at disappearing when I was angry. We'd lick our wounds and let time pass filing one more unresolved interchange in those festering file cabinets in our subconscious. The price I paid for not "letting go of it" or learning how to deal with it more satisfactorily was anger and a lousy sense of my own self worth.

In our time together I lingered between anger and sadness and a thirst to get home to my little farm where I felt safe and allowed to be myself. The fear was that my discontent would follow me home and from time to time it did. Hugh and I had a joke where we always asked the other one how long it took to become seven years old when we visited the parents. I could be up all night fishing in a storm, piloting my boat through treacherous seas, pick fish from the net all night, fix a hydraulic leak with ingenious effort, come home to the little farm I built to happy laughing children, drop by my parents' house and within six minutes I felt like I was a seven year old.

Chapter 30

Visiting the Elderly Parents

My mother lay on a hospital bed like a colorless leaf, waiting, pushing pain around, her mind so preoccupied in her struggle she didn't notice me for a while as I sat next to her. A rare visit from the sun in December drenched the living room like an aquarium filled with warm water. The room was quiet and she lay silently just taking in the day, eventually opening her eyes smiling at me, but was quickly distracted by the gnawing beast of pain.

She has the relentless hounds of pain on her trail and has no idea of how to shake them. In her groggy delirium she tells me the cleaning lady found a bowl of flies underneath the sink and that having her visit was the high point of her week. She interrupted herself to try and sit up and adjust her legs for more comfort. It's like I was watching an animal writhing while being stung to death by angry bees. It feels perverse to just sit and stare. I feel desperate. If she were my dog, I'd shoot her as an act of love and a gift to her dignity. She wants to die, she knows there is no way out, no getting better, no miracle cure and now she's too threadbare to give a rip.

She looks across the room through half opened eyes at a well-choreographed regimen of framed photos of her grandchildren and softly says how beautiful and dear they all are. Words from her heart. There is no posturing or pretense, only the bare heartfelt truth. I have been here before as this desperate struggle has lingered now for many years. I am without words and full of prayer. Prayers that I feel astonished to be asking.

My father can be heard down the hall like a hedgehog rustling through shredded newspaper. He's got documents and data that give him (an old broken warhorse surgeon) a thread of hope and a swan's song that his research might bring some relief. He is manic in his medical inquiry, but if he can pull her off the tracks before the freight train of death arrives, it may repair some of the miles of the long broken road of their marriage.

On entry without greeting me, looking down his nose through half glasses, he begins to blather on about hermaticrit and other foreign language terms. They go over my mother's and my head like a jet plane leaving nothing but a vapor trail of questions. He's limping like an old logger but, with the help of furniture supporting him, he makes his way to the couch and descends through facial grimaces never missing a beat as he gushes medicalese.

His hair is a fog bank coiffure from three days of no sleep and no comb. Shaving cream is dry crusted and yellowed on his left sideburn; his jaw jutted and sticking out like the Duke of Earl, he goes on and on and on. He's hardwired in the nomenclature of medicine.

I don't think my mother or I knew to whom he was speaking, but hoped the other was absorbing the facts like a couple of overwhelmed schoolmates. His data developed into questions for my mother who struggled to answer correctly to relieve his incessant pressure and anger if she might suggest that she didn't understand. She tried to give answers she thought he'd want to hear, but between the cocktail of morphine and unrelieved pain she was unable to pull it off. He was frustrated and angry and scared and spoke in a voice he'd developed as a four year old.

Just as I was considering leaving due to my increasing discomfort, he realized he was fighting with an already beaten enemy. The room fell into an awkward silence. My childhood and my wiser self struggled and I felt compelled to try and fix it, to help him, to relieve their frustrations.

I hate myself when I try and do this, letting my nervousness attempt to help and get stuck between them in the process. Besides, their frustrations are much bigger than any few words that I might offer. I had only been in the house now for about ten minutes and I realized I was starting to feel real depressed, not just a little but a sadness that felt like a lifestyle, precisely my whole life with these two. I fished in my mind for redemption and hope that it was my presence that brings on such angst between them so I could at least fantasize them happy when I was not around.

I remember reading how marauding male grizzly bears, who want to kill their own offspring, are fought off by protective mothers. "Hell hath no fury like a sow guarding her cubs" except in our house where these two old bears are worn thin and their teeth ground flat from chewing relationship rocks most of their lives. Their sun is setting and although they struggle to higher ground for glimpses of its warmth, their time is short and they know it.

They're writing the conclusion of the story of their life, what they made of it and what they were dealt. And now the rendered down soup of their lives has them in a desperate place. One will no doubt live on without the other for a while, but after 50 some years my guess is that one will only be putting in time.

My father limps off to the kitchen talking presumably to us. The floor is wet from a fresh waxing that he doesn't notice. I try to warn him so he doesn't slip and fall but he claims he's just getting something from the kitchen and seems annoyed that I am interrupting; my words drift away. My mother searches the back of her eyelids for the place the morphine is hidden and begins to barter with the gods for relief. I get up and walk out quietly, except to say, "Goodbye, I love you, Mum." There is no answer, only a combination of deafness and distraction.

Outside their dog is high on oblivious concerns and bounces around like he's just finished a helium breakfast. The ground is wet and the sun pours down warm on my face. I inhale the fresh coolness long and slow. I file my visit in the back of my mind like so many others.

Chapter 31

A True Story

The phone rang at midnight. I found the receiver in the dark to hear my father's voice say that my mother was in her final hours if I wanted to come spend time with her. This was it. He was a doctor and he knew the signs. He hung up and returned me to the silent darkness. I quickly pulled on crumpled clothes and made my way to the truck. My thoughts raced in semi-circles as I considered what was going to happen.

It was time. I had wanted her to die for her own sake. Her suffering had reached the realms of faith lost for any empathetic higher power. She had pushed pain around, fought with it, tried to deny it, and yet the relentless hounds of cancer had bit and gnawed at her from the inside out. I thought of the times I'd imagined placing a pillow over her head and helping her escape this cruel world. I struggled with such notions and agonized over my visualizing actually doing it. I'd shot my old suffering dog once and he wagged his tail as life drained away, seemingly thanking me for helping him along. It was so complicated with human suffering. I would go to jail, my daughters grow up without a father, and the sadness would never end.

The lights flashed in the trees as I drove up the driveway, tunneling the road to their home on that dreadful rainy night. The house was silent; a dim light or two did little to lift the sullen demeanor. My father sat on a couch across the room from the hospital bed where my mother lay. He was talking on the phone in a controlled official voice.

My mother was sadness in a plain white sheet. Her long skinny body lay motionless, her face old wrinkled and pale. Her breath was the the confused Cheyenne-Stokes arrhythmia of a life at its end. She looked nothing like the vibrant capable woman who had brought me up. The gentle eyed mom whose strong athletic body could swing up on a horse and ride like the wind. She had lost so much weight she barely made a lump in the neatly made bed. I pulled a chair up next to her and leaned toward her.

"Hi Mum. It's me, Jim." I was ambushed by the moment and felt my throat knot and tangle. "I love you, Mum," my voice trailed away to whispers as I stared at her face. I knew what was coming, and I wasn't prepared. I still had the open wound of my brother's death weeping into my heart and it just seemed like too much. But it was going to be.

My father hung up the phone and came over to her side. I didn't look up as I was feeling tears on my face. He said he'd call the doctor and have him come and "pronounce her". I stared forward and didn't answer. My mother's breath jerked and paused as it had been doing.

His voice was strong and clear and matter of fact. He'd spent a life in the rooms of the dying and this was being handled as a professional, not as a husband losing his wife of 54 years. It was our relationship personified. He professional in difficult times, his brain functioning towards control and problem solving. Mine unraveling, seeking pity and sprawling toward tears. Our eyes avoided each other.

Hours passed and I sat in prayer. Not prayers in a bargaining grocery list with god or a repetitive murmuring of hallowed phrases but a swarming of my thoughts with good memories and thankfulness. A prayer of meditation and thanks as the clock drooled toward the inevitable. My mother's breaths struggling in a crescendo-decrescendo pattern from within her comatose near lifeless body.

The light struggled through the clouds and rain rattle tapped the window sills. My father shuffled papers and talked doctor to doctor with the attending physician. I could hear the veneers of his voice cracking as reality began to wedge him apart.

At 11:30 a.m. there was no real change except my wife Lisa arrived and quietly pulled up a chair on the opposite side and we both held my mother's hands and waited. I looked at both of them and was thankful they knew and loved each other. These two women had a big piece of my heart. They shared a love of our children, of me and both had always had a keen interest with all things equine. Stealing away to ride horses. Time spent together and with horses was time loved.

The antique grandfather clock in the living room started clanging high noon. I counted under my breath as I was losing track of time. At the 6th beat my mother's eyes opened, her head pushed slightly forward and she stared out into the room briefly and then the last half-ounce of life drifted from her body. Lisa and I looked up and took turns saying goodbye out loud. I spoke across the room to my father and told him she had passed.

His struggle not to believe it would be true collapsed within him and he acted startled and disbelieving. "Oh god, where is she?" He crumpled on the couch and the attending doctor took the professional's role and consoled him as he could. There is that moment after death when it's so unbelievable. My brother's death several months before hadn't prepared me. It all felt hollow and lost. Vacant and alone.

Lisa rubbed my shoulders as I sat in the recesses of the living room. Nurses and help filed in. My sister arrived moments later and helped with my mother's body. They all uttered kind words and spoke as if she was aware of their empathy. That confused me a little but I let it pass.

Moments later there was an enormous crash out in the barn some 100 yards north of the house. It sounded as if a truck had lost its brakes and bashed through the side of the barn. We were all momentarily startled but too preoccupied to go look. I guess every one figured someone else would and no one did. Several minutes later my mother's horse, Moon, trotted on to the front lawn and came over to the large picture window where she lay. We were all astonished as Moon stood there breathing on the glass.

Lisa ran outside and found him shivering and shaking, acting disoriented and confused. She called me out and we haltered him and led him toward the barn. At the time I remember feeling baffled and somewhat annoyed that this big horse was interrupting our mournful day. There is a cosmic unreality around death and I felt like I was plugged into a different circuit board when I looked at Moon and then said out loud, "This horse is all but dead. Life just hasn't left his body yet."

Lisa and I took turns leading him around trying to steady his nerves and figure out why and how he had lunged through a solid wall in his stall. He was 17, not particularly old for a horse. He'd been used for endurance races covering 50 to 100 miles and was in particularly good condition. That and the fact that I'd never witnessed a horse getting out and running towards the house. Usually they missile off down the county road looking for that lost voice they heard whinnying in the dark. Lisa pled with my dad to call a vet but he didn't want any more people around and denied her request. He was wrapped up in grief and he couldn't deal with it. I too was lost in my own thoughts and didn't feel like confronting the situation.

I led Moon out into a pasture where he eventually lay down. His body quivered and he threw his head from side to side. I sat and pulled his large boney head into my lap and talked to him as to console his fretful white eyed look of terror. We sat for 10 minutes and he calmed, his big lunky head heavy on my thighs, the wet of moss seeping up my backside.

Then two large mature ravens flew a low tandem pattern over our heads, gliding up from behind and swooshing quickly past.

One did a perfect barrel roll and let out a loud resonating "ROO-OUK". In my dazed and addled brain I realized they took that horse with them. Not physically but his spirit was gathered and taken away. He died later that day.

As I sat on the wet ground, annoyed to have to deal with the horse moments after my mother's death, it occurred to me that she took him with her. The ravens had delivered my mother's horse to her as she galloped off for adventures unknown.

Chapter 32

Dog Story and Father Hunger

My mother has been dead almost ten months, my brother several months longer, the emotional bullet hole still weeping and my sense of trust in this world still shaken. My father called and sounded worried although he camouflaged it as best he could. He had the results of the latest visit to the medical center, and wanted me to come to his house so as not to scare my children. After a 50 year marriage he'd not found a lot of reasons for being and I could tell he was accepting his plight with some sense of relief.

He sits in his nightshirt on an over-stuffed chair sipping a cup of instant crystals coffee loaded with non-sweetener. His hair, slept on hard, looks like a still life sand storm, his body hunched and his face the worn out version of handsome.

He spills it out like a hard knocks grocery list. Cataracts in-operable due to an infection, and PSA (the thermostat for prostate health) soaring exponentially. The wild grizzlies were out of their cage and gonna ravage his body. He seemed ready for his ice floe, ready to cut himself loose from his world and join the ever increasing number of family members who had gone before him. He tells me daily he doesn't really have anything to live for and largely seems to get in an argument with most of life around him and seems to increasingly lose the arguments. He seemed glad to know the last march was beginning. The words delivered from the surgeon's mouth like gravel from a truck, cold and hard.

My mind was fighting off the nightmare of more loss, confused by our complicated relationship. It so seductively pried its way into my thoughts, well practiced from my recent experiences.

My father and I, never close, had waded nervously into the cold waters of relationship for the first time in 48 years, since my mother's and brother's deaths. As the playing field finally cleared enough of alcohol, 80 hour work weeks, crippled family merry-go-rounds, genetic hand-me-downs and my own anger, we struggled toward a few conversations. War-wounded and gut-shot, we took the periodic chances that I was starting to get used to.

I had begun to once again realize the vastness of the missing realm of my life without my father, and the desire to quench the primal need for this relationship. All my life I had suffered from this father hunger. And although part of me was able to step slightly off-center of the comments that he'd nothing to live for, I was feeling the final opportunity was about to slip away. The hope of a miracle that he'd be interested in me was unraveling with every word.

He had two primary concerns. He'd decided to sell his sailboat, and he'd written up a document earmarking part of his military pension of $10,000 for his dog's future without him. The dog, I was reminded, was the one thing that had given him pleasure since my mother's death and, with tears struggling in his eyes, he worried about the canine's future without him.

This dog did not have the mellow obedient disposition of a Golden Lab who'd fetch slippers and follow a master with blind faith into fire, but was an over-bred Chesapeake Retriever with a personality of a nuclear warhead with a fetching disease. The dog hallucinated intruders, barked at the wind and jets passing 25,000 feet overhead, and was in constant search of fetching objects, the latest being a drool covered six pound zucchini. Buster deemed this as choice fun, delivering and redelivering it in a continuum at my feet, never entertaining the idea that I might not be interested after several hours of zero eye contact and a refusal to play. A true manic. Good looking as Robert Redford and the warmness of a love child born to the Ayatullah and Gidget. Trying not to show my real feelings, I promised him as executor that there would be no problems. The dog would be cared for.

I slumped in my chair, nodding to his discussion and feeling the sadness of a million questions that were probably not going to get answered. Questions of connection, place, and okayness. I am a little boy at the foot of the king and he decrees that all young boys will be sent out into the woods alone for eternity to fend for themselves, to experience life without a father.

I give him too much power and I struggle with wanting his approval of my existence. He doesn't know the language nor do I believe that he knows one exists, no doubt a non-gift from his father and his father before him.

I think of my teenage daughters and our periodic alienation and the scrambled airwaves between us. How, when I am talking, the voice or non-voice of my father comes through me. I had sworn a 1000 times in my youth not to ever act this way. But in the grips of impending battle, I feel his presence. I hate myself and the erosion of our love. I've done miles of therapy and wonder if I've begun to erode the chain of disconnection.

How did this dog end up with the zucchini and me with all the questions? He will die no doubt with a lot of untold stories and we will have missed our opportunity of knowing each other.

Chapter 33

Talking With Hugh - 10 Years After

My truck rattles across the wide expanse of the alfalfa field and parks on the small bridge crossing the full flowing irrigation stream. Water on both sides and underneath me, a fisherman's dream. I crawl into the back of the truck, under my canopy, as the last shafts of light turn the water surface into a long silver saxophone that bends toward the bridge. I pour two fingers of Stoli into my cup and snuggle deep into my bag with a flashlight and some poems of Pablo Neruda. Sipping and listening to the water, poetry and the first menacing taps of rain, I drift off to sleep.

Morning comes and the rain taps like the relentless finger of an angry schoolteacher, stealing dreams and forcing me into a gloomy day. I make coffee from the irrigation water, hoping I have boiled away any bad bugs, and sit staring at the diamonds of rain on my windshield as the radio calls for rain and the truck heater blows lukewarm air into the cold cab.

I begin a conversation with Hugh. Although he's not here, he's here. I have many talks with him when I'm alone doing the things we used to enjoy together, especially when I need courage. It's my way of spending time with him, the intimate language of brothers adventuring. This despite the fact he's been dead ten years. I sound absolutely deranged as I utter the words out loud into the cold empty cab alone, but it makes all the sense in the world to me. "Well, are we gonna do this fucking trip or not?

It's as black outside as the inside of my sleeping bag and the rain nitters and spatters as a cold reminder of the day to come. "Yah, man. Let's go stand in a freezing river all day in the rain and catch no fucking fish." I'm glad I'm not alone. I shift the truck into drive, rattle back across the field gyroscoping my coffee cup over the bumps to the edge of the field, turn left on the gravel road and head for the river.

After an hour of driving, I begin to get excited and nervous about the steelhead that my imagination conjure up. In my thoughts they lie in wait, with a ravenous appetite, as they bump their wide shoulders in the beautiful deep clear pools of the Grande Ronde River. I will hike up river where no one ever fishes and have a day the record books will never forget. As I roll to a halt, the first glimmers of light begin to appear and the adrenalin is coursing through me as I don my waders and vest. "Let's get this bitch started," I say to Hugh in his vacuous non-presence.

I am acutely aware of the hike that crosses the old orchard as I head up river and the copious amounts of bear shit I usually encounter. I clip the canister of pepper spray to my suspenders and have a not so humorous dialogue about needing a salt canister too, because bears don't just like pepper on their hors d'oeuvres.

Lots of nervous giddy discussion as I lock the truck and head off road to find the trail in barely lit morning rain. "So did you ever see the cartoon of the polar bear with his arm reaching down inside the igloo? He turns to the polar bear standing next to him and says 'These are my favorites—hard and crunchy on the outside, warm and gooey on the inside.'" I can see Hughie smiling nervously back at me. He's usually a little less brave than I in these situations, but I gather courage knowing he's my big brother and he's with me. He's always kept me safe and I've always trusted he would, even after he died.

Once while camping with Lisa and daughter Mara in Australia, we were held up in the middle of the night by two deranged miscreants who shoved a gun barrel into my chest through a shattered window. It was in the middle of a violent thunderstorm and as the rain and lightning flashed, an enormous man screamed he was gonna kill me. I could all but feel the blast of the gun into my upper right chest, when suddenly he and his drool-faced partner turned and left. It was a horrible screaming match that escalated well beyond reason, laced with primal terror, as we knelt on a bed of broken wet glass trapped in our van like fish in a barrel. But it stopped and the two madmen vanished without a trace. No explanation.

As we sped away from the scene, as fast as we could drive on the winding muddy roads, I had a sense of divine intervention. Like when the bully at recess in elementary school is about to bloody your nose and your older big brother shows up and defuses the situation. He had saved my family and me that night when logic and explanation were missing and he would protect me from the startled bear that I might stumble across as I tramped through the overgrown forgotten orchard on my way up the river.

I stepped over several piles of fresh bear shit that looked like large handfuls of ground apple leftovers from a cider pressing. They are around but not to be seen. I feel I am being watched. I mutter beneath my breath, half aware that I am in my lunatic mode of talking out loud to my dead brother, but I am content to do so. "They're either eight bears or one who sure shits a lot." My voice is pounded to the ground, where no one can hear me, by the strength of raindrops.

I am relieved to find the river's edge and in the smoldering dawn I can see the wide expansive canyon where eons of time and water have cut a most beautiful gap for the melting snows of the high country, waters that now feed the Grande Ronde River as it makes its way downhill to its union with the Snake. The silver blue of first light reflects across a pool at the top of some rapids as I make my way along the edge of the boulder strewn shore. The calls of the water ouzel drift in and out of the sounds of the river.

A mile from the truck I arrive at some small rapids that have deep lumbering shoulders and tail out over a rock garden of boulders. "This is a steelhead hotel if I ever saw one," I say out loud as I excitedly tie on a fly with buttery wet fingers. Water drifts from my nose as I step into the river at the high end of the run.

The morning is gray wet and perfect. I roll cast to the top of the fast water and let my fly swing. I love seeing my line move across the water smoothly to the soft edges where currents and morning steelhead rest. I let more line out and cast deeper into the current. I am content. I am happy on the most basic levels. I am here with my brother, hundreds of miles from home and a mile or so past the bears in the orchard, standing in my most favorite river.

The rain is pelting the river into a matted dimpled gray and I can feel with my hunter-gatherer primitive spirit that there are fish around. It's a sense that percolates through an intuitive layer when I'm away from the human process. I am a hunter and today I hunt steelhead.

I take a careful step downstream and cast again. The line straightens in the strength of the current and angles toward shore and the slower water. I feel a pluck on the line and I stand, quiet as a heron, my line hanging downstream. Was that a trout or steelhead? I wait and after no response recast and wait again as my fly drifts. Suddenly my line yanks tight and there is a tremendous pulling. I step back and raise my rod.

"That's what I'm talking about!" I know he's listening despite his jealousy. The fish pulls a pulsing thunder and pushes its way to deeper water, then reverses and shoots to the surface launching himself above the river in a headshaking display of arrogance. I stumble to shore, rod held high, fingers reeling in and releasing, as the fish makes a run downstream and the spool of line in my reel whines the music that fisherman think about all year, waiting for this moment, this time and place.

After ten minutes he begins to tire and I reel him closer to the calm water on shore where he is only feet away and I get a closer look. I am always in awe. This primitive wild animal with bright silver sides and an emerald, moss green colored back slips through the shallow waters tethered by my line and within reach of my left hand. I talk to him as I slide my grip around his tail, thanking him for letting us meet. I feel honored to touch him. His eye stares baffled with some sort of resignation. I unhook my barbless fly from the side of his mouth and hold him and gently push and pull him in the calm shallow waters letting him regain his strength. He pulls toward the deep and I let go, thanking him again.

He is gone and I move to a boulder where I sit and ponder my good luck. For a moment my spirit buckles and I wish Hughie was here. Really here. He would be proud of me and a bit jealous as well. Jealous as a man whose little brother just outfished him, but proud of me despite that. We had saved each other's life in that way. This self-pity was all too familiar and I tried to brush it aside. "I miss you, you son of a bitch." My stomach reflexed tightly as tears blurred my vision. "Fucking eh, what did you go and die for? Fuck you. Fuck you for dying." The rain began to slow and I sat on my rock and had my annual cry. It always leaves me sort of flat and empty.

There was the phone call the day I was in my kitchen cleaning flats of strawberries with a friend. Hugh's wife was crying on the other end. She said they'd been to the doctor and Hugh came home to take a nap and several hours later he wouldn't wake up. The fear in her voice filled me with a fear I'd never known. Hughie's sick. It had always been me. He wasn't supposed to get sick. I couldn't relate.

Within 24 hours it was discovered he had a brain tumor and was scheduled for surgery. I felt panic in every step. People die from brain tumors. Hughie can't die; he's my brother. He has a wife and two little children. It can't happen.

We drove to the hospital to see him the day before his surgery. The word had spread and dozens of people came to see him. We all held camp in the main lobby. Stories and prayers, discussions of healing, and panicky tears that brought love to the eyes of all. My mother, also gravely ill, showed up and was confused by the crowds. It was a private grief for her and she wanted to be alone with her first- born baby. The first child in one's life is what makes you a believer and they always hold that special spot. We all wanted it to be a private time with Hugh. But people heard and people showed up.

Here was their friend, 47 years old, too young, too handsome, too vital to be sick. It was disrupting our vision of the world and the way we needed it to work. It reminded us we weren't in control, that we too were vulnerable, which was no comfort at all. The tension we felt that day, and the sadness that accompanied it, festered and left scars with hidden benefit that remain throughout our lives.

"He has a glial cell astrocytoma, level 3," the surgeon dropped the words off like a drive by hand grenade loaded with indifference. We all scramble for understanding. What did this mean? Is this bad or good? Will he be okay? The surgeon had disappeared down the hall before anyone knew what was happening. He didn't want to be the one to explain that this was Hugh's death sentence and time was limited. Eight months. Of course it was never explained that way. The medical world likes to keep hope alive but his chances were best left to miracle workers. My father, the doctor, knew. And without saying it, my mother could tell by looking at his shifting eyes, his words that he wrapped up in medicalese to keep him from having to say it. He'd known medicine his whole life and he knew the prognosis. We all reacted.

My father wanted to be in charge. He wanted to be the doctor who was at the podium delivering the daily reports. He wanted control and respect. My mother was on death's door with her 25 year battle with cancer and it was a cruel and unjust blow to the threads of life she hung on to.

Hugh's wife, Lisa, was the rock to which many of us clung. In moments of desperation, a certain few have the instincts of survival. Lisa grew to be the conquistador of common sense that led many of us through dark nights and confusion.

My sister and I crumbled and had a hard time finding where we fit in to his care. The community took charge and cooked, prayed, sang, drove, did laundry and changed bed pans. My sister eventually moved to the farm and found a way to fit in.

For me, it was the most difficult time of my life. I too wanted to be involved. I wanted Hugh to want his brother at critical times to be close. But that was not how it worked. He shut himself off from me. Told me to go live my life and he seemed angry that I should get to live and that he would not, some brotherly competitive concession of defeat. This added to my devastation. He would die and he would turn me out when I wanted to be close. I spent a long time grappling with the whole situation.

Several weeks before he passed away, he had someone dial the phone and we talked. He was looking for me. He was going to die and he knew it. It was spring, around the beginning of April. I had worked all day in the orchard and now sat in my house listening to the quiet dark outdoors. We were saying goodbye for the last time. I lived in the right side of my brain. Later I wrote a poem.

I thin blossoms in an orchard of millions
I swim in this haiku ocean, bees buzzing,
spring in my eyes, on my tongue.

The sun pours down like yellow milk
and licks the wounds of winter.

A tree frog summits a green tendril leaf
a proud baffled gaze.
The world is renewed.

My back sucks on heat,
hands of warmth renew forgotten skin.

I'm reminded of that phone call that etched my memory.
A robin's call in the dark, a pause, and your voice.
You struggled with the beast of tumors
and the words to say it.

You called your brother to say goodbye.
There would be no reference to the future, no regrets,
pauses congested with anguish.
You brave, resolved to your last adventure alone.
I terrified, drowning in fear.

A robin calls from the outside in the dark night,
mingled with a chorus of peepers.
We share this pristine moment.

And now on my orchard hillside
staring down over my world
a world I wish we could share.
You are now all these things.

A few days later, while visiting him at his house, we spoke
in French together. He was a remedial version of my big brother,
more like a seven year old in pajamas. He said let's go to France
together, just you and me. We'll travel and we'll work. He lurched
up from his chair and as we passed our wives sitting on the couch,
he looked at me and said, "Ou lala, regard les jeune filles. Ce beaux
ca." He wiggled his eyebrows and carried on about our trip and
the animals we were going to take. A trip where we can spend
time together. "God, I've missed you man."

The phone call came the next morning. He had fallen asleep
and passed away in the middle of the night.

And now I go fishing to be alone and to talk to Hughie. In a
place I know he can hear me.

The Power of a Dream

Since the death of my father, mother and brother, all in relatively rapid succession, I began to feel like at any moment my number was going to come up. After all I had been the sick child with unlikely chances of a very normal life or for that matter a long life. Why was I left standing when others who'd seemed so healthy got tangled in the net of a fatal disease?

Fright ran just beneath my skin as I waited. I went in to see the doctor for every hangnail and odd feeling trying to catch my turn at bat with the grim reaper early enough so I could perhaps diagnose early and be the lucky one. My life was a sepia tone movie of me in the cockpit of an old fighter plane and it was spiraling straight down. I would die soon if my logic had anything to do with it.

Then one night I had a dream. For me dreams generally pass like curious movie shorts in a thin wind. I usually don't pay too much attention. But this dream soaked in deep and stuck like a tattoo to my psyche.

It is dark and I am in a long wet tunnel of soft membrane struggling through the darkness toward a light. Yes, a light at the end of a tunnel and I push my way out and drop free to the ground below. I had been delivered to this place, on to this dusty road below, through the bowels of a gigantic cow. I look up to see a tail switching at the relief of the event.

I hit the ground in a heap and slowly, painstakingly collected myself and began to walk the dusty dirt road. I was old. Very old. My hair was white and I was smaller and bent over in a painful hunch as I limped along. I noticed a young man walking toward me on the road. His step was strong and he walked at a good clip.

As he got closer I could see it was my brother Hughie. He walked right up to me and with a smirk said, "Fuck you." I was aghast as I had not seen him in many long years. Startled I asked what he was saying that for and with a little brotherly envy and an

301

equal dose of affection he explained, "You got 50 more years than I did on earth." And I immediately shot back, "Well, fuck you, you're young, handsome and healthy and don't hurt all over." Then we looked the other in the eye and with a smile had a long hug. At the same paused moment we both uttered, "God, I missed you."

After the dream everything changed. I was going to live to be an old worn out man with white hair. Death would come from some bizarre farming accident with a cow I guess. I would live 50 more years. I had a purpose and I was meant to stick around for a while. I was the family elder and that came with a dignity. I haven't worried about death again.

Chapter 34

Farm Smart, Don't Just Farm

I do not have to go
To sacred places
In far off lands.
The ground I stand on is holy.
Here, in the little garden I tend
My pilgrimage ends.
The wild honeybees
The hummingbird moths
The flickering fireflies at dusk
Are a microcosm
Of the universe.
Each spade of soil
Is full of love
Living in place
In this place.
For truth and beauty dwell here.

Mary de La Valette

When I thought of the rough weather, the seasickness, time away from my children, junk in my nets and long nights with no fish and no sleep, I was glad to leave fishing behind. Other than those things, it was like the parts of farming that I loved. The independence, the hard work, the multitudes of necessary skills, along with that primal desire to procure food were all very similar.

Now it was time to trade in the blustery nocturnal winds of a commercial fisherman for our 30 acres of trouble and weeds. I was glad to have my farm. My body has always ached for land, the soil, the pastoral contentment of purposeful work in small scale agriculture.

I visited friends on different small farms and tried to glean as much realistic information as I could, now that I had re-entered the Ag World with the reminder I had a wife and two children I needed to support. The odds were stacked strongly against me.

I came to know a couple who lived in the pristine Similkameen Valley in British Colombia and grew organic apples. We walked their lush orchards where the fruit hung heavy and their caring wisdom poured forth. I bombarded Brian with questions and my observations about other farms I'd seen and his response was a simple, "Farm smart, don't just farm." In other words, think it through and make everything count. Say goodbye to your romantic notions and treat yourself like a legitimate business.

It sounds easy and obvious but I have to admit that I was drawn to the images of grandpa on his old tractor, with his crumpled old straw hat, with the old cow and the "golly shucks" reasoning for why nothing ever worked. It was all so likeable.

Pastoral fields of freshly baled hay were beautiful to look at on a late August evening, but the bottom line was if that hay wasn't making a profit, it wasn't making it. It was all so colorful and harmless; it just wasn't going to work for my situation, so through time I developed a reaction to my inclination for the romantic backdrops of the Walt Disney version of small scale food production.

The economics were pretty gaunt when adding up a garden of vegetables sold, even at retail prices. The dairy business was moving out of western Washington and therefore raising replacement cows went with it. I needed my own niche.

Lisa and I started with blueberries. We transplanted several hundred adult plants in a small area in front of the house. I shoveled the compost and mulches on and spent hours pulling weeds only to find the soil was too claylike for them to thrive. We planted an acre of strawberries in loamy soil across the meadow on our hands and knees and weeded and watered and sold flats around the island.

We had a very old John Deere 60 to do our primary tillage. It rattled and coughed but it pulled like 16 mules. It was a dangerous old faded green pile of metal and tires and on the days it felt like working was a formidable beast. This was an improvement.

America is a free enterprise system and anyone can compete in the market place. With no real economic desires in mind my father, only a hop, skip and a jump down the road, decided to become a strawberry farmer. Perhaps seeing my moderate success, he took his retirement time and ample funds and bought new tractors and implements and was determined to become the strawberry farmer of the island. I hated competing with him, largely because he so loved to battle with me.

He loved to win, to control the podium, to be in charge. It wasn't the winning or losing as much as the sadness I felt from his dominating anything I was doing. He needed to farm like he needed a hole in his head. It wouldn't be hard to out compete me. I felt indifference was the best way to handle the situation so I plowed the strawberries under and moved on and said nothing about it.

About that time we sold our fish boat and felt lucky to do so at all. The fishing industry continued to plummet and, through time, many boats sank at their moorings as the lack of money and neglect pulled them toward the bottom.

We took the money and built a greenhouse. Initially we developed a wholesale salad greens business, but soon realized salad greens grew well outside and switched to tomatoes inside. This was a great combination for small farm production. After a good year we could afford a second greenhouse and our little business was under way. We were producing several hundred pounds of greens a week and selling five to six hundred pounds of heirloom tomatoes.

We experimented trying different crops, from artichokes to ginseng. Panax Quincefolia (American ginseng) was selling for $169 a pound when we planted our first crop and an acre produced 3 to 4,000 pounds. It was as hard a plant to grow and keep healthy as anything I'd ever tried. It was grown under shade cloth canopies that were suspended on elaborate networks of cables and posts eight feet off the ground. This dynamic created an environment ripe for various fungi that could kill off the little seedlings. The common doctrine was to spray with all sorts of very strong and toxic fungicides.

The Asian market, that bought most of the root, didn't seem to mind its non-organic status; but it felt to me like I was entering the wrong church, so I began to experiment with natural fungicide teas made from nettles and chicken manure compost. My farmer/chemist experiments worked and I was able to certify my crop as organic.

According to the state agent who visited the farm each year, Thirsty Goose Farm was the first to organically certify a cultivated crop of ginseng in the U.S. It was a great achievement but the market plummeted to a mere $9 a pound in the four years it took to produce my first crop, and my best estimates calculated it was costing closer to $20 a pound to produce. I sold enough root to pay my expenses before the market totally bottomed out, but it joined the list of niche products that ended up being crossed off the list.

After the cows left, I'd switched to sheep as much to keep the fields mowed as anything. A local resort was developing a lamb sausage with our meat which gained enough popularity that a national TV show came to the island and did a promo on both our farm and the resort. We thought our 15 minutes of fame and fortune had arrived and we set up web pages, USDA labels, and shipping facilities to accommodate the onslaught of business. For the several weeks before we were filmed, we ran around and cleaned and mowed the farm into a model looking facility. There's nothing like a few cameras to get the farm in tiptop shape. The only other way it ever gets that clean is with about 16 inches of snow that covers every unfinished project and pile of rubble.

My daughters were staged as the tomato pickers and they spent hours fixing their hair and choosing the right outfits for the big day. There were shoulder held cameras, sound men that hovered boom microphones like dead crows over our heads, and a director who fired questions and then asked us to repeat the answers. "But this time could you stand over here and look to your left, and when you see sheep, swing the gate open."

It all felt awkward, and misrepresenting the way the farm normally functioned. We didn't even have a TV so before it aired, we not only bought a TV, we signed up to have a dish that was bolted to the side of the former Luddite's little house. And then the evening came when the show was aired.

We had a party, clicked on the TV and there it was, Thirsty Goose Farm, seven minutes of fame looking like a responsible effort, shining through the luminous screen from somewhere in deep cable. It had theme music and all the bells and whistles along with credits and our phone number if you wanted to order sausage.

The phone immediately began to ring. "Hello, this is Thelma Thornwhistle in Nowhere, Delaware, and I saw the show on TV and could you send me some, please." The phone rang all day and we took orders and mailed sausage to every corner of the U.S. Our demographics were elderly shut-ins who watched deep cable shows, didn't have a computer, didn't use a credit card and liked to tell you at least half their life story when ordering sausage. But most of their checks cashed and for several years, whenever the show was aired, our phones were jammed.

At the best of times the farm has found footing so we are able to survive, along with a respectable income from Lisa's job off the farm. One crop led to another and eventually we put in five hundred apple trees, have a small herd of sheep and raise over twenty varieties of heirloom tomatoes. The experiments continue as do the piles of inventions and crops that do and don't fit in.

It's not a job for the mild hearted who discourage easily. But I have found great contentment at the end of a warm day at the Farmers' Market where I am honored to be shoulder to shoulder with other island farmers and the line in front of my booth is full of smiling faces. We are providing people with sanely produced food, rich in nutrition, while knitting our community ever closer in a fundamental way.

The work is both hard and honest, yet steeped in a strong life force that can't be found in your local grocery store despite the smoke and mirrors used to buffalo consumers into believing they are getting fresh food. There is no comparison between a tomato or an apple grown five miles down the road from where it is sold to the fruit grown in Mexico or Ecuador. This says nothing about the carbon footprint of the tramp steamer that delivers it and the substandard wages that grew and picked it, not to mention the trucks and the grocers and all the middlemen who take their cuts. Each of these steps takes excessive time, food value, and carbon that a local farmer minimizes.

There is no mystery to the origin of my apples, tomatoes or lamb, no deceptions as to how fresh they are with little comparative demands on our ever fragile planet. I am proud to have found a revolution that I can feel good about, one tomato, one crisp apple, one honorably raised lamb at a time. It's merely a rekindling of what humans have done for thousands of years.

Afterword

Thirty-five years later I walk out on the deck. The spring sun is warm and bright on my eyes, and the farm in front of me lies generous and fertile. Three black horses dignify the hillside and a small flock of sheep look like white caps on a green ocean of grasses. The orchard of 500 apple trees has just finished its blossom set and a new crop of apples looks hopeful.

The wonderful dog that traveled with me lived 15 years and made it to see my first-born child. Several more dogs with great spirits too have passed, names that are forever etched into teary memories: Tally, Diesel, Honey, Frida and Elsa. The VW bug that I lived in was sold but lasted to see the farm and I continued to sleep in it the first summer after selling my tipi. Many more cheap, poorly running cars and trucks that have left their balding tire tracks on this great piece of land are gone now as well. To this day I love taking naps or sleeping in my car. It feels basic and safe and full of important memories.

My parents' living down the road was a continual test of our tolerances. My father was never able to acknowledge his children's successes and generally tended to compete with us. Their tenure on the island ended with their deaths. After 50 years, in their old age and infirmities, they seemed to have found peace with each other.

My inflamed intestine cooled off and I was told I was normal after 40 years of struggle; this occurred within six months of the death of my father. The untimely death of my brother was a loss of extreme proportion and is an unhealed scar in my heart and probably always will be.

My ability to read never really clicked in. To this day it is a struggle and the challenge forced me to learn the world with my hands, ears and eyes. Despite all this, I do love to write. When the words come out it feels more like painting words or carving a story than it does writing. My thievery fortunately ended about the time I bought land as I was feeling the luck of my good fortune

My farm all came together from such obtuse directions and it all feels blessed. It is no longer my farm but our farm, my family's farm. My wife, Lisa, and our two tall strong daughters, Natalia and Mara, and our strong and courageous granddaughter, Charley, consider this place a sanctuary in a world that seldom makes sense. The dream is as important all these years later as it ever was then. The learning curve was and still is enormous, as the earth always seems to be shifting beneath one's feet.

It's a story of survival, of loss and growth and, between the lines of these words and the rows of apple trees, of finding one's spirit. The losses and costs humble and fill me with tears from time to time, but the joy and love of important work in a rich soup of family and community leads me to say that "kings could have no more."

Acknowledgments

On a list of self-dares in my life, writing a book was one of the scariest and most difficult. My scholastic experiences in life created a disdain and avoidance of such dubious exercises. But I was drawn in by the challenge and with the help of good people, perseverance and the good fortune of cooperative constellations, I struggled through.

I found a circuitous route to getting my butt in the chair and pounding out the words. Late in the afternoon I would don a wet suit and plunge into the icy waters that surround our island and swim the shoreline sometimes for an hour or more. With endorphins coursing through my veins I'd rush home, zip up to my little office, turn on the music of Greg Brown and almost physically feel my brain shift from the left to the right. To that place where the poetry mixes with the memory, my body relaxed and my mind was at play.

A great deal of thanks to my editor, Emily Reed, who read and reread and helped form my dyslexic misspellings into a more universal language. My computer refused to tackle the job. It emitted a low bumping growl and a puff of smoke whenever I endeavored to employ the spell check and grammar buttons.

To Janet Thomas for her worldly understanding of the process of writing and her careful and kind words that encourage and foster the strengths in all her students.

To Shaun Hubbard who is as talented and willing with a Photoshop program as she is with a fly rod.

To my wife, Lisa, who is patient with my shenanigans in life, and is a loyal and loving adventurer. To my beautiful strong daughters, Natalia and Mara, who inspire and make me feel lucky. And to Charley because she is everything about hope and beauty.

I am eternally thankful for the good fortune of living on this island, a place where I found sanctuary and peace.